GIFTS AND POISON

PAVILION SERIES

General Editor: F. G. Bailey

GIFTS AND POISON

The Politics of Reputation

Edited by

F. G. BAILEY

Professor of Social Anthropology
University of Sussex

PAVILION SERIES

SOCIAL ANTHROPOLOGY

OXFORD
BASIL BLACKWELL

ISBN 0 631 13800 5 Cloth bound edition
ISBN 0 631 13830 7 Paper bound edition

Library of Congress Catalog Card Number: 78–149138

Printed in Great Britain by
Western Printing Services Ltd, Bristol
and bound by Kemp Hall Bindery, Oxford

Contents

vi *Contents*

Acknowledgements

I am happy to set down our thanks for financial assistance in carrying out the research, some of the results of which are reported in this volume, to the Nuffield Foundation, the Social Science Research Council of the United Kingdom, the University of Sussex and the Wenner-Gren Foundation.

For their skill and patience in preparing the manuscript I am most grateful to Yvette Ashby, Susan Durr, Margaret Heywood and Pat Sinclair. The index was prepared by Nanneke Codd.

F.G.B.

1
Gifts and Poison

Valloire is a village in the French Alps. It has a population of around 400 and you can walk from one side of the village to the other in a few minutes.

Housewives in Valloire avoid being seen talking to one another. In the winter, when the snow lies deep and one can walk only along narrow cleared pathways, these women stay indoors. If they need something from the shops, they try to find a child who will run the errand for them. There is no reason why the husbands should not go to do the shopping, and if they happen to be around, they do so: being men, they combine the shopping with a visit to a café, and in fact one is said to *aller boire le shopping*. For men to sit around in public and gossip is quite acceptable since, it is generally assumed, this exchange is *bavarder*: a friendly, sociable, light-hearted, good-natured, altruistic exchange of news, information and opinion. But if women are seen talking together, then something quite different is happening: very likely they are indulging in *mauvaise langue*—gossip, malice, 'character assassination'.

Even when the spring and summer come and the snow has cleared away, and women go out more and will more frequently be willing to run their own errands to the shops, they still observe some caution and restraint. Since the snow has cleared away, one can reach the shops by following pathways around the backs of gardens and houses and across fields and so lessen the risk of meeting other people. There are three reasons for not wanting to meet people: one is that you might bump into someone with whom you are not, at the moment, on speaking terms, and this would be very embarrassing for both of you. Secondly, if you do meet someone with whom you *are* speaking, then good manners require you to stop and stand in the street and exchange some remarks about the weather (remember that this is mountainous country and the weather is no less interesting than in England) and about births, marriages and deaths and other bits of family news. This has two disadvantages. Firstly, anyone who sees you talking in this fashion is likely to make assumptions about *mauvaise langue* and so your reputation suffers. Secondly, everyone knows almost everyone else, and many of them are relatives, and at least some of them are on speaking terms with one another, so that a trip to the shops through the streets could turn out to be very time-consuming. If you try to cut the meetings short by being brief, or, worse still, by ignoring the other person, then you deliver a deadly insult, for your behaviour signals that you consider the other person very much inferior to yourself. You earn yourself a reputation for being *fière*, that is, 'stuck up'. There is, however, one device which allows a woman to hasten past her acquaintances, calling out a greeting but not stopping to chat: this is to wear an apron. The apron indicates that there are pressing tasks at home to which she must get back and that the people whom she meets need not think that she is cutting them because she does not stop and talk. In other words, the apron signals that the woman is politically 'off-stage'.[2]

To understand this vignette, it must be seen in several contexts. It is about small politics; it takes place within a community; behind it lie both a set of shared ideas about how life and people are and how they ought to be, and a code for communicating these ideas; it concerns power and solidarity as variables in human interaction; finally it is about exchanges of information and courtesies, one might say, about accepting and offering the gift of good manners and therefore, since (as the reader will see) no gift is wholly uncontaminated, about the poisoning of human relationships.

I take each of these topics in turn.

SMALL POLITICS

The small politics of everyone's everyday life is about reputations; about what it means to 'have a good name'; about being socially bankrupted; about gossip and insult and 'one-upmanship'; in short, about the rules of how to play 'the social game' and how to win it. This is not just a question of how to do people down: one needs also to know how to influence people and to make friends. It is a matter of knowing how to live in society, how to manage social space so that one is neither lonely nor overcrowded, how to preserve one's individuality and identity and self-respect while at the same time serving the interests of the community to which one belongs.

At first sight the investigation of 'small politics' seems a trivial enterprise, one that is, perhaps, unworthy of intellectual attention. Reputations and gossip and one-upmanship are the small beer of small people, while our destinies lie in the hands of great men— cabinets and shadow-cabinets—who deal or would like to deal grandly with great issues. This view is mistaken.

The 'great man—great issues' argument is weak because it confuses description with analysis and ignores the fact that the same principles serve for political competition and political alliance alike in great issues and small. Certainly the content of the rules may differ from one level of power to another, just as they do from one culture to another. Cabinets and town councils and the committees of tennis clubs clearly deal with different matters: but, by and large, they deal with these matters in the same way. The repertoire of political management is limited, so that if our object is to explore regular patterns in social behaviour, the activities of small people provide evidence no less useful than the actions of statesmen. To believe otherwise is to be deceived by the façade which men in power put up in front of themselves, and if the exploration of the politics of everyday life happens to take the shine off statesmen, it does not matter.

A more serious objection might be that such an exploration ignores fundamental questions about man-in-society. By concentrating upon trivial everyday manoeuvring, it loses sight of the great—essentially religious—enigmas, which confront those who study society. Such an objection, if true, would indeed be serious, but in fact it turns out to be invalid. Our interest in how to play and win the social game in the one-time peasant communities of Europe brought us very quickly to dilemmas about the individual and society; egoism and altruism; equality and inequality; even original sin and man's perfectibility.[3] Moreover, we came to these problems not because we have a collective religious and metaphysical bent, but because these are rocks that lie very near the surface of that sea of petty manoeuvring, which we found ourselves studying. Indeed, a central concern of the enquiry has become definitions of the moral being: finding out and explaining where people think it proper to draw the line between treating man as an instrument and granting him the status of a human being. We did not set out with the intention of solving through field research the many problems that arise in the conflict between egoistic and altruistic behaviour. But the people whom we studied sometimes engaged in philosophical and religious discussion at that level, frequently invoked these themes to justify or condemn someone's conduct, and constantly used dichotomies of this kind to formulate plans for interacting with one another. In this book we discuss these problems: they lived them—as, in our everyday lives, we all do.

COMMUNITIES

Everyday life is lived in small communities, where everyone knows about everyone else, or, if they do not actually know about a particular other person, they know who will be able to talk about him. These are 'face-to-face' or—as a cynical Indian anthropologist has put it—'back-to-back' societies. These phrases do not mean that everyone is constantly in everyone else's presence: only that there is a fund of common knowledge about all the members of the community, and that it is not too difficult for anyone in the community to have access to it. This fund, in fact, is made up of reputations.

A man's reputation is not a quality that he possesses, but rather the opinions which other people have about him. It matters who these other people are. My reputation is one of the factors which control the ways I can interact with other people and manipulate them to gain whatever ends I have in view. Therefore only the opinions of those with whom I am likely to interact are important to me. If people on the other side of the world learn from a newspaper what a fine fellow I am (or what a cad), this is of no concern unless I come into contact with those people. The importance of one's reputation diminishes as the intensity of interaction also diminishes. Only in front of those with whom I interact frequently must I take care to manage the impression which they gain of me.

Life in long-settled rural communities has this quality of intimacy. It is very hard to mind your own business if you live in a village. It is hard even if you were not born there and have come to live in the village as a stranger. It is impossible if you are local born and bred, and if half the village consists of your kinsmen and the other half went to school with you. The villages about which the contributors to this book are writing have much of this quality of close living. But the conclusions we reach about the strategies of reputation management do not apply only in the former peasant communities of the mountains of Southern Europe. The problem is a universal one and the reader should be able to carry from this book at least a set of questions to be asked about his own life, wherever that happens to be lived.

It is sometimes said that town life is different. The man who lives in the town can be anonymous, can be lonely, can have privacy, is freed from the sanctions of prying neighbours, lives miserably in a bed-sitting room, and so on, according as to whether you wish to praise or condemn urban living. Research has shown that urban neighbourhoods are not always like this:[4] villages, so to speak, exist inside long-settled urban neighbourhoods and the warm embrace (or suffocation) of community-living is found there no less than in the countryside. But even people who inhabit those fragmented English suburbs where you speak to your neighbour-of-25-years only on the night the bomb drops and never again afterwards, must have some degree of community life.[5] The reason is that community life does not depend on neighbourhood alone. It may be found in churches, in factories or offices, in pubs and other places of recreation, in fact in any kind of association, formal or informal. Those who live the so-called anonymous life in the facelessness of urban surroundings, nevertheless derive their identity, find their reputations and so find themselves in interaction with a circle of people who know one another, who talk about one another and who therefore matter (either for good or for ill) to one another.

Of course, there are degrees of entanglement in and intensity of community life. To measure this by counting the number of occasions on which people interact, becomes impossible as soon as one envisages anything more than a handful of people in a social psychologist's laboratory. Moreover, there is a formidable problem in discovering a unit of interaction, which can be counted. The problems become less formidable if one looks not at individual acts of interaction but rather at the patterns which these interactions reveal. A civil servant should treat all clients who come to his office as a member of the public and refuse to take into account the fact that they may have been to school with him, that they may be Roman Catholics like himself, that they may want to speak Welsh with him, and so forth. This is universalistic behaviour. If, on the other hand, the civil servant recognizes the client as his cousin and for that reason gives him favourable (or unfavourable) treatment, then he is behaving in a particularistic manner: he is identifying him as an individual, whom he knows to have other roles besides the one he is currently playing. A similar distinction is made by the word 'multiplex' in contrast to 'single-interest' relationships. In a society like our own, and living where I do, and being of the age I am, it is likely that my ties with my neighbour will be nothing more than whatever we silently establish to be the right standard of 'neighbourliness'. That would be an example of a single-interest relationship. But if I happen to have been born in the village of Bisipara in India,[6] where I once lived, my neighbour would almost certainly have been a close kinsman, perhaps a brother or a first cousin related through my father; we would have attended many family ceremonies together; even if we did not own fields in common, we would certainly own neighbouring fields; we would sit together on the village council; in short, we would interact with one another over a great many different kinds of issues, sometimes in a friendly fashion and sometimes as rivals. We would have a multiplex relationship, one made up of many different roles, just as a rope contains many strands.

Multiplex ties, then, are not found everywhere to the same degree. This makes it possible for us to scale communities. Roughly speaking, the more people do a wide variety of things together, the more they treat one another in a particularistic fashion as whole persons, and the more intensive is community life. Where this intensity of interaction shades off towards single-interest relationships, that is the point at which a man needs to be less careful about his reputation, if only because he has to manage it, so to speak, only on the one front. If you are both determined to deal solely in the single-interest relationship of customer-to-shopkeeper, then it can matter to neither of you if one is a saint and the other is an adulterer. All you need take care of is your reputation in the specific transaction of buying and selling.

It follows that the more often and the more different ways in which you interact with another person, the more will be the occasions on which you have an opportunity to assess the other's performance, to evaluate it and so to arrive at a judgement about his reputation. But this does not mean that a community only exists where there is consensus about particular reputations. A reputation is a many-sided thing. On the surface it is summary and solidary—'a decent chap', 'a good man', 'a rotter' or even just 'a man'. But this single judgement is reached by taking into account many different aspects of his behaviour, and the process by which one averages between these different aspects always seems to be arbitrary and obscure. It follows that other people, even if they agree about 'the facts', may yet weight them in quite a different way: the person whom you rate as 'a decent chap', they may write off as 'a man on the make'.[7]

Membership of a community does not depend upon having a *good* reputation: only upon having a reputation. Those who are judged to be poor performers, whether in particular roles or in the summary comprehensive judgement, are nevertheless part of this same community. To be recognized as bad and anti-social certainly puts someone apart within the community, but he or she remains a part of it and indeed it may be argued that no community could get along without its negative examples. Anthropologists use the phrase 'moral community' to refer to those who are prepared to make moral judgements about one another. The immoral man is no less a part of his community than is the moral (i.e. good) man, for he is being judged by the same moral standards. He is treated as a human being, with human standards of fallibility. To err is to be human. To have a reputation allows one to be a member of a community,[8] even if the reputation is bad.

But those who are outside the moral community have different kinds of reputation. They are likely to be judged in an instrumental fashion, not 'in the round'. They are not human beings to the same extent as those of us who belong within the community. This is the world outside, the world where moral judgements become less important, where fewer holds are barred, where men are not to be treated 'in the round', where they are to be used instrumentally, where they are mere objects to be destroyed or employed in whatever fashion serves our interests.[9]

This phenomenon—that 'civic sense stops at village boundaries' —has most clearly been noticed among villagers in underdeveloped countries dealing with an alien, usually colonial administration. One can find examples in India and Cyprus and, indeed, in the regions discussed in this book.[10] But only the most unintelligent and perversely ethnocentric among us would pretend, after reflection, that the same kind of attitude is not also found among us: we all live in the centre of a moral community, the force of which diminishes, like the ripples from a splash, as the circles grow wider. How much more readily will people resort to aggressive justification of what they only partially recognize to be dishonesty, when they are talking about cheating the customs officials or fiddling on the income tax, than they will if they have been caught out swindling the church, or a masonic lodge, or their own family or any group in which they have a multiplex tie! Dishonesty, in other words, does not always mean dishonour:[11] breaking the rules matters most when one is also 'letting the side down'.

VALUES AND CATEGORIES

The 'side' or the community (or for that matter the large entity, which does not rest on face-to-face relationships, which we call 'society') is defined by a common set of values and categories. Communities and societies are made up of people but we only recognize them as a community or as a society, because the people who belong share some ideas about how things are and how things should be: they have a common set of categories with which they 'word' the social and the natural world around them and they share a definition of the good things and the bad things in life. From this point of view a community is a set of shared values and categories.

These values and categories are matters of faith. It is true that they form a hierarchy so that some may be derived from others: but, in the end, there are sets of final values which people never question, and never think of questioning, and these form the boundaries and fixed points in the game of politics which we shall be discussing.

To find out the rules for maintaining or undermining a reputation in any particular culture, one must also understand its categories and values. Without knowing this, one cannot know why one reputation is reckoned good and another bad. Fortunately the task is not so formidable and comprehensive as it sounds. The relevant values and categories are near to the surface: they rise to people's lips, when they pass judgement upon one another.

There seems to be a great pressure, in arriving at the decision which makes a reputation, towards simplification, towards the yes/no, black/white judgement, unqualified by considerations of 'more or less'. But this simplicity is only on the surface. The analysis which anthropologists make of the way in which different values within any one culture relate to one another can be exceedingly complex. But the people who live in this system and operate it are frequently unaware of this hidden complexity. In just the same way most readers of this book will obey, when they speak, the rules of English phonology, without being able to say what the rules are.

We should not expect the same values and categories to be found in different communities and cultures. We have to take particular care not to impose our own ideas of what is 'naturally' right conduct on the people whom we are studying, by imagining that they hold the same notions about the world and people as we do. Sometimes the good man is he who accepts evil done to him with equanimity, turns an endless succession of other cheeks, and is ever-forgiving: sometimes the good man is the man quick to anger, the man who boasts that no-one who harms him goes unpunished. Certainly, there are some things which look like universals and which extend across many cultures: but these are more often the patterns which we discern in the logical relationship between values and categories, or the patterns which we find in the process of political competition, than the values and categories themselves. For example, neither egoism nor altruism are to be regarded in themselves as universals; but the two taken together as the ends of a dimension, allow us to ask questions about communities everywhere.

B

CODES AND SIGNALS

When you play a role—leaving out of that phrase any suggestion of sincerity or hypocrisy—you need to signal to the person with whom you are interacting, and perhaps to the members of an audience if they happen to be around, what role you consider that you are playing. Sometimes this signal seems to be, so to speak, built into the action itself and you are not at all conscious of creating an impression. For a person who is not particularly shy and does not feel the terrors of the market place, a casual purchase is likely to be of this nature: the buyer does not worry too much about what the shopkeeper thinks of him. There are other occasions when the actor goes to great trouble to send out very clear signals, in order to make sure that he is giving off the appropriate impressions. A candidate being interviewed for a job, a barrister pleading a case before the courts, and—the case from which we take our metaphor—the actor on the stage are all likely to be very conscious of the signals they are emitting to the interviewing board, the judge and jury, or the audience. Handsome, in fact, is *not* as handsome does: handsomeness lies not in the doing but in the communicating. This must be so, for handsomeness is not an objective quality: rather it is a judgement about the quality of an interaction, and the judgement lies with everyone concerned, not with the performer alone.

We signal our way through life and, from one point of view, society and community are an endless exchange of messages. Exchange is the essence of social interaction: society exists in that men give each other deference, challenges, pieces of information, money, tribute, service—even marriage has been construed as the exchange of women. Messages are conveyed in a variety of ways: the spoken word, the gesture, the nod, the failure to greet, the banging down of coins on the counter, the timidity of a knock at a door and other slight cues of this kind, which may well remain invisible to someone not familiar with the culture concerned.

One is struck again by the almost terrifying process of simplification which human interaction seems to require. We find ourselves reading off a whole personality from the gesture which a man uses to smooth down his hair. We glance at a set of clothing or the texture of the skin on a man's hand and read into it a class, an occupation, and a whole way of life. We are apt to take instant likes and dislikes on the slenderest of clues in dress, speech or demeanour. Of course we are frequently wrong, but that is not the point. The point is that a very small signal leads immediately to a large judgement, a pigeon-holing of the other person, which is a gross act of over-simplification. Moreover, we deal not only with individual persons like this, but with whole situations. We know a crisis, when we see one, or think we do. We pick up an 'atmosphere' from a few behavioural clues: from the expression on a face, from how people are standing, from the distances between them, and so forth. This is no more than to say that we have to think in categories; we cope with the wild diversity of the real world by abstracting, by reducing differences and so ignoring them. This jump from the small clue to the large judgement is nowhere more apparent than in the field of making and breaking reputations. Moreover, to repeat, your simplification of a complex set of facts may be very different from the simplification which I choose to make.

Yet it would be wrong to think that we are wholly free-movers in making our judgements and communicating them. At its simplest, we are never free to communicate anything we wish. We can only convey a message successfully if the other person will understand it and our judgement of his comprehension limits our ability to express ourselves. In a quite literal sense, we have to speak his language and we can only say the kind of things which are possible in that language. One can say things in the language of mathematics that cannot be said in poetry: and a poem written in mathematical symbols is at best a joke comprehensible to a few people. Things said in one language can be translated into another: but the translation always has some degree of approximation, and there are some concepts which cannot be translated at all. This is one reason why we find in any language terms which have been borrowed from some other language. Language, in short, sets a limit to the kind of things we can communicate to someone else.

To communicate with another person, you need to have something in common with him. I have so far been calling this 'language', but the reader will appreciate that this word is used in a very wide sense to include not only all the non-verbal ways of signalling, mentioned above, but also the set of values and categories which are coded in the signals transmitted. Let me draw a metaphorical picture of the human mind.[12] From a few items of behaviour, we are ready to build up a picture of the whole man: in this we are like the archaeologists who, from a single bone, are said to reconstruct the whole skeleton. How do we do this? We look at the way a girl is dressed, at the way she sits in a chair, at the way she uses her eyes and her hands while she is talking. We then draw certain conclusions about the class into which she was born, about the kind of school at which she was educated, and possibly about the way she is likely to behave in the presence of males. From the fact that she belongs to a certain class and has been educated in a certain way, we can make predictions about the way she will behave in situations which are different from the one in which we first see her. Whether or not we are right, does not at present matter: the point is that those initial clues trigger off extensive stores of information which we carry in our minds. This process consists of two steps: firstly we decode the signal to arrive at the concepts or images or categories (all these words are in use) for which the signals stand; secondly we start linking one image with another, by saying, for example, that being female and middle-class and being relatively highly educated mean that she is more likely to be found in a concert hall than a dance hall, when compared to someone who is also female but working class and less highly educated. Three things are involved in this. One is the code, the set of rules for linking signals to concepts. The second is 'elements': these are concepts like 'middle class', 'female', and 'educated' in the example given above. Thirdly, we also carry in our minds sets of rules about how these elements may or may not be combined with one another. These rules are called 'operators'. In short, we receive a signal: we relate this signal to a category: then we link this category, either positively or negatively, to other categories.

We began this section with codes and signals and we have now linked them to the values and categories which were discussed earlier. It remains to say some obvious things about how these connect with communities and with reputations. Those communities in which relations are relatively highly personalized, in which people treat one another 'in the round', in which relationships are multiplex and roles are particularistic should also be the communities in which the signalling system is most efficient—that is to say, in which the signals can be most laconic. This is a commonplace of everyone's everyday experience. With those who are intimate, you do not need to spell things out. They know what you are thinking, before you say it: of course they only do, because either they have seen you in this situation very often before, and/or you have already revealed what is 'in your mind' by some facial expression or bodily gesture. It is one of the difficulties of anthropological field-work that, even if you happen to know the language well, you can still listen in to a conversation and not know what is being said. The conversation consists of allusions, hints, fragments, all of which serve perfectly well as a means of communication for those on the inside: but effectively they rule the stranger out of comprehension.

Secondly, besides efficiency and lack of redundancy (that is, repetition) in their signalling systems, communities also consist of persons who, to a very high degree, have in common a single set of categories and an agreed set of rules for linking these categories with one another. In other words, they have a common culture. It is because the elements which make up this bank of information are shared, as also are the permissible patterns which these elements may make, that the signalling system can be so laconic. Just because it is laconic, there is that much more room for manipulation and manoeuvre, for punning and innuendo, for messages hidden within other messages, for the apparently inno-cent remark that punctures an overblown reputation—in short, for all the civilized subtleties in communication that are possible between those who are masters of the same language. The relationship between the clues and what they stand for is one of gross simplification. But the tactical use of these clues to convey an impression, to manage a situation, to boost a friend or to bring down a rival generates a quite formidable sophistication and complexity.

To understand what is going on in encounters of this kind, one needs to know not only which particular behavioural clues relate to which particular categories or concepts, but also who the speaker is and at whom he is directing the message. We do not really know what a man is saying, until we know who he is and to whom he is speaking. All this follows from the fact that inter-actions convey messages about status: part of the job of under-standing the message is to understand what statuses are being signalled in it.[13]

POWER AND SOLIDARITY

The word 'status' has its own difficulties, since it is used in several senses, both in everyday speech and in technical discussions. In everyday speech, it can mean that one person is high and another low. When we ask of someone employed in an organization, 'What is his status?', we are asking where he is placed in a hierarchy. Is he on the board of directors? Does he have a managerial post? Is he an administrator, or a clerk, or a workman, or the boy who makes the tea? On other occasions the word is used in a way that is very similar to 'reputation'. If we say of someone that his status is very high in the profession, we mean that other people in the profession accord him a good reputation. We also talk of people 'seeking status' and this can be equivalent to either or both of the meanings already mentioned: 'status' in the sense of 'reputation' or in the sense of 'rank'.

In sociological writing status often means the bundle of roles which a particular person possesses. Consider the 'head of the family'. When we talk of this as a status, we mean that it contains several different roles: husband, father, possibly grandfather, and so forth. The head of the family also may have a variety of roles which are concerned variously with the management of family property, representing the family towards the outside world, socializing children, and possibly arranging and performing acts of worship. Status, in this sense, is a bundle or cluster of roles. The process of thought involved here uses elements and operators, for it consists of stating which roles may be combined with which others (and which may not) in order to make up a particular status.

So much for the word itself: now back to the argument.

I have so far stressed the homogeneity which exists between the members of the same community. They share the same outlook on life; they want the same kinds of things; they have the same ways of 'wording' the world; they share an allusive, laconic and economical system of signalling and they conceive of themselves as an entity, ruled by law and regularities and standards of morality, and ranged against a non-moral world outside. But there are also ways in which the members of a community may be *unlike* one another. The fact that they are so is the reason why a message cannot be understood until you know the statuses of sender and receiver. People simplify their social universe by allocating one another to a small number of statuses. Indeed, this is one part of the meaning of 'reputation'.

I am going to look at the ways in which status (or modes of interaction) vary along two dimensions: power and solidarity. These are illustrated in the diagram below:

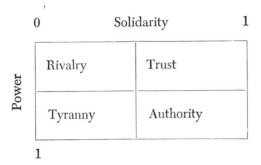

Diagram I: Power and Solidarity

The words in the squares of the matrix indicate modes of inter-action. They could have been verbs, or nouns referring to persons, or adjectives, or adverbs. Whichever grammatical form is used, the words indicate the same basic variations in political inter-action. If one has exchanges[14] with another man in the sphere of politics, then he is an ally, or a rival, an accepted leader/willing follower, or a resented tyrant/reluctant subject. This is not a claim that precisely this pattern will be found in every culture. Rather it is a list of questions which one may take to a culture and ask whether and in what manner there are modes of inter-action which fit into one or another of these four compartments.

To a surprisingly large extent people can be ruled only in so far as they are willing to accept orders. Of course there are many examples of duress. But there have also been many recent ex-amples, for instance in the universities, which demonstrate quite clearly that only a very small number of people need to flout authority systematically in order to bring down the whole system. Many kinds of regimes, even those which are apparently most powerful and most authoritarian (one might instance the British in India) rest on consent (or apathy, which is tacit consent).

Consent, of course, means more than merely willingness to

accept a particular command. It means accepting the pattern of statuses which divide people into high and low, those with the right to give orders and the duty to take responsibility, and those with the duty to obey orders and without the burden of responsibilities. In their turn these statuses connect to ideas about man's place in the world, about God and our duty towards Him, about the nature of men and women, about their origins, about the existence of evil and suffering—in fact with all those things which we lump together under the heading of 'religion'. The pattern of stratification is likely to be validated by a wide variety of beliefs about man and divinity and nature, all of which are connected in the manner of and with the strength of a net. Through these sets of beliefs the difference between the status of those who lead and those whose duty is to obey are made comprehensible and acceptable.

In this way the monolithic uniformity and homogeneity of the community has been broken by separating the leaders above from the followers below. Thus there are two cultures or sub-cultures. Each differs from the other by having a distinctive way of life; that is by having at least some (but not all) elements which the other part does not have. Before the First World War almost everywhere in Europe, there was no difficulty in distinguishing between gentry and peasants. By the style of their houses, by their demeanour, by the clothes they wore, by the offices for which they were considered eligible, distinctions were made obvious between the literate and the illiterate, between those who worked with their hands and those who did not.

The two strata or classes (or three, or whatever is the number) are not wholly separated from one another.[15] Firstly, while some elements in their culture divide them, there are other elements which they have in common and through which they can communicate. Moreover, each side is joined to the other by a network of reciprocal rights and duties, although this is different across the boundary from what it is within either group. Both sides belong to the single moral community, at least when one compares them with anyone outside. It would be a mistake to be so affected by present day egalitarianism as to think that the tie between a leader and a follower cannot be accepted by both sides as a moral one: both history and one's everyday experience provide examples which are proof of the contrary.

'Tyranny' is the slightly archaic word which I have chosen to represent the Italian word *prepotenza* or the French *puissance*, for which the English word 'power' seems too undecided a translation. These are the situations in which the less powerful person does what he is told, not because he thinks it is his duty to do so, but because he is afraid of punishment if he does not. The claims of the more powerful person to moral superiority are not accepted and to this extent tyrants become part of an outside world to be exploited, cheated, outmanoeuvred by whatever means are possible, without considerations of morality. In other words, a community within which there is a struggle between strata, between classes, is to that extent becoming two communities. Yet at the same time the break is never as complete as this and, as some of the studies later in this book will show, the very intensity of interaction, even when it is in the mode of hostility and conflict, goes along with a great deal of discussion about reputations and a great many claims and counter-claims to be acting in the right, in a manner very similar to what goes on within a single community, which is not divided into different strata.

The quality of trust (or its absence) makes the division also within the kinds of interaction possible between those who consider each other to be equal in status. It is as if every man in society lives in the middle of a series of concentric circles of trust. He is at the centre: those nearest to him are those who are never in competition with him and are always his allies. Those beyond the furthest circle are those who do not belong to his moral community, so that when he comes into conflict with them, he need have no consideration about what is right and what is wrong. In between these two limits are categories of people with whom he has different degrees of confidence. This is not fanciful. Campbell writes that a group of Greek shepherds, the Sarakatsani, divide the world of mankind as follows: at the centre are the family, those related by blood, in whom trust must be implicit and with whom one never fights; next there are the families who are related as in-laws, with whom there is some degree of trust but it is far from being total; beyond them are other Sarakatsani who are classified as 'strangers' and these are the people on whom one's back must never be turned, for their intention is always to increase their own reputation by diminishing yours.[16] If we think of examples from our own life, clearly there will be differences according to the upbringing and outlook of the person concerned, but everyone has some people whom he trusts more than others, so that, even though we may not discuss strangers in the manner of the Sarakatsani, we nevertheless are likely to sort out people into those whom we can trust absolutely, those who have no reason to harm us but also no reason to harm themselves by helping us, and, very likely, those who will do us down if we give them the chance.

As in the case of tyranny, the fact that there is an element of 'no holds barred' in one's relationship with rivals, should not lead us to think that rivals are outside the moral community. There is indeed an intensity of interaction between rivals, who are by definition close to one another in rank, both in the communities which we are discussing in this book and, one would guess, within any kind of community-like group of people. This intensity of interaction, and of competitive interaction at that, is only possible without bringing the whole community to the point of disaster because the competitors accept a common framework of rules, which allow some moves and forbid others, agree that the prize for which they are competing is worth having, and agree upon a common set of signals about issuing challenges and deciding what shall constitute a win or a loss. This game-like quality is exactly what distinguishes transactions with rivals from conflicts with people outside the moral community.

These are four basic ways of categorizing political interactions: trust, rivalry, leadership, and tyranny. It is a very simple picture —and indeed a very well-known one—but it can be used to generate interesting questions.

One such set of questions arises from the possibilities of movement from one compartment to another. Trust may give way to rivalry: or move in the reverse direction. Leaders may turn into tyrants: tyrants may somehow legitimize themselves. Those families who are in the same stratum in one generation may find themselves in different strata in the next generation. What causes the movement in any of these directions. Where have people acquired the resources to bring about the shift? How are these resources applied most efficiently? How do you start to signal to someone who was formerly your rival that you now wish to become his ally? How can you pressure him into doing so? How can you bring back into line a leader who is showing signs of becoming a despot? How, in that particular culture, do you signal to the leader that he is reaching the point of no return? Once again we see the possibilities of manipulation, arising this time not only from complexity but also from the possibilities of change.

GIFTS AND POISON

Much of this book is about people competing to remain equal. Sometimes the threat is imagined and, like an armaments race, the whole affair seems wasteful, and therefore tragic. A little more knowledge and a little more trust would have resulted in a lot less sacrifice. It is this that gives the sense of tragedy, the bitterness which we see in conflict between those who are equal and who therefore might have been friends. The fight against a tyrant also may eventuate in tragedy but it carries its own nobility. But the fight between equals tells only of frustration and the waste of human endeavour. When brothers fight, when friends fight, the winner loses no less than the loser. It should not take place: but it does take place, and with vehemence.

Equality exacts its price. With equals—with peers—you are a man relaxed and uncompetitive: or so you think. But in the villages and in the communities, described in this book, this is true only for a few of those whom you consider equal. With the rest, equality is the reward for constant vigilance. The prime competitor—the first enemy—is frequently the man nearest to you in rank. The Oriyas have a proverb, which hurts: 'Your brother is your enemy'. Like most proverbs, this one is founded in reality: when the father's land is shared out, adjoining estates belong to brothers and they quarrel about the placing of boundary lines. Those nearest are also those with whom you interact most frequently and, therefore, those with whom you are most likely to have a cause for contention.

To put it metaphorically, competition takes place mainly between those who are in the same league.[17] It takes place between people who are equal, or almost equal, to one another. A gross difference in power and in status usually has the effect of putting people so far apart, that they cannot compete (although they may, of course, seek to use one another). Hence the paradox and, I suppose, the tragedy: people remain equal because each one believes that every other one is trying to better him, and in his efforts to protect himself, he makes sure that no-one else ever gets beyond the level of approved mediocrity. Equality, in communities like these, is in fact the product of everyone's belief that everyone else is striving to be more than equal. Equality comes about through the mutual cancellation of supposed efforts to be unequal.

Are there, then, also people who do not stand as competitors? Firstly, there are those with whom a man has a relation of trust: with them he should not compete, although, as we know, in the real world these relations too may degenerate into competition. Secondly there are those who stand outside the moral community. One does not compete with them: one comes into conflict, the distinction being that in such conflict, as is not the case in competition, there are no rules of fair play. Thirdly, there are people still within the moral community, who nevertheless do not stand as competitors. These are people whom one considers to be in the 'league' above or below. In some ways this system resembles the traditional system of caste in India. To enter into relationships of competition—and therefore a kind of intimacy—with those below one, brings one down to their level. So one ignores their challenges and provocations, for to take them into account would be to demean oneself. This is splendidly described by Pierre Bourdieu, who writes about a people in Algeria.[18] One has to consider very carefully whether to issue or to accept a challenge when the potential competitor might belong to a different rank: to make a mistake might also be to put oneself, accidentally, into a lower league. Our own culture contains plenty of examples to show that a gentleman who engages in a fight with a non-gentleman, puts at risk his reputation as a man of honour and breeding.

There are two other categories of people who stand aloof from the competition, who are of great theoretical interest but who do not seem to feature very largely in the material that we have gathered in Europe. Competitions of this kind may have specialized roles for people who act as referees or umpires. The culture defines them as being ineligible to take part, themselves, in the competition: but they stand by, and sometimes they are equipped with sanctions, to see that the competitors observe the rules and do not cheat. This is, of course, frequently the task of a person in authority and one would expect to find someone in an upper stratum refereeing the competition of those in a lower stratum. But it seems to be one of the conventions of systems of this kind that those who stand above it close their eye—at least their official eye—to the squabbling and elbowing that goes on in the stratum below them. Of course, in cases where the competition reaches the standard of acerbity at which people take one another to court or manage to bring such public resources into the quarrel as to jeopardise public interests, then the lord of the manor or the priest may intervene to restore some kind of peace and may lay down a settlement. But very often there is no single authority figure of this kind, and the last word is left with something much more vague, public opinion. This public opinion, quite certainly, belongs within the stratum in which the competition is taking place.

Secondly, there are sometimes personages who exempt themselves from the competition. The sense of tragedy and futility which I mentioned above is not confined only to the observer, but is a sentiment which is also frequently voiced by the competitors themselves. They want harmony—or say they want it: if people quarrel, that is because people are sinful. Consequently, there may emerge certain figures who stand outside the competition and symbolize the common desire for communal harmony. These are Christ-like persons, whose reputation one would expect not to be assailed and who therefore should have no need to protect it. One of the striking things about the material we have collected is that very few of these figures have emerged, and when they do they are mocked: to be 'too good' is also to be stupid.[19] It may also be that no man can be a prophet in his own country and that in small communities people know too much about one another, about one another's antecedents, for it to be possible to find someone pure enough to remain, respected, outside the competitive arena.

Such Christ-like figures would stand for the community: they would stand for altruism as against egoism. They would stand for the general interest in defiance of self-interest. The feeling that this quarrelling, this bickering, this petty manoeuvring is futile and a waste of human energy and a waste of human life arises partly from a conviction that co-operation could bring benefits to everyone. If everyone acted in the public interest, then everyone would be better off. Yet there also seems to be a deeply felt human conviction, attested once again in the pages that follow, that although this would be a desirable state of affairs, in fact everyone acts for his own interest or the interest of his family and the man who claims to have acted in the public interest is, usually, a hypocrite.[20]

In this field, as in many others, we cannot talk of motivations, for there is no means of knowing what are the 'real' springs of human action. The debate between egoism and altruism, between private interests and public interests, is in fact not part of the study of motivation but rather a part of the language of claims. You are one up on your rival if you can convince other people that you have acted in the interests of the community, while he was selfish. Ideas of egoism and altruism become part of the public language of public justification of conduct: they become political resources.

For this reason it seems, at first sight, that egoism always prevails. Everyone seems to believe that all the other people are working for themselves and an air of cynicism hangs over claims to work for the community and for the general interest. Yet this cannot be entirely the case. Firstly, there is a limit upon the degree to which claims can diverge from actions: in the last resort someone is going to say 'handsome is as handsome does'. Secondly, and more importantly, there is a sense in which the individual actor can never be a free agent steering his own course towards his own best advantage. His own best advantage depends upon his reputation: his reputation is not something which he can create in and by himself. He depends upon other members of a community granting it to him. This is one paradox in the situation. Even those rules which appear to enjoin cynicism and self-interest, which praise the man who is able to look after himself and protect his own property and his own family and his own honour, spring from and are sanctioned by the community: that is, by other men and other families. The 'sturdy individualist' is able to respect himself only because the community in which he lives itself respects sturdy individualism. In the end egoism does not win: the community sets the standards and it is only by conforming to those standards that the supposed individual attains an identity and a sense of self-respect.

A self is a set of reputations, and these reputations spring from belonging to a community. The reputations arise from the interactions in which a man engages and from the messages which these interactions signal about him. These signals, in their turn, are triggers which set off in the mind values and beliefs, which are linked to one another, not simply as aggregates but in patterns of inclusion and exclusion. Within any moral community there are four kinds of political interaction, summarized in the terms 'friends, rivals, leaders, and tyrants'. In this last section we have concentrated upon people who consider themselves to be equal, that is upon friends and rivals. To this arena the individual must devote some political resources and skills and energies. The result is a kind of competition for precedence. Yet, paradoxically, for all the effort that goes into the competition, the result seems to be that the strivings cancel one another out and, with few exceptions, everyone remains equal to everyone else. This is, I suppose, literally democratic society: in such a society, careers are not open to those with talents. Skills and energies go into keeping people in the place that they have always been: they run hard in order to stand still. It is the kind of world which stamps heavily upon change and innovation. To pause before acting in order to work out what other people will think, will often mean not to act at all. This is a characteristic not just of the one-time peasant communities, which we have studied in Europe, but also of tightly knit communities anywhere. This is depressing, but to be depressing does not make a conclusion false.

There remains one last paradox in face-to-face relationships. It is a commonplace of contemporary folk psychology that only misery results from failure to 'communicate', inability to 'relate with' other people, exclusion from 'meaningful exchanges'. Of course those who are shy suffer for it. But it must also be stressed that there are limits in the other direction and the behaviour of housewives in Valloire—and people everywhere—demonstrate this. People want space around them. A warm embrace may remove the misery of loneliness and constitute the nicest kind of 'meaningful exchange' but it has meaning only because some people can be kept at arm's length.[21]

The very nature of social exchanges assist one in doing this. An exchange is a message. Messages have to be interpreted. But the line which separates co-operative from competitive messages is remarkably fine and delicate. This is the irony of man's existence in society. If you make no exchanges, you do not belong;[22] if you make the exchanges, the messages which you intend to invoke solidarity, may be interpreted as a challenge. The gift requires the counter-gift, and the inappropriate return constitutes a challenge. *Gift*, as Mauss points out, is a German word for poison.[23] No-one can doubt this, for it is a feature of everyone's life. The overgenerous gift, so big that it cannot be returned, becomes a humiliation. In short, it is not that some exchanges are co-operative and others are competitive: *all* exchanges have the seeds of both these opposed things within them.

From the apparent triviality of housewives in Valloire wearing aprons to go shopping, from the petty competition to keep a balance in obligation and preserve one's good name, from the malice of tiny manoeuvres to spread gossip emerge the fundamental dilemmas of being human and living in society. The two left-hand cells of Diagram 1 stand for competition, disorder and self-interest; the right-hand side embodies the rules which point men in the direction of co-operation, altruism and service to the community. On the right is duty, the community, the society, *dharma*, continuity and stability: on the left is *artha*, self-interest, the individual, change and uncertainty. But only on formal occasions do people resolve this conflict by the simple assertion that what is on the right is good and what is on the left is bad: when it comes to planning their responses and initiatives, all four modes of action are taken into account.

NOTES

1. This vignette was given to me by Susan Hutson. See Chapters 3 and 4.
2. This phrase, like many of the ideas in this book, is taken from the work of Erving Goffman. See references.
3. I am happy to acknowledge the stimulus to think along these lines provided by *Burridge* (2).
4. The most illustrious example of this is in a report on research in Bethnal Green. See *Young and Willmott*.
5. The reader will perceive, if he has not done so already, that the primary meaning which we are giving to 'community' is not geographical (for which the word is 'neighbourhood') but rests upon the criterion of intensity of interaction.
6. See *Bailey* (1) and (2).
7. See especially Chapter 3.
8. The reverse is not true: others besides members of the community have a reputation, including those who have nothing to do with the

community and never visit it. They may be significant in being used as examples and models.

9. This distinction, which is of fundamental importance to the analysis, is here made in a simple fashion. Later it will become obvious that one has to think in terms of gradations. See also *Bailey* (3).
10. For India see *Bailey* (3). The example of Cyprus is one among many which have been taken from *Peristiany*.
11. See the article by Pitt-Rivers in *Peristiany*.
12. On this question there is an extensive and interesting literature in ethnolinguistics. The terms used here are taken from *Sanday*. See also *Burling* (1), *Hymes*, and *Frake*. See also *Tyler*, section four.
13. This point is taken up again in the concluding chapter.
14. The bible for the sociology of exchange is *Blau*. See also *Homans*, 1961. For us, the enquiry starts with *Mauss*.
15. The most elaborated example of stratification is provided by the caste system of India. See *Dumont*. See also *Bailey* (1).
16. See the essay by Campbell in *Peristiany*. See also *Campbell*.
17. In the strict sense competition takes place only between people who are equal in status and they compete for the same prize. There can also be contests between people of different status, but this is a contest to make use of one another or to avoid being used, and compared to competition between equals, it lacks the notion of fair play.
18. See the essay by Pierre Bourdieu in *Peristiany*.
19. See the essay by N. T. Colclough, Chapter 10 in this volume.
20. See especially the articles by Loraine Blaxter and Paul Adams, Chapters 6 and 8 below. The dilemma of altruism and egoism is also the well-known 'prisoners dilemma'. See *Schelling*, pp. 213–14. See also *Boulding*, pp. 92 ff.
21. The need for privacy is keeping pace with the menace of pollution at the top of the charts of popular sociology. See *Hall*.
22. The word applied in France to people who avoid the company of others is *sauvage*. See Chapter 3.
23. See *Mauss*, p. 127 (note 101). The disabling element in gift giving is noticed in English in phrases such as 'being overwhelmed with gratitude'.

C

2

Changing Communities

For thirty years the people, whose philosophy of life we are describing, have been a headache for the governments of their countries. They draw large subsidies to make good deficiencies in agricultural techniques. The villagers live in a world where reforms are thrust upon them and where new ways of making a living, either by going away or by introducing new industries and enterprises to the mountain areas, are put before them with varying amounts of subsidies and assistance. As in all cases of development, much depends on the willingness of the people concerned to accept innovations. This in turn depends on how well they understand what is being offered them, and still more it depends on how well the designers of these innovations understand the social and cultural milieu into which their reforms must be fitted. Relationships with outsiders (that is with government agencies, with political parties and so forth) become channelled by the notions of trust, rivalry, legitimate and illegitimate power. It follows that one must know about the world of status competition in order to select policies and strategies of economic and social development.

Certain characteristics are held in common by some or all of the communities described in this book. All of them have until recently been part of the peasant world. All of them are now going—or have gone—through a series of crises, the termination of which is either their demise or their rebirth in a different form. All have problems of economic development and community development, and all are undergoing changes, both planned and unplanned.

This recent history provides a background to our analysis of small-scale politics. Also, questions of economic development and the progressive integration of small communities into larger nations are important in themselves. At one level we will be discussing specific communities (even specific people in them) at a specific period. But to do this and nothing else is to fail. Our interest is primarily in problems. We want to raise questions (and answer some of them) which far transcend villages in Europe in the middle of the twentieth century, because they are questions which can be asked about change and development in many parts of the world, at all periods in history, and about human assemblages of other kinds besides the peasant village.

WHAT IS A PEASANT?

These villages, at least up to the beginning of the First World War, were all peasant communities. They are no longer so, but some of the peasants and many of the features of peasant life and attitudes, still are present on the scene.

'What is the village', asked Ambedkar, in a sentence that echoed scandalously around the newly independent Gandhian India, 'but a sink of localism, a den of ignorance, narrow-mindedness and communalism?'[1] The peasant, in other words, is mean, narrow-minded, heedless of his neighbours, suspicious, crafty, wholly bereft of a sense of the public weal, the common good. He quarrels with everyone, trusts no-one, and shows towards his neighbour the meanness and malice that nature seems, all too often, to show to him. The grim, unsophisticated, uncivilized and punishing routines inflicted by the seasons on man, when he makes his living from the land, are lived again—like handing on punishment—in the social life of peasant communities. That is one stereotype of peasant life, and it is not wholly the invention of the 'civilized' town-dweller but also forms part of the image which villagers have of themselves. The selfishness and the lack of public spirit is a kind of original sin against which a man should struggle, but of which he cannot hope to be innocent.

There is another stereotype, which uses the same set of qualities to draw different conclusions. The peasant is sturdy. He has a robust sense of his own independence. Each man or each family fights its own fight with nature. They produce things from the soil without depending on other people, they respect their land and they care for it through the generations. Both in the material and the psychological sense, peasant life means security. Peasant societies cannot go bankrupt: peasants cannot lose their jobs, and even if the market fails them, they can still grow their own food and weave their own clothes. Furthermore, unlike the restless city dweller, they have no doubts about their own identity: they do not torture themselves by asking what they are doing in the world, whether their life has a point and a purpose to it, and all those other questions which the rich use to make themselves unhappy. Peasant life is unhurried, deliberate, redolent with that sense of continuity, of eternity, which is for some people a source of deep satisfaction. Life in an industrial city is the final affront to human dignity: that dignity is most finely brought into reality in peasants and their communities.

This romantic view of the peasant life is found in opinions which range from a wholly serious philosophy (exemplified in the Gandhian ideals against which Ambedkar reacted so vehemently) to a picture post-card, musical comedy, light opera set of themes about sturdy lads and apple-cheeked buxom girls, free with their favours on carnival nights, picturesque and ever so healthy. Both as a policy for the way things ought to be and as a description of the way things are or have ever been, this picture is wholly bogus. In our researches we have found evidence of people regretting a vanishing way of life, but we have never encountered a pretence that sweetness and light is exclusively the product of an absence of modern conveniences.

These two opposed stereotypes define the peasant by identifying qualities both of the person and of the community in which he lives. A third set of definitions also makes use of distinctive qualities to identify the peasant, but lays more stress on the relationship which he has towards non-peasants and the part which peasant communities play in the total society.

Anthropologists were once concerned to separate tribesmen from peasants. The distinction—like all distinctions, inevitably theoretical—was that tribes could be seen as units in themselves, little worlds that were self-contained and wholly independent of that world which was unlike themselves—nations and governments and civilizations. The peasant community, on the other hand, was always part of a civilization. There were two kinds of connection: firstly the peasant marketed his surplus produce in a town, and therefore in the wider community; secondly there was some kind of flow, never very precisely identified, to and fro between the 'high' cultures of the cities and the 'little communities' of the countryside.[2]

Peasant communities are in fact in exactly this position: they stand out as a distinct element within a nation, but the degree of difference which identifies them is not so great that it becomes a complete barrier to communication with the world outside. They are isolable for study but not literally isolated. We have then to say what it is that makes them distinct. The gross and oversimplified descriptions of peculiar attitudes discussed above do not serve the purpose, both because they lack subtlety and, more importantly, because these characteristics (toughness, obstinacy, pettiness, generosity, and so forth) are also found in other sectors of the population.

We have to focus upon the style of farming and the way the farm enterprise is run. Production for a market will distinguish peasants from tribesmen, but it will not distinguish peasants from farmers. We begin, therefore, by asking what is distinctive about a peasant enterprise.[3]

Firstly, the peasant makes his living from the land. The farm he runs is a small one: small enough to be worked by members of the family. He may grow a staple crop, either for himself or for the market, like potatoes, wheat, rye or sugar beet, but he also mixes his farming, so as to provide for his own needs as widely as possible. The result, especially in the mountain areas which we have studied, was a farming programme of fantastic subtlety, which made a harsh and apparently unpromising environment yield a living for what nowadays seems to be staggeringly large populations.

Peasants, then, have small farms and go in for mixed farming. But there is something more important to be said. A peasant farmer is distinguished from a non-peasant (that is, a 'capitalist' farmer) by the fact that the peasant attempts to maximize work opportunities and not production. The farm does not exist to make a profit, to get the greatest possible money returns from the market. Certainly the peasant wants the largest return available to him, but this aim is secondary: most importantly, the farm exists to provide a living for the family. The farmer who buys machinery and in so doing puts his sons and daughters off the land, is not behaving like a peasant. It follows from this that peasant enterprises are labour-intensive: they find work and they make work for everyone in the family. The very subtle farming programmes mentioned above depended upon having many pairs of hands working long hours.

One can see from this why the peasant way of life should be associated with security. The workers in a peasant enterprise cannot get the sack: a new machine or a new technique that will raise the level of production constitutes no threat (as it would in capitalist farming) because the objective is not the highest level of money return per unit of capital, but the provision of work for everyone in the family. There was once a time when those who worked on peasant enterprises were never exposed to the uncertainties and insecurities of those employed in capitalist enterprises, whether farming or industrial. Of course there may have been famines and other kinds of natural disaster, but the cunning peasant, other things being equal, was likely to be the last one to starve.

In short, given the way economies worked in the pre-Keynesian era, one can readily understand why peasants stayed on their land, when they could. The land provided security: they could never be unemployed: barring a famine, they could always eat; the land insured them against changes in the value of money; the farming enterprise, continuing in the hands of the family, provided for their old age.

Furthermore, just as the farm provided work for the peasant's family, so, for many years, peasant farming provided a living for the nation's population. Until the last two decades statesmen could look calmly on rising populations, not worrying about where they would work, because peasant farming was there as the, so to speak, residual occupation. It is still true that the peasant sector is a (now rather costly) sponge which mops up what would otherwise be a pool of unemployables.

For centuries the peasant sector has performed this service for the nation. Like everyone else, the peasant provided tribute or taxes, but also the peasant communities constituted a reservoir of labour and of soldiers to be conscripted into the nation's armies. This phenomenon resembles migrant labour in Southern Africa in the past few decades. The nation (or industry) has the benefit of able-bodied labour without having to meet the cost of the labouring population before and after it is productive, and often without even having to pay for the sustenance of wives and children. Even if we leave aside the abuses which arose from land tenure systems—and southern Italy used to be a striking example of the degradation which this can bring—it is still true that until recently the relationship between the state and its peasant sector was a predatory one. If the peasants seemed to the outsider to be mean, self-interested and suspicious, that must to some extent have been because experience with outsiders had taught them to protect themselves by such attitudes. This, of course, is not the whole story: it is one of our contentions that those who live in a close-knit community inevitably are suspicious of those beyond its boundaries.

MIGRATION

Particular techniques of farming can only be maintained within limited ratios of population to land: the balance is particularly delicate in mountain areas. If the numbers in a farming family fall below a certain size, they have to close down some of their farming activities; this puts other activities at risk. Such families are particularly in need of the co-operation of others within the community. Examples will be given later of the strain caused by declining population.

Clearly there is also a limit at the other extreme. No matter how much the head of a family wants to support it and find work for all its members on the land, he cannot do so beyond the capacity of the land to carry them, without lowering the standard of living at all: and to this lowering too, there is a limit set by conventions at a level above the hypothetical notion of starvation. Before that level is reached, people do something about the situation.

The solution that men of our generation are seeking to this problem—and it is a world-wide problem—is directed towards improvements in the techniques of land management and land exploitation (and, more recently, population control). This, it is hoped, will raise the level of production and so provide enough for everyone to eat. What it does not do is provide enough work for people who are not trained by their culture to manage leisure sensibly. Indeed 'leisure' is a very small element in the cognitive map of mountain peasants.

Mountain peasants have always taken the other solution to the problem of over-population. The techniques of land-exploitation are left intact: the surplus population gets out. The solution lies in one or another form of migration.

For centuries seasonal migration has been a feature of the mountain communities of Europe. For the most part this took place during the winter months, when the land is under snow and when there is little work for members of a farming family. Sometimes the mountain men had distinctive skills which they took down to the towns and cities of the plains and sold during the winter months. They went as masons or carpenters; sometimes they took herds of sheep or cattle to winter pastures, literally hundreds of miles away on the plains; sometimes they went as salesmen or entertainers; sometimes they went as teachers. Then, when the snows began to melt, they returned to work the farms through the summer and autumn, until, in October or November, the winter again closed in.[4]

The trades and skills which were carried down to the plains and sold there during the winter months constituted a secondary economy, supporting peasant farming, by relieving it of surplus members for a time at least, and by providing an income from the outside world which did not depend upon producing a farm surplus to be sold there. Sometimes these skills did not involve migration and in some parts of the mountains there is a long tradition of crafts (often in wood or in metals), the most famous being Swiss watch-making.

Seasonal migration provided a fund of contacts and expertise, which has led, for at least the past hundred years, to an ever-increasing flow of emigrants from mountain areas. These are people who have gone to find a living in another place, often in another country, and they return to their mountain villages, sometimes after a long absence, sometimes only when their working life is finished, and often not at all. The same process of emigration took place from lowland areas, where, as in southern Italy, there was great poverty.

Such people went away. For a generation, or perhaps two, they kept in touch with the family members still on the farm. In some areas the system of land inheritance gave them at least a nominal stake in the family property, and this has produced a very complicated land tenure problem for those who wish to develop and change farming in the mountain areas—and else-where. But until the Second World War, at least in the mountain areas, this process remained one of emigration; it was not yet de-population. The surplus population went away from the moun-tains in great numbers, but it was still a *surplus* population. Sufficient people were left on the land and in the families to keep the family farm going and to maintain the highly complex labour-intensive farming programme. The mountain communities, at least, were left intact.

But since the end of the Second World War all this has changed. Emigration has turned into depopulation: the end of peasant farming in mountain areas—and in many other areas too —is now in sight.

PEASANT FARMING TODAY

Always to some extent and increasingly so nowadays, the peasant enterprise was managed so as to produce not only the family necessities but also a surplus which was sold on the market. The returns from these sales enabled the peasant to pay his way in the world outside, both to give the tax and the tribute required of him and to purchase those things which he needed but which could not be produced by the family enterprise itself. So long as this market was supplied by other peasant enterprises like his own, family holdings comprising a small area, labour-intensive and with little farm machinery, and above all directed towards work for the family rather than to producing at the most competi-tive rate, the peasant had little to fear.

But the markets in which peasants have to sell their produce nowadays are no longer like this. The goods which they produce —potatoes, grain, and so forth—come into competition with the same produce which has been grown on 'industrial' farms. The latter commonly cover large areas, are highly mechanized, and grow one crop only (or at least very few crops) and so are able to produce at a price which far undercuts that which would enable the peasant to continue in business. These industrial farmers, un-like the peasant, manage their enterprise and judge its efficiency not by the work it can provide for the family but by the size of the profit per unit of input. The peasant cannot compete.

This is particularly true of arable crops grown in mountain

areas. The growing season is shorter than on the plains and the soil is generally poorer. Sometimes the terrain makes the use of machinery, even if the peasant could afford it and wanted it, either impossible or uneconomic. Even where nature appears to be on the side of the mountain farmer, as in the abundance of pasture which the mountainsides provide for sheep and cattle, he is still unable to compete because his enterprise is still too small in scale and because the terrain is not, in any case, decisively favourable when compared with pastoral areas in less precipitous regions. Left to themselves, peasant farmers anywhere in Europe, let alone in the mountains, would today find it impossible to make ends meet.

These difficulties are compounded because the expectations of those who live in the countryside and in the mountains about their due standard of living are rising. This has come about because, particularly since the end of the Second World War, communications are very much improved. This applies both to transport and to the means of mass communication. Because they can and do travel easily to the towns and cities, because they read newspapers and subscribe to magazines and listen to the radio and watch television, both the peasant farmers and their sons and daughters know that people outside the peasant sector achieve a higher standard of material comfort for, so it seems, less work and less arduous work. The factory-hand begins at eight in the morning and finishes at five in the evening and does this, perhaps, only for five days a week. The peasant farmer works from dawn until sunset, and seven days a week. It is true that some industrial work is dangerous and difficult, but there are safeguards and compensations. The mountain peasant faces dangers of terrain and weather, against which even the experience of many generations fails to provide complete safeguards. Even now in Italy the kinds of insurance available in the case of sickness or injury are much less advantageous for the peasant farmer working on his own land than for someone employed in industry.

It is said that the comparative advantages of employment outside farming are even more apparent to women than to men. Women in Losa whose house was what they call *aggiustata*—that is, modernized—spoke with feeling about the changes in their lives which came when their husbands or fathers ceased to be farmers. Without cattle in the stalls the house could be made clean and easily kept so. Moreover the wages which a factory worker can earn provide such comforts as central heating, clothes-washing machines and dish-washing machines, not to speak of a family car. Women, for two decades, have not wanted to marry into farming families, for these both fail to provide the comforts of modern life and inflict upon the housewife the arduous routine of cattle, hens and heavy manual work on the farm or on the mountainside.

In short, at the very moment when the market prices deny the peasant producer the surplus required to buy consumer goods, the demand for those consumer goods becomes more insistent. The result is that the sons and daughters of the peasants leave the land and go to work in the towns or in rural industrial enterprises (including sometimes farming, but not peasant farming). Some go away altogether: others find work at a distance which makes it possible to commute. When this happens, the peasant's difficulties in marketing his goods in the face of competition from non-peasant farming enterprises are compounded by the desertion of his labour force—which, as we have said—is the *raison d'être* of a peasant enterprise.

The other main advantage of peasant farming, from the point of view of the family members, was the security which it provided. Right down to the twenties and thirties of the present century—and especially then—workers in industry lay under the shadow of unemployment. Today this seems no longer to be true, for the old pattern of boom and slump is under control. Furthermore, as I have just said, personal security arrangements in the shape of sickness and accident benefits, in Italy at least, differentially favour the industrial worker as against those who work the land. This is true also of pension arrangements. The old person, providing he has been employed in industry, is cared for in his old age, and therefore does not need the security of a family enterprise. Moreover, at the present time, these enterprises are in such a bad condition that their chances of providing security in old age are seen to be very low. Here again we see another part of the foundations of peasant life removed: security can be found elsewhere.

All those difficulties which have descended upon the peasant farming enterprise—its produce being undercut in the market, depopulation, demands for a higher standard of consumption, and its loss of a monopoly in the provision of security—have come from outside. At the same time, its own difficulties which arose from over-population, were solved by emigration to the outside. At the present day emigration both provides the solution for the individual, who wants to raise his standard of living and provide himself with the security which farming once did, and it intensifies the difficulties of those who remain on the land.

This is more than just a problem of not having enough people to run a satisfactory farming programme. The mountains, particularly the higher valleys, have been depopulated. They are depressed and denuded areas. In the higher reaches of Val Maira in the Cottian Alps I have walked into hamlets of ten or fifteen houses, all standing, all with their doors locked, some still furnished, with electricity cables laid on and an apparently new concrete water tank, and all deserted. Around any village in the lower valleys as in the higher, you will find the mountain huts, once in use for storing hay or for overnight or month-long stays during the summer to exploit the upland pastures, now deserted and crumbling. These pastures too are reverting to a wild state. Some have been planted with pine trees. The homesteads that were built beside them and were sometimes lived in the year round (perhaps cut off for three months by the winter snows) are fallen in, for at this height the Alpine winters make short work of a building that is not kept in constant repair.

I have stood with an old woman and listened while she pointed to the mountain slopes above, where I could see the remains of terraces, and told me how, when she was young fifty years ago, these fields were planted with barley and rye. In those days there were fifteen or twenty people in the household: now there were two. The village school, which now had three pupils, used at that time to have more than fifty. A community had died.

Only in the higher and more inaccessible valleys does one find the land and the villages abandoned. Those lower down are groping their way towards other solutions. But everywhere in the mountains the mark of death has been put upon peasant farming. Those who still make a living from the land are aged forty and upwards. In Losa, the Piedmontese village in which I lived, out of about forty men who were engaged more or less dominantly in agriculture, only two were under forty years old.

The rest worked in quarries, factories, offices or had gone away. In another twenty years, unless the direction of change is radically altered, farming will no longer be an occupation in Losa. People there take a gloomy pleasure in predicting that in ten years' time there would be no one in their village who kept a cow. Once everyone kept sheep and goats: now there are only two or three modest flocks of sheep. Farms are kept going by old men and women, supported mainly by remittances from migrants and pensions earned when employed outside the valley. It is clear that the future lies elsewhere than in farming.

This also constitutes a problem for the nations. Their dilemma is this. Modern methods of farming produce enough to feed the people. The agricultural problem, as an economic problem of how to allocate resources so as to produce sufficient food, has been solved. But it has left behind a considerable social problem. The effect of the new agricultural technology, out of which industrial farming has grown, has been to put the peasant farmers out of business, without incorporating them into any new kind of enterprise. The younger generations from the countryside, and particularly from the mountain areas, have found their own solution by moving out. But there is left an ageing population, roughly from forty upwards, which continues the old way of life and which is unwilling to move and, in any case is almost certainly too old to be trained for a new kind of occupation.

Various kinds of national solutions have been tried. They all amount to paying some kind of subsidy to peasant and family farmers. Sometimes these are direct subsidies in the form of 'social price' for the goods the farmer produces, rather than an 'economic price'. In other words, the less-efficient producers have to be kept in business by keeping the price of food high. They have to be kept in business because there are many of them and because they have votes: and because, in France and Italy at least, the unemployed and under-employed rural proletariat has found its leaders and its spokesmen and is able to make the rest of the nation pay compensations for the discomforts brought about by changes in the peasant way of life.

The peasants and the nation are each other's headaches. A Stalinist solution—wipe them out or let them die—is everywhere considered wrong or impractical. There are in all these countries sufficient peasants, sufficiently well organized, to make it plain that a total disregard of their problem would bring about national insecurity, the fall of a government or even the fall of a regime. Certainly peasant culture will die. But the peasants themselves are sufficiently robust to ensure that their death will not be a sudden one and will not be too painful. They cannot win: but they are going to lose in comfort. Their produce earns them not an economic market price, but a 'social' price. Governments spend large sums of money in attempting to develop the rural areas by improving farming techniques, by enlarging and consolidating holdings, by encouraging various forms of co-operation, and by promoting the development of industries (including tourism) in the rural areas.

CHANGE IN RURAL AREAS

Franklin has argued, in a recent book, that the ambitious land reform programme in the south of Italy, in so far as it has succeeded in producing a class of peasant family farming proprietors —one of its aims—has done so just in time to see these men driven out of business by the more efficient techniques of industrial farming. In the mountain communities described in this book, this process is almost completed. Certainly there is *talk* of agricultural improvement. There are attempts to consolidate landholdings and to distribute them more efficiently by doing so. There are extension services. There are loans for development. Even in Losa, new crops and new techniques occasionally become subjects for conversation.

But at the same time it is clear that most people believe that mountain farming has no future. Other ways of making a living have to be found, and are being found. In Losa the younger half of the population work outside agriculture—in a cement factory lower down the valley, in the state electricity organization, or in the factories and offices of Cuneo, which lies fifteen miles away. One section of the people of Losa was interested in developing tourism, but seemed unable to do anything effective about it. In many places there is, as in Valloire, a 'myth of development'. This myth says, in effect, that there are resources available in the valley which, if properly managed, will bring, or restore, prosperity to everyone. In the higher valleys the myth had to do with tourism, often with the development of a winter sports station or facilities for summer tourists. In two of the valleys known to me in the Italian Cottian Alps, there was a rumour that work would soon begin, or would start again, on driving a road over the mountains into France and would thus open the valley to tourists.

Both those who would welcome change and those who resent it, know that change is inevitable. Either these villages will find some new way or ways of making a living; or else they will die. When one talks of reputations and of gossip and of scandal, and when one sets these activities in the context of small close-knit communities, then the reader must remember that the battle for status and reputation is taking place at a time of change and uncertainty, of regrets for the past and hopes for the future. Whether you are a reactionary and want to keep as close to past styles as is possible, or whether you are progressive and want change, this is the time to assert yourself. Over a large area of life, situations arise for which it is not easy to find precedents. Established definitions of good and bad become blurred, because they are applied to new situations. Our interest lies in the fact that much of this debate is carried on, so to speak, behind the hand: it passes through channels of gossip and it concerns the behaviour of individuals and their reputation, rather than being worked out in open discussion as matters of public policy and public interest.

In this affair there are several kinds of transactions, both of the inimical kind and of the friendly kind. Some of these transactions take place between people of the community and agencies and persons outside it: others are exchanges of acts of co-operation or of hostility within the community. All these interchanges, both hostile and friendly, make use of the language of micro-politics. This language provides a constraint on the strategies and tactics open to any side on any occasion. We can only understand and predict the kind of choices that are likely to be made, the reaction to new forms of leadership, the response to offers of development aid, and so forth, if we first understand the language.

NOTES

1. See *Avard*, p. 25.
2. The *loci classici* for this range of discussion are *Redfield* (1) and (2).
3. In the discussion which follows I have taken my lead from *Franklin*.
4. An excellent account of the culture of the so-called 'circum-alpine' region is given in *Burns*.

3

Social Ranking in a French Alpine Community

The village of Valloire is situated in the French Alps, near the Italian border. At the turn of the century it had a population of 1,000 people, supporting themselves from subsistence agriculture. As contact with the outside world increased, agriculture declined and many villagers migrated to Marseilles. The population dropped to 400. In the last twenty years both the population and the economy have begun to stabilize through the growth of tourism. Although many old people still farm, the young people have opened shops, small hotels or work as building labourers and ski instructors. Ninety per cent of the present population were born in the village and are connected by ties of kinship.

THE EMPHASIS ON EQUALITY

When asked by an outsider about differences in wealth and power, most villagers emphasize the equality of all. In several different contexts I was told: 'No one commands here; we are all *copains*.' In answer to the question: 'Who is the richest man here?' I was told: 'No one is really rich here. Anyone who wants to be really rich will move to the town.' However, in another context, they say: 'No one is poor here. We all have our own houses and our vegetable plots and so we can all live very nicely.'

This ethos of equality is based on the idea of felt common kinship. Ideally, kin are social equals. Close kin share in common property and a common reputation. Kin are expected to exchange services, give support and to be sociable. Until recently, most marriage has been within the commune and villagers feel that they are all *cousins* or *petits cousins*, although exact links are not traced beyond second cousins.

D

Women do little visiting outside the family. Friendship amongst women is considered 'dangerous' as it threatens family solidarity. In Valloire there are few formal associations such as abound in some English villages,[1] through which status differences could be expressed.

Equality in the village is also based on a feeling of common culture, distinctive from the outside world. Until recently, distinctive language, dress and customs have marked villagers off from outsiders. The villagers' dependence on the land has created universal poverty in relation to town dwellers. Villagers say: 'Outside a class system exists. But here it is different. We all have the same origin.' Until recently, villagers were seen by outsiders as belonging to a single class, a homogeneous 'peasant' group.

Felt equality is based on the fact that Valloire was traditionally a community of peasant proprietors. All families owned land. The traditional economic unit was the family farm, self-sufficient in labour and produce, except at harvest and other peak labour times when help was exchanged with kin. There were thus few opportunities for control over others through control over economic resources. Today the ideal economic unit is the family business—shop or hotel—which is similarly self-contained and independent.

In an economy where many goods and services cannot be bought for cash, villagers depend on non-cash exchange in the idiom of help or *rendre service*, where a more specific contract is made. Villagers are only willing to ask for or offer help or *rendre service* from or to those whom they feel to be their equals. Only in this way can debt be avoided, independence and equality maintained. Thus villagers emphasize their equality in order to ensure this free flow of goods and services.

Equality is linked with the feeling of obligation villagers have to help and support other villagers. This sense of solidarity is illustrated at a funeral when each family in the village sends a representative. This feelings of obligation towards fellow villagers is based on the fact that, as they say: 'Here, we know each other.' This norm is linked with the Christian teaching, familiar to all, that everyone should help his neighbour.

In a face-to-face society, where the same people meet in different roles, it is a wise tactic to accept and emphasize the

equality of others. Any temporary situation of command or inequality is likely to be played down because, in another sphere,
the positions may be reversed. When it is necessary for a command to be given by one villager to another, it is often given in
a joking form. Because nothing 'serious' has been said, it cannot
cause offence.

In a village where the same people interact in different roles
and are linked by numerous, cross-cutting ties, it is difficult to
vary behaviour. For example, a villager cannot be haughty in
the shop but pleasant to the shopkeeper's mother-in-law who takes
her children out for walks. Under these conditions, people tend
to behave in much the same way to everyone. As one villager said,
explaining the difficulty of interpersonal relations: 'One must be
polite to all, or polite to no one.' Specialist roles, which could
create positions of authority, are played down. For example, in
the village shop, the shopkeeper, her assistants and village customers pass the time of day, gossip and interact as villagers.
The employer/employee and shopkeeper/customer roles only
come into play in the tourist season when work is so busy that
commands must be given quickly and village customers ignored.
Since the tourist seasons are short, opportunities for the expression of superiority/inferiority, implied in the new specialist roles,
are few. Behaviour would be different in a busy all-year-round
resort.

In Valloire a high value is placed on being polite to all,
respecting the person and independence of others. This *politesse*
hides any felt inequalities and maintains a façade of good relations. A villager who acts proudly (*fier*) is sharply criticized.
The importance of manners is illustrated by the evaluation of a
girl from Marseilles who had been living openly with a village
man. This girl was condemned, not for her breach of sexual
morality but for her rudeness and haughtiness in her relations
with other villagers.

There are, however, differences in the way villagers behave
towards each other which imply respect and authority. For
example, there are different ways of naming (the use of the title,
surname, Christian name or nickname); the *vous* or the *tu* form
of address can be used. Villagers can speak correct French, slang
French or patois. The contents of the conversation can vary from
personal jokes and gossip to 'neutral' topics such as the weather or

'culture'. In each other's presence, villagers may take more or less care in presenting their image—in the clothes they wear, their bearing and *toilette*. These variations in behaviour can be seen to range from formal to informal behaviour, echoing Goffman's distinction between 'front' and 'back region' behaviour.[2] Formality in behaviour implies lack of knowledge, respect and can imply inequality. Informality in behaviour implies equality, familiarity with and knowledge of the other person.

The degree of formality in behaviour between two villagers is determined largely by the ascribed statuses of age, sex and kinship. Respect is shown by younger to older people. Mutual respect is expected between the sexes. Behaviour is most informal between children and towards children. If people knew each other as children or were known as children then it is likely that the informality of behaviour will continue throughout adulthood. For this reason a person's origin—where he was born and brought up—will influence people's behaviour towards him. Knowledge of others, which influences the formality of behaviour, is passed along lines of kinship and origin. Common activity, which can create informality, is most likely between people of the same age and sex or within the same kinship group. Thus, although differences in behaviour, implying inferiority/superiority do exist in the village, they are generated by differences in 'ascribed' statuses such as age, sex, kinship and origin rather than by differences in 'achieved' statuses such as occupation, class or wealth.

In Valloire deference based on differences in power is seldom seen. No-one throws their weight around or cringes. Power-seeking within the village appears to be deliberately limited and leadership positions are avoided. There is a commonly held dislike of *politique*, by which villagers mean the pursuit of power and influence in public affairs. All people who 'play at politics' and set themselves up as leaders are suspected of dishonesty, deceit and of profiting themselves. This suspicion of leaders was easily aroused in the efforts at tourist development and accounted for the downfall of the only active mayor Valloire has seen. Because leaders are so unpopular and open to criticism few are willing to take on leadership positions and village politics are generally marked by apathy and avoidance.

The ideal of village unity and equality is seen in village

ceremonies and public occasions such as funerals and fêtes. In these people play parts allocated according to age, sex, kinship, and origin rather than to wealth or power. For example, the building contractor and his labourer carry the coffin side by side as '*hommes du village*'. There is an avoidance of secular village occasions which need organization and therefore leadership. The chief secular occasion—the summer fête—is organized by the young men of the village who are united, through their youth, across family rivalries and hostilities. Thus possible conflict over organization is insulated from wider village society. Moreover, the young men are not expected to act 'seriously' and so are less open to criticism.

RANKING

However, despite the protestations of equality and the emphasis on equality in much day-to-day behaviour, villagers appear to rank each other. Criticism and evaluation of others, which involves ranking, is the subject of gossip, said to be the chief pastime in the village. Villagers often speak of the *jalousie* which characterizes their particular *mentalité* and which implies constant competition for prestige. The biting criticism of others behind their backs does not accord with the *politesse* offered to their face.

Criteria for ranking

A villager may be ranked according to material attributes, the most important of which are wealth, education and manners. Wealth may be calculated on the amount and quality of land, livestock or other property owned; or on income; or on the possession of consumption symbols such as clothes, furniture, cars and so on. A man may be praised or criticized for his education which is valued in itself and for the better job and more cultured manners it brings with it. Education can also be disparaged for the pride and the dangerous political views it can bring. A man may be praised for his cultured manners or criticized for his country uncouthness.

Villagers may also be ranked according to moral characteristics.

For men and women, honesty, helpfulness and generosity—in fact all the qualities which emphasize the equality of others—are highly valued. Someone who works hard is praised. Dishonesty, hypocrisy and meanness are condemned. In a society where the sexes are frequently segregated, different standards are applied to their behaviour. A man can build up a good reputation on his openness, friendliness and ability to joke. Women, however, are expected to keep to themselves and to refrain from gossiping. A woman who has friends and is frequently seen out of the house is suspected of telling family secrets and gossiping maliciously.

Villagers also rank each other on intelligence, which is seen as a moral characteristic. A basic distinction is made between those who are *dégourdi* and *engourdi*. The latter usually exhibit some noticeable mental defect, often coupled with a physical defect. This usually makes them unsociable, unable to follow the normal pattern of behaviour, and so morally inferior. They are often treated with suspicion and fear. Villagers are praised for their intelligence which leads to good management of their resources. However, a man who is too clever and calculating is thought to be dishonest.

An individual may be ranked according to his individual standing in relation to these criteria or his ranking may be strongly influenced by the reputation of his family—for example, the wealth, education, morality of his ancestors, relatives or children. An individual's reputation may rest on the number of relatives he has in the village as these people are expected to speak well of him and defend his reputation as their own reputation depends on it.

Villagers are chiefly concerned with ranking other villagers or *gens du pays*. My questions on the relative rank of women who had married into the village were frequently dismissed by the phrase: 'But she is an outsider'. Outsiders cannot be ranked with villagers because the same criteria are not known about them. Although villagers may comment on the clothes and manners of outsiders, they do not show the same absorbing interest which they have in other *gens du pays*.

Resolving the contradiction between equality and ranking

This apparent contradiction between the emphasis in behaviour and in comment on equality and the ability and willingness to rank other villagers in gossip can be resolved in three ways.

Restoring Equality
   The chief occasion on which ranking occurs is when a villager or outsider, through words or behaviour, challenges the ideal of equality. Such claims to superior status are rejected and annulled through the introduction of different ranking criteria by which the offending villager is brought down and, if possible, the status of the speaker raised. For example, in asking one villager the question: 'Who is rich here?', I volunteered the name of M. Chienno, a second generation Italian migrant who has built up a large contracting firm in the valley which now employs 150 men. The villager, a retired employee of M. Chienno, comes from a local farming family. He replied: 'Oh no, M. Chienno is not rich. He is dependent on others for his wealth—on the labour and custom of others. What makes a man rich is land. It is the large *propriétaires* [and by implication himself] who are rich.' Similarly, I have heard the wealth of a bar- and hotel-owning family dismissed by villagers saying: 'They are not wealthy. They must be up to their eyes in debt.'
   Ranking also occurs in the opposite situation when anyone, particularly an outsider, puts a villager in a marked inferior position. The status of the villager is restored by introducing different ranking criteria. For example, I have heard the reputation of the alcoholic owner of a bar, which many say expanded through dirty dealing, defended by the fact that he had been a *bon garçon* and came from a *brave famille*. His present degeneration and the bad reputation of the bar was blamed on his wife, an outsider.
   It is possible for a villager to reject and annul almost any bid for prestige or accusation of low status because of the diversity of ranking criteria. For example, an individual's status can be altered by reference to the reputation of his family. It seems most common for a man's moral character to be played off against his material attributes. Both in the past and the present, the

wealth of rich and successful men is often dismissed as having been gained through cheating and the rich man is put in his place by accusation of low moral status. Several writers have mentioned this characteristic of peasant communities.[3]

This would seem to contradict the commonly held view that different criteria of rank tend to coincide. *Campbell*, for example, clearly shows how amongst the Sarakatsani an 'honourable' man needs wealth, manpower and other material attributes in order to defend his 'honour' or moral worth. On the other hand, wealth and numbers without honour is 'a prestige which is at best equivocal'. But in Valloire there is, apparently, an inverse relationship between moral and material attributes. This is the result of several particular circumstances. The community is obsessed by equality; the ability to play off material and moral attributes against each other helps to maintain equality. In Valloire, as we shall see in the next section, material wealth seldom leads to power over people. Villagers can, therefore, afford to criticize and challenge the morality of the wealthy. Lastly, in Valloire, these criticisms of a man's moral worth are not open challenges but go on behind his back in gossip. Valloire does not have the same atmosphere as many Mediterranean com-munities where men strut proudly in cafés and knives are quickly drawn.[4] A man does not need wealth or supporters to protect his honour, when it is never openly challenged.

In Valloire, as in many peasant societies, moral characteristics are particularly important in ranking. In Valloire one hears comments on moral character more often than on material attributes. Much work on Mediterranean communities brings out the emphasis on 'honour' i.e. moral worth.[5] There are several reasons why moral characteristics are so important. Firstly, in a face-to-face community, where people have lived most of their lives in close interaction, all details of their own and their family's behaviour in the past and the present are known. Material is thus available on which moral evaluations can be made which is not available, for example, in many urban societies. Secondly, in the past in Valloire the material attributes of a family or individual were largely a matter of chance. Where property is divided equally between all children wealth will depend largely on demographic accidents and the point of time in the develop-mental cycle of the family. An only son will be wealthy; many sons will start with little. Where the chief lines of solidarity are lines of kinship, the number of supporters a man can muster will also depend on demographic factors. In an economy open to risks, wealth may depend on good weather, well-placed fields, lack of sickness and other factors largely outside a man's control. On the other hand, a man is felt to be responsible for his moral character. To evaluate a man according to his moral worth is to evaluate what he himself controls. Thirdly, moral character, which is evaluated by judgements rather than objective measurements such as number of fields, examinations passed and so on, is most open to different interpretations. This way of ranking is most suitable in a society where many disparate ranking hierarchies are constructed and where ranking expresses the speaker's relationship to the man ranked rather than being the expression of a unified hierarchy. Lastly, the emphasis on morality can be used to illustrate the ideal equality of all. All men are born morally equal even though they may be born into different material circumstances.

Lack of Consensus

Although villagers rank each other there is no consensus, which would be necessary for the establishment of a single-ranked hierarchy. In general villagers will attempt to place themselves at the top of any hierarchy—as with the large landowner who belittled the wealth of his *nouveau riche* employer. Villagers will generally claim high status for their relations as the social status of a man is closely connected with that of his family. Villagers expect their reputations to be defended by those with whom they have close relations—for example, relationships of exchanging assistance, common activity and gossip. For these close relations to continue, equality and trust must be maintained. Extreme criticism would destroy both. On the other hand, families who have quarrelled (are *fâchés* with each other) are expected to spread scandalous stories about each other, to destroy each other's reputations.

What we are in fact seeing in this process of ranking is competitive bidding for prestige. Villagers compete verbally for prestige rather than for power expressed in the deferential behaviour of others. Because equality is the norm, claims to prestige are never accepted. Because this is a competition, each villager produces a different ranked hierarchy of others according to his own particular position and relationships. This competitive element in ranking explains the lack of interest shown by villagers in the relative rank of outsiders. In general, villagers are only concerned with their own ranking *vis à vis* other villagers.

As I mentioned above, disparate hierarchies can be produced through the manipulation of the many cross-cutting criteria for ranking. Another significant factor is the way in which the same behaviour can be interpreted in different ways. This can be illustrated by looking at wedding ceremonies. Villager weddings are watched by all the village and are topics of great interest. They are occasions when village families put themselves on show and notice is taken of the size of the wedding and who is asked. Villagers distinguish between two main types of wedding —the *grand mariage* and the *mariage ordinaire*, or *du pays*. They vary according to the length of the bride's dress, the number of guests, the quality and length of the festivities.

Last summer two weddings were held in Valloire in the same month. One was the marriage of the son of the rich café owner who married the rude and vulgar girl from Marseilles, mentioned above. The couple had been living openly together for the last six months. A *grand mariage* was held. There were 100 guests; the food was lavish and the celebrations went on all night. The other wedding was between the son of a farming family and a girl from the valley. A *mariage ordinaire* was held. There were only twenty guests and the celebrations were modest.

When asking about weddings in general, I was given six main reasons for giving a large/small wedding. The reasons were: (1) the wealth of the families involved; (2) the *situation* of the familes; (3) to *faire honneur*, i.e. to impress others, generally implying that they were snobs; (4) the number of relatives living locally and therefore likely to come to the wedding; (5) whether or not either family was in mourning and (6) the personal preference of the couple. Thus there are reasons for the size and grandness of a wedding which can give or belittle status— for example, wealth, *situation*, to *faire honneur*; and there are reasons which claim that finery at a wedding is not connected with status seeking—for example, the number of relatives, whether or not the families are in mourning, the preference of the couple.

At the time of the two weddings, I asked many people why, in the first place a *grand mariage* had been held and, in the second case, a small wedding. The reasons given varied according to the relationship and existing attitude of the speaker to the families concerned and also the way in which the evaluation would reflect on the speaker's own status. For example, a woman who came from a similar background and was on friendly terms with the second family said that the wedding had been small because the family was in mourning. Two other villagers told me with a sneer that the wedding had been small because they had 'little money'. Several guests and relatives of the café owners told me that the wedding was large because there were many relatives, thus rejecting claims by others that the wedding was large because the family were snobs and wanted to appear rich. Others villagers who had a low opinion of the family concerned, contrasted the show of finery with the bad manners and immodesty of the bride. No villager changed his existing attitude to the families—whether it was favourable or unfavourable—on account of the marriage ceremonies.

Differing Contexts for Ranking

What a villager says of another will depend on the context i.e., with whom the speaker associates himself and his opponent. A villager will not run down another villager in front of an outsider as this would be to belittle his own status as a villager. Similarly, a villager will not run down his brother in front of another family as this would be to belittle the status of his family and therefore himself. Thus, as the context changes, someone placed as an equal can be considered an unequal. This explains how a village can appear, at the same time, to be a united community of equals and a collection of competing hostile individuals. It is because, in relation to the outside, villagers maintain equality; but, between themselves, they emphasize differences.

So far I have been concerned with how and why ranking occurs in a community of 'equals'. Now I will make the picture more complex by taking an historical approach and looking at the effect which increasing and differential contact with the outside has had on social status in the village. Contact with the outside has introduced difference in wealth, power and style of life. I will consider the extent to which these differences have been translated into power and prestige within the village. Contact with the outside has also led to the introduction of new criteria for ranking into the village. I will look at the effect which this has had on the process of ranking.

THE TRADITIONAL RICH FAMILIES

Around the turn of the century, there were seven or eight families in Valloire who are now called the *familles riches* or the *clique*. These families owned the best flat land in the village. As farming was the chief form of livelihood, good land meant wealth. They could work large farms through employing casual labour in the village. As this was the only form of cash employment in the village, they controlled the market and could pay low wages.

Several of these families were helped in their rise to fortune by demographic chance. For example, where there was only one child it meant that the family lands were not divided on inheritance. At this time there was a conscious effort in most families to consolidate their wealth through marriage between cousins and other relatives; and through migrants and the many unmarried siblings not claiming their inheritance but leaving the land in the hands of one brother who would continue the family name. Some families were luckier than others. One rich family began its rise to wealth by a lucky inheritance from an unmarried uncle and later consolidated the family property in an uncle/niece marriage.

However, the position of these families rested largely on sources of wealth and power available to them as middlemen controlling contact between the village and the outside world. All the rich families ran some kind of commerce in the village —a café or small shop. This trade gave them an income in addition to agriculture and, more important, often put villagers in debt to them. Goods were sold for cash and ten per cent interest was charged on credit and loans. Dealing in cash, these men were the chief moneylenders in the village. Often, when debts could not be paid off, property and animals were confiscated.

These families maintained their wealth by intermarrying between themselves. As they could afford to give their daughters large dowries, they could make good marriages. Because of their early contacts with the outside, these rich families were the first to marry outsiders and bring them back to the village. (Poorer villagers who migrated at this time often married outsiders but seldom had the means to bring them back to the village to a standard of living they expected.)

The rich families held official state appointments in the village —for example, the post of lawyer, J.P., tax collector and postmaster. They gained these posts through their good education and contacts. These positions gave additional cash incomes and also power in the village.

These families monopolized the council and the position of mayor. As one villager said: 'We had to vote for them. They had the *puissance*. If we didn't do as they said they could make life difficult if we wanted to buy things at the post office or in the shops.' Holding these positions was profitable. The county administration gave the village grants to repair flood damage, build roads and so on. Today villagers say that these grants went into the pockets of the councillors. The rich families often had links of kinship and friendship with the officials in the *département*. As one descendant of a rich family said: 'We knew everyone then.'

These rich families set themselves apart from the village by adopting a different style of life. A villager, not herself rich, but friendly with a woman who had been, said: 'They were real *bourgeoisie*. They knew how to live (*savoir vivre*). I used to go to tea with this lady. She would receive and entertain me in a way that you don't see now. We would talk of books, the wireless and other general topics. Now women only know how to gossip.' Most of the rich families spoke French rather than *patois*. This was often because, when an outside marriage was made, French was the language of the household and the language learnt by the children. The houses of the traditional rich are distinguishable from those of other villagers even today—in the presence of easy chairs, rugs on the floor, old furniture in the local style, pictures, books and so on.

These rich families were treated with respect in the village. Villagers used the *vous* form of speech when addressing them and, more often than not, called them by their surnames. A villager told me how one man would strongly reprimand young men who did not raise their caps and say '*Bonjour Monsieur. . . .*'

The villager concluded that now the young men have no manners and one does not see such *politesse* in the village today. *Whymper*, an English climber writing of Valloire in 1860, describes a fire breaking out in the village saying, 'my old friend the mayor was there in full force striking the ground with his stick and vociferating "Work, Work"'. Such orders from a mayor today would be unacceptable.

Thus limited and differential contact with the outside gave new resources of power and wealth to a few village families. These families set themselves up as a village aristocracy, translating their wealth into power and prestige, demanding respect and deference.

After the First World War the rich families lost their wealth and influence in the village. Several rich families were left without a male heir after heavy losses in the war. Families dwindled as members migrated. Migration was particularly heavy from the rich families who had better education, contacts and skill in dealing with the outside world. Those who remained usually stayed because of misfortune, illness or lack of ability. Being more choosy in their marriage partners, several remained unmarried and the family died out. As agriculture declined in the village, those rich families who had invested in land found their wealth unproductive. As more opportunities for wage labour were opened in the village, the rich families could no longer find cheap labour to work their land. Cash incomes, bank loans, government grants and social security meant that ordinary villagers no longer depended on these families for loans or goods. The professional posts of lawyer, J.P., tax collector, were moved to the nearby town as the rural population declined. As ordinary villagers learnt to read, write and speak French, and themselves had contacts outside the village through migrant relatives, the influence of the rich families declined and their way of life became less distinctive. The rich families lost their political contacts in the county administration as local aristocracy were replaced by 'experts' from Paris and Marseilles. Because of this, their declining influence, and various political upheavals resulting from tourist development, the rich families lost their seats on the council and position of mayor.

The present-day position of the descendants of these rich families can only be understood in the light of this history. Today the descendants of five of these rich families live in the village. They are accorded certain signs of respect. Most villagers when speaking to them use the *vous* form of speech, use their surname and talk about such 'neutral' topics as the weather. They are not on familiar terms with other villagers. Their menfolk are seldom seen in the bars and there is little visiting or exchange of help between them and other villagers. This respect accorded them and the social distance which exists between them and other villagers is often the direct result of having spent much of their life outside or, in the case of women married into the rich families, of being outsiders. This is an indirect result of 'rich family' status. In many cases social distance exists between previous rich and ordinary families because of the lack of kinship ties. This is important as much mutual aid, familiarity and visiting runs along lines of kinship.

Although they are treated with respect, everyone realizes that these rich families no longer have any influence in the community and are not as wealthy as the new shopkeepers. They generally dress better, speak more correct French, are more at ease with educated outsiders and live in some of the largest and best furnished houses in the village; but many ordinary villagers and their migrant children have adopted a style of life similar to these rich families. They are treated to their face as superior but the grounds for their superiority have disappeared.

Changes in the power structure and loss of status make it possible for ordinary families to prove themselves as good, if not better, than their past superiors. They often accuse the traditional rich of gaining their wealth through dishonesty, cheating and exploitation. It is said that they made false agreements, taking advantage of the illiteracy of others; that they held back the development of the valley in order to maintain their own monopoly of wealth and power; that they embezzled village funds. Their present-day poverty is explained, in terms of their past wickedness. Villagers cite the saying 'Dishonesty flowers but does not seed itself', pointing to the high number of spinsters in the traditional rich families in contrast to the prestigious and fruitful marriages made by children of ordinary villagers. In this way accusations of immorality annul claims to wealth and high status.

The descendants of these rich families, when speaking of social rank in the village, stress their superiority by emphasizing their education, better manners and traditional family standing. They mock at the 'put on' bourgeois accents of the *nouveaux riches*, the lack of 'culture' in the village and the 'stupidity' of many villagers illustrated in the political muddles of tourist development. They often tell of the dishonesty and double-dealing employed by the present rich in acquiring their new wealth.

The ambiguous position of the descendants of the traditional rich families in the village today often leads to the withdrawal of these families from the social life of the village and a reliance on outsider friends and relatives for company. The daughter of one of the rich families, who was brought up in another village, says that she prefers to go to her natal village where everyone calls her *tu* and treats her with familiarity. She feels that, in Valloire, villagers avoid her as they do not know how to address her. However, three families, descendants of the traditional rich families, do take considerable part in the village: one keeps a shop, another a café and hotel and one is secretary to the mayor. These people are treated with familiarity—primarily because of their everyday contact with villagers through their work. However, the families from which they come are only mentioned occasionally in the tales of the 'wicked rich families'. Perhaps they have been able to play a more active part in the village because their association was marginal or perhaps, on the other hand, the 'difference' and 'wickedness' of their families in the past are played down because of their social acceptance today. Prestige depends not on characteristics but rather actual transactions.[6] The separateness of most traditional rich families in the past is emphasized because of their present-day withdrawal from the village scene. Criticism is possible today because few villagers have much to do with them.

THE 'ÉVOLUÉ'/'NON-ÉVOLUÉ' DISTINCTION

Differences in power and wealth were produced in the past through limited contact with the outside world. Today each villager has extensive knowledge of and contacts with the outside and differences between the way of life in the village and the outside are being eroded.

Contact with the outside world and increasing cash incomes

have led to the adoption of a modern pattern of consumption in the village. Many houses have been converted inside. Heating and cooking by wood is being replaced by coal and oil. Most houses have washing-machines and television. A few families have planted flowers around their houses. All young people own cars. Brightly coloured, modern-styled, shop-bought clothes are replacing the predominantly black, home-made, endlessly repaired clothes. The traditional country diet—in which few food items were bought and meat only eaten occasionally—is being replaced by the modern urban diet. This adoption of a modern pattern of consumption, with its emphasis on comfort and appearances, contrasts with the traditional pattern of life where a high value was placed on thrift. The butcher in Valloire indicated this distinction when he said that change in Valloire could be summed up like this: 'Before the war we had a sum of work to do; now we must have a sum of money.'[7] Before, work was an end in itself. Now, work is for money and the end is the things that can be bought with money. In Valloire, the adoption of a modern consumption pattern divides the village into two visibly distinct groups—those who have a modern comfortable way of life who are called *les évolués*; and those who continue to live in the traditional manner who are called *les non-évolués*. These two groups differ in their pattern of consumption; the language they speak—French or *patois*; the ease or discomfort they feel in the company of outsiders; and in their values and expectations.

In general the distinction between *évolué* and *non-évolué* corresponds to differences in age. Most people born in the last century live or lived according to the traditional pattern of life (except, to a certain extent, the 'rich families'). Now all young people in the village have much the same life style, which differs little from outside, urban France. It is within the middle age group of 40–70 years that differences exist between people of the same age and the distinction between *évolué* and *non-évolué* is relevant. Here the style of life is largely determined by the degree of contact with the outside world. Villagers returning to the village in retirement continue to live in the style to which they were accustomed outside. Where an outsider has married into the village, she may bring changes in behaviour directly into the family. Villagers who have children living with them may modify

E

their standard of living in accordance with the expectations of their children. Shop- and hotel-keepers, whose work brings them into contact with outsiders, are most likely to adopt modern standards of living. Those who continue to work the land are most likely to maintain the traditional pattern of living, which was well adapted to farming. Farming means dirt which is incompatible with many of the new consumption symbols; and farming gives a lower cash income with which to buy these things.

In Valloire, it is the women who bring the greatest changes in the style of life and behaviour. Women have most to gain from the comforts of modern living—a more comfortable house, labour-saving gadgets, and so on. In general, the wife has the greatest say and considerable autonomy in household expenditure. Women are concerned with the future and education of their children and often press for change for their sake. Women more often move on marriage. In the last ten years several wives have come from urban areas bringing with them an urban style of life. Wives are more often 'strangers' in their husband's community. Where less is known of them, they will be more concerned with the appearance of things and so with consumption symbols. For the last fifty years, few women have been prepared to marry a farmer with all the hard work it entails for the wife. Thus many people who work the land in Valloire are bachelors. These '*vieux garçons*' form the traditionalist core of the village. They have no wives or children demanding change.

Today it is widely acknowledged that the richest people in the village are the tradesmen who run the three hotels, three bars, four shops, two bakeries and one garage. The ideal future for a young married couple in the community is a small business. In 1968–1969, four additional shops were opened in the valley by young couples from Valloire. However the present-day *commerçants* are all second-generation tradesmen as only they have the sufficient capital and experience to start in trade. Commerce is heavily dependent on family labour and trade expands as the children of tradesmen marry and are given their own business. There is thus a concentration of wealth in a few families. For example, one family, with four sons, controls three bars, a hotel and restaurant; another family, with three sons, controls a hotel, two shops and a garage.

However, in general, the *évolués* and the newly rich tradesmen have not attempted to translate their wealth into power and prestige within the village. In behaviour, there is an emphasis on equality, which I outlined earlier. Although the *évolués* have adopted a modern way of life, more urban manners, and are easily distinguishable by their clothes and possessions, they do not command any respect or deference from others on account of this. Transactions between villagers and tradesmen are largely on a cash basis. Tradesmen give small favours in return for a customer's patronage, but no large debts are accumulated as in the past. The new rich do not play a noticeable part in local politics. Many deliberately keep out of politics because the criticism which it invariably invokes could damage trade. The decline of the 'rich families' has resulted in the removal of the traditional village leadership level. This means that villagers, who consider themselves equal, are forced into positions where decisions must be made and enforced and leadership has to be assumed. This could lead to political competition for power within the village but, in fact, leads to apathy and an avoidance of decisions. The new rich have not succeeded the traditional rich as the village aristocracy. The differences between the *évolués* and the *non-évolués* have not led to the formation of two distinct classes or status groups. There are several reasons to account for this difference in behaviour between the traditional rich and the *évolués*.

CONDITIONS UNDER WHICH POWER AND PRESTIGE ARE SOUGHT

People who set themselves up as superior are often criticized and their wealth or claims to prestige are rejected and belittled by according them a low moral status. The force of criticism levelled against someone who sought power and prestige is illustrated by the career of a returning migrant who, as mayor, introduced plans for the development of a large ski resort at Valloire. He was active as mayor, taking control of plans and often acting in a superior manner towards other villagers. Soon after taking office, stories began to circulate about his dishonesty, deceit and the extent to which he was out for personal profit. Many villagers talked of his 'wickedness' in much the same terms as they talk of the traditional rich. This personal criticism and scandal was a major factor in his downfall. He, together with his plans for development, was thrown out. He left the village and today 'does not dare show his face there'.

The sanctions imposed on those who offend against the norm of equality can go further than critical gossip and can lead to a withdrawal of sociability and help. Villagers are only willing to ask for and give help to those whom they feel to be their equals as, in this way, their own independence is safeguarded.

Thus, an important factor accounting for whether or not an individual (or a group) will seek deference and power is the extent to which he can withstand criticism, illwill and the withdrawal of mutual aid and sociability which can only flow between equals. The traditional rich could afford to remain aloof. They depended for their wealth largely on outside sources of income. They had friends and kin outside the village with whom they spent their time and whose opinions they valued. The new rich can less afford criticism. They are dependent, to a certain extent, on the goodwill of village customers in shops and in bars. Their concern with public opinion is illustrated by the baker who, economically, might have profited from supporting the mayor but said that he had sided with the majority against him because he did not want it said that he had sold out and cheated other villagers, especially as his sons would continue to live in the village and so suffer for his action. In addition, the present dislike and distrust of the traditional rich act as a restraint on the new rich who do not want to follow their example or to be associated with them.

Power and prestige in the village will only be sought if it brings further profits. Visible power in the community was profitable to the traditional rich. It gave them cheap labour in the village and helped them secure grants and professional appointments from the outside. Today, with improved communications and wider contacts between the village and the outside world, many are not concerned with their prestige in the village. The new rich tend to withdraw from village life rather than assert their superiority there. This is linked with a general decline in community activities which is due, in part, to a declining and ageing population.

An important factor accounting for the extent to which differences in power and prestige will lead to distinct status groups is the extent to which there is a coincidence between the different components of high status. The traditional rich were both wealthy and powerful. They had the *puissance* to exact cheap labour, to demand repayment of debts. Their economic control of others meant that few dared vote against them when they stood for political office. They had the power to demand respect and the independence to avoid the sanctions. Through intermarriage amongst themselves and marriage with outsiders, they managed to limit kinship ties within the community; such ties could have acted as levelling factors. There are several cases where kinship connections were and still are claimed by ordinary villagers. These were laughed at and rejected. Today no-one in Valloire has high status in all spheres—wealth, power, good manners, family connections and so on. This means that any claim for status on one count can be easily discredited by the introduction of another factor. Present differences in wealth and style of life are relatively recent. Detailed personal and family histories are known and from these evidence can be drawn to annul claims to superiority.

Differences in wealth, power or style of life are cut across by other factors such as age, which implies inferiority/superiority or kinship which implies equality and unity. Differences between *évolué* and *non-évolué* are cancelled by kinship links which are very important in a community where kin share in property and reputation. Children acknowledge the values of the traditional way of life and do not claim 'modern' superiority, because they respect their parents. There is little conflict between the two ways of life, which could be expressed in prestige competition or power seeking, since parents share in the modernity and success of their children. Moreover, an *évolué* claiming high status on account of modernity can easily be cut down by others pointing to the backwardness of his old uncle.

The difference between *évolué/non-évolué* is largely a division between young and old. Thus any superiority attached to being *évolué* is limited by the traditional deference which is expected to be shown by the young to the old. Although many younger people may be more 'successful' and have more technical knowledge than the old, in many face-to-face situations this superiority-through-modernity is played down. The young and the old have always been expected to keep their own company, organize their

own affairs and young, unmarried men have always formed a
jeunes group which has been primarily a leisure group but
played a noticeable part in village affairs. For this reason, the
two ways of life—the modern life of the *évolué* young, and the
traditional life of the *non-évolué* old[8]—can exist side by side
with the minimal degree of conflict.

On the other hand, at the time of the traditional rich, differences in wealth and power ran along family lines. The family
was and still is the basic competitive unit in village society.
Thus, differences between families were not cross-cut and so
could be more easily emphasized.

NEW CRITERIA FOR RANKING

The adoption of a modern pattern of consumption introduces
new criteria on which wealth can be evaluated. In the traditional
village system of ranking, wealth was evaluated in terms of land
and stock, i.e. the factors of production. These can only be
evaluated if a man and his property are known well. In modern,
outside terms, wealth is reckoned in terms of consumption, i.e.
cars, furniture, clothes. These criteria of wealth are immediately
noticeable to a stranger. In the traditional system, a man's status
is evaluated in relation to his family; this makes his status relatively static. In the outside world, a man is an individual, ir-
respective of the occupation, wealth or reputation of his family,
because these are generally not known. In the traditional system
of ranking, moral attributes are of great importance for reasons
discussed earlier. In the traditional system, status is reckoned
according to many attributes which are known, and therefore
relevant. In the outside world, status signals are more likely to be
accepted for what they are. In short, according to the traditional
village system of ranking, a man is evaluated for 'what he is'.
According to the modern, outside system of ranking, a man is
evaluated for 'what he does'.

In a French village considered by Pitt-Rivers,[9] these contrasting ways of evaluating status were held by two groups—the
farmers who evaluated themselves by the traditional method
and the non-farming villagers who ranked by modern criteria. In
Valloire, however, all villagers operate in both systems. Extensive personal knowledge of others exists in a community where

ninety per cent of the population was born in the village and are joined by close ties of kinship. Such personal knowledge forms the basis for the traditional manner of ranking. However, many people have adopted the modern pattern of consumption and so can claim status in relation to this, and often like to signal this modern status to outsiders. By increasing the number of ranking criteria, the process of ranking becomes even more confused. It is even easier for anyone to prove himself as good as or better than another. For example, a villager may emphasize the traditional reputation of his ancestors or the modernity of his children according to the scale on which he scores the best.

INCREASING APPEARANCE OF INEQUALITY

Although the *évolué* do not exact deference with their wealth as did the traditional rich, differences in wealth and status symbols are becoming more noticeable in the village. Differences in wealth between ordinary villagers undoubtedly existed in the past but were not emphasized as they are today, for three reasons. Firstly, where thrift and non-consumption was the norm, there were few ways of signalling wealth. In the past, when villagers were economically interdependent, relying on each other's help and where differences in wealth were temporary, a villager would play down his present fortune and give away any surplus as an investment for future help. Today, differences in wealth are based on different occupations and have a greater permanence and so are more likely to be signalled. The extension of the cash market into the village and specialization of the economy make villagers less dependent upon each other's help. They are thus less anxious to distribute or hide their wealth as their ancestors did. Lastly, status symbols are often displayed in order to impress outsiders and, as outsiders are seen more frequently in the village and are beginning to marry and retire into the community, modern status symbols are increasingly displayed. Although this display does little to change the reputation of the individual or the family in the village, it is possible to impress outsiders. In an earlier section, I mentioned a grand and costly wedding that was given by one family. The reputation of this family did not alter in the eyes of the other villagers, whose comments were determined by their previous opinion and relationship to the family. However, the lavishness and modernity of the wedding may have been designed to impress the bride, an outsider, and the outsider guests. In the tourist season almost everyone puts on smarter clothes, clothes being the easiest symbol to change. An increasing show of these modern status symbols can give the impression that inequality is increasing. Villagers see this themselves, saying: 'Before, we were all equal because we were poor. It is these modern differences in wealth which have caused the present jealousy and *animosité*.'

Villagers also point to the increase in formal behaviour in the village as an indication of an increase in inequality. In general, behaviour in the outside world is more formal and expresses greater social distance than in the village, where behaviour is informal and familiar. For example, outside the village, the *vous* form of speech is often used, there is little joking or gossip and there is greater concern with one's image. The main reason for this difference is that, outside, people have less personal knowledge of each other. In the last decade, behaviour in the village has become more formal, especially between women, for two reasons. Firstly, some villagers, especially those who have spent some time outside the village, try to behave more like outsiders as they feel that this is the proper way to behave—true *politesse*. Secondly, knowledge of others has declined as more outsiders have come to live in the village. An increase in formal behaviour can give the impression that the former equality and familiarity are declining. Formal behaviour can be thought to indicate superiority/inferiority as it did when the traditional rich behaved in a more formal way. The table below shows the different reasons for using the *vous* or the *tu* forms of speech. It can be used with any other element of formal/informal behaviour:

Vous form	*tu* form
1. good breeding	ill breeding
2. respect	lack of respect
3. inequality	equality
4. to be *fier* (proud)	to be *familier* (familiar)
5. indicates lack of knowledge	indicates personal knowledge

This table shows the slippery path that each villager must tread between being neither *fier* nor too *familier*. If a villager acts formally, for whatever reason, he may be accused of pride, of denying equality and familiarity. If a villager acts informally, he can be accused of rudeness, lack of respect or illbreeding. This table also shows, as did the earlier description of weddings, the way in which behaviour can be interpreted differently according to the relationship between the speaker and the actor. Also, from the table, it can be seen that if formal behaviour in the village increases because of (1) (knowledge of, and a desire to have, better manners), or (5) (people in the village knowing each other less well), then villagers can accuse each other of (3) (asserting inequality) and (4) (being proud).

CONCLUSIONS

I began by examining the apparent contradiction between the lack of deferential behaviour and the assertions of equality on the one hand and the willingness of villagers to rank each other on the other hand. The emphasis on equality is based on common kinship; a common culture distinctive from the world outside; universal ownership of land leading to self-sufficiency, together with exchange of help between equals; feelings of solidarity arising out of common knowledge; interaction of the same people in different roles; and the allocation of roles and positions of authority according to ascribed rather than achieved roles. This emphasis on equality was apparent in local politics and on public occasions. However, when villagers spoke about each other, they readily made judgements, frank in a way, which would seem to contradict the emphasis on equality.

This apparent contradiction was explained in three ways:

(a) much of the verbal ranking that occurs in the village is, in fact, an attempt to restore equality, following a claim to superior status or an accusation of inferior status. These claims or accusations are rejected and annulled by introducing other criteria for ranking by which the offending villager is brought down or raised up. Ranking is thus a mechanism by which equality is maintained.

(b) Although villagers rank each other, there is none of the consensus necessary for the establishment of ranked status groups. Each villager will rank others in a different way according to his relationship to them. Each villager, when setting up a status hierarchy, will attempt to put himself at the top, followed by his family and friends. He will try to put his enemies at the bottom. This type of ranking is a form of competition for prestige. The competitive bids are, however, not accepted. No prizes, in the form of deference, are given. Ranking is thus a jostling for position through which equality is maintained.

Many disparate hierarchies can be set up and dismissed because there are diverse ranking criteria which cut across each other, and because there are many different ways in which the same behaviour can be interpreted—as I showed in the description of weddings and later in the analysis of formal and informal behaviour.

(c) What a villager says of another one depends on the context, i.e. with whom he identifies himself and the person of whom he is speaking. This means that, in relation to the outside, villagers will maintain equality but, between themselves, they will emphasize differences.

It is important to distinguish between material and moral attributes of rank. In a peasant village, moral attitudes are particularly important since the evidence on which such evaluations can be made is well known; a man is felt to have more control over his moral characteristics than over his material attributes; and, above all, moral character is most open to different interpretations and so can be manipulated to construct the desired ranked hierarchy. An inverse relationship is commonly found between material and moral elements in so far as a successful man is often accused of dishonesty. This is an important mechanism for the maintenance of equality and is possible in Valloire where material wealth seldom leads to power over people and where accusations of dishonesty do not constitute open challenges.

However, these arguments are not sufficient to explain ranking in Valloire, where increasing contact with the outside has introduced considerable differences in wealth, power and style of life into the village. By contrasting the position of the traditional rich and the *évolués* or new rich, I attempted to show the conditions under which these differences are or are not translated into power and prestige in the village. The process is effected by:

(a) The extent to which the wealthy group or individual is

economically and socially independent and so can withstand the criticism and the withdrawal of mutual aid and sociability customary only between equals;

(b) The extent to which visible power and prestige bring further profits in the form of increased resources or influence;

(c) The extent to which there is a coincidence between the different components of high status; and

(d) The extent to which differences in wealth, power or style of life coincide with or are cut across by other lines of solidarity or social distance, such as kinship or age.

The different configuration of these factors, largely a result of the different positions of the traditional rich and the *évolués* in the contacts between the village and the outside, accounts for the difference between the former, who set themselves up as village aristocracy and the latter who do not constitute a distinct status group.

Finally I considered the effect which the introduction of new criteria for ranking, through the introduction of a modern pattern of consumption, has had in the village. There is a difference between traditional (village) and modern (outside) criteria of ranking. The former emphasize factors of production to indicate wealth, morality, family reputation and all aspects of status; the latter emphasize factors of consumption to indicate wealth, appearances and the individual. In Valloire because personal knowledge remains, traditional criteria are still relevant. But, because a modern pattern of consumption had been adopted and villagers wish to impress outsiders, modern consumption symbols are used to signal wealth.

This more visible signalling of wealth through consumption, together with the adoption of an outsider and so more 'formal' way of behaving, and increased economic and social independence give the impression that former 'equality' is being replaced by 'inequality'. But in Valloire each villager can lay claim to status in traditional terms through their ancestors and to status in modern terms through their children. This produces confusion and means that it is even easier for anyone to prove himself as good as or better than another.

NOTES

1. *Stacey* and *Frankenberg*.
2. *Goffman* (1).
3. *Foster* (3). See also *Banfield*.
4. *Campbell*. See also *Simic*, p. 89.
5. *Peristiany*.
6. See also Chapter 10.
7. 'Avant la guerre nous avions une somme de travail à faire. Maintenant il nous faut une somme d'argent.'
8. The contrast is overstated but is in line with the sharp distinction the villagers make themselves between the traditional and the modern.
9. *Pitt-Rivers* (1).

4

A Politician in Valloire[1]

Valloire is a small mountain community in the French Alps, showing signs of the contemporary malaise of peasant farming, described in other parts of this book. The limited resources of the agricultural system did not permit competition on an open market and the result was a steady depopulation that has drained the peasant enterprise of its essential resource—labour.[2]

However, the family production unit, self-contained and self-sufficient—where the chef de famille *is still the* chef d'entreprise *—remains the ideal. Agricultural development has been unsuccessful both because of considerable climatic and physical disadvantages and because of the villagers' belief that farming is finished and will never provide an acceptable income or livelihood.*

Regional industrial development provided the villagers with some employment between 1918 and the outbreak of the Second World War, when an aluminium factory run by hydro-electric power was built in the town at the bottom of the valley. However, labouring jobs constructing dams and conduits for the factory, and other labour opportunities in reconstruction work on river banks, roads and bridges financed by the government after severe flood damage, were only temporary stop-gaps. It was not until after the Second World War that an economic future of any stability or permanence was opened up to the inhabitants of the valley. With improved transport facilities, the introduction of the paid holiday and the increasing popularity of camping, mountaineering and skiing, tourists began to come in increasing numbers to the valley in both summer and winter. Those very things that had made life difficult for the villagers and stood in the way of efficient farming—mountains, snow, and hot sun—

*assumed a positive value in the eyes of outsiders who were eager
to enjoy these natural resources of the valley.*

*As villages in other valleys of the region became skiing or
climbing resorts where land and house prices soared, the people
of Valloire began to visualize a new future in similar terms. A
myth of development grew, suggesting that there were resources
available in village and valley which, if managed in the right
way, would bring or restore prosperity to everyone. The attitude
developed that these future opportunities ought somehow to
be shared because they offered a chance to sustain and revive a
dying community whose members shared a common set of
values.*

*The excitement at stories of successful development in other
villages was increased by the success in Valloire of a few villagers
who let houses to visitors, sold land for building or opened guest
houses. However, the majority had neither the resources nor the
ability to negotiate sales or start up businesses. For them the new
life remained just a hope, an aspiration which all shared but few
were able to articulate in terms of either policy or action. Their
hopes, fears and jealousies found expression only in rumour,
gossip and local politics.*

*The situation was such that while there was no consensus about
either the desired end itself or the policies by which it should be
achieved, the expectations surrounding it were clearly spelled
out in terms of shared values, but these norms were not sufficient
to provide an explicit answer as to how to handle, or initiate
action in, a novel situation. As a result, any steps that were taken
towards development became matters of controversy, and those
concerned suspected of furthering their own ends through using
immoral strategies that threatened the opportunities of other
villagers less wealthy or less cunning.*

*The majority of villagers looked to the local leadership some-
how to make their dreams come true, to solve the problems of
fitting the norms of equality and independence which they valued,
into a policy of innovatory action. And in Marcel Martin, many
people thought that they had found someone who was of the
right moral character and personal acumen to fulfil their ambitions.*

MARTIN'S CAREER

Marcel Martin was born in Valloire in 1909 of a family long established in the commune—*gens du pays*. He left the village when he was sixteen and made his career in the French Air Force. He was successful, becoming a senior officer[3] and marrying the daughter of a prosperous businessman in Provence.

All the members of the family lived outside the village by the early 1950s, only returning to their house there for holidays. Martin was a keen skier, and when skiing in neighbouring resorts after the war, he had ideas about developing facilities for the sport in the Valloire valley.

A small ski-lift and ski-run had been constructed at Valloire in 1954 by the *Syndicat Intercommunal*,[4] a society set up to further tourist development in the valley. Though it had been a controversial project, it had been successful in attracting outsiders and increasing the trade of local hotels, so that after the lift had proved its worth for several years and the early controversies had died down, many villagers were in favour of further developments in a similar direction. Thus, Martin decided that the time was ready for him to put his plans into action, and he drew up a *liste*[5] for the sessional Municipal Elections of 1959.[6] Through seeking support in the right places and some hard canvassing on the right issues, seven of his *liste* were elected as councillors and he himself elected as mayor. The general view of villagers today is that he was successful because his propaganda fitted the needs and mood of the moment. Both influential leaders and the majority of villagers believed that Martin would achieve what they wanted. Martin was also elected to the presidency of the *Syndicat Intercommunal*, thus securing the authority to act at both communal and inter-communal levels.

Martin initially had the idea of starting a land co-operative for the group ownership and consolidation of land to be laid out and resold as building plots. However, this plan was unacceptable to both the villagers and the outside financiers whom Martin had hoped to interest. As a result, he was forced to seek the help of the local government development board, after failing to raise funds from private backers. This local board, S E D H A, was a branch of the Paris-based S C E T, in turn dependent on financial grants from the *Service du Domaine* to develop problem areas.[7]

S E D H A agreed to help but imposed certain conditions and a delay of one year. Martin used this year to set up a camp site, build a new road and provide other amenities for tourists. In both the things he chose to do and the manner in which he did them, Martin built up a certain amount of unpopularity for himself as well as putting the commune under mortgage, or as many saw it, into debt.

In early 1962, S E D H A turned it interests towards Valloire. S E D H A was now being instructed by S C E T that the valley was to be developed as one of the major ski resorts of the southern Alps. Martin's original plans for Valloire were to be supplemented and overshadowed by the creation of a resort with accommodation for about 10,00 visitors.

The scale of the development Martin now found himself committed to, as mayor and President of the *Syndicat Intercommunal*, was very much larger than anything that either he had proposed or the villagers had anticipated. However, the new resort itself was to be higher up the valley and well away from the village of Valloire, so that the new plans did not seem to threaten the village directly, and could even be advantageous to it through opportunities for increased trade. Though Martin came in for some criticism from other communes in the valley directly affected by the proposed resort, his plans for Valloire had received official sanction, and his political support in the village remained strong.

However, when in the summer of 1962, the *Service du Domaine* finally approved the purchase of land in Valloire for Martin's original plan, they only offered 50 centimes per square metre.[8] Since other land was selling privately at the time for between 10 and 40 francs the square metre, this caused an uproar. A few months after this shock, came a second blow when S C E T announced its determination to build a co-ordinating centre for all the new developments in the valley. The centre was to be sited on the Plaine of Valloire, and the necessary land purchased at a price of one franc per square metre. The Plaine was a triangular area of flat land lying between the village and the convergence of two rivers. It was not only the best agricultural land in the commune, but also an area of great natural beauty with orchards and lines of poplars along the river banks. Both the project and the price were entirely unacceptable not only to the villagers, but also to Martin and the S E D H A officials who realized the villagers' feelings.

However, S C E T was adamant, the plan was confirmed and scheduled to come up before a public enquiry early in 1964.[9] On the result of this enquiry depended the future of the development in the valley as a whole as S C E T was determined not to have development without the centre, and as a governing body acting in the public interest, it was unable to undertake development where an enquiry showed public opinion to be against it.

Martin's future also depended on the result of the enquiry, since he had become increasingly identified with the plans of S E D H A and S C E T. His political survival depended on his convincing the electorate that he too was being manipulated rather than being a manipulator. However, the villagers increasingly saw him as the scapegoat for failure, and opposition against him and the plans fused together.

In March 1964, a month before the enquiry, six councillors, three of whom had been on Martin's *liste* in 1959, resigned and formed the *Syndicat de Défense*.[10] The atmosphere became very tense with inflammatory speeches and threats of violence made by both sides—'It was like the revolution . . . with sticks (*batons*) in the streets.' Both sides held meetings and, in one, S E D H A's representatives were shouted down and were unable to speak.

In May 1964, the results of the enquiry showed an overwhelming majority to be against the centre. S E D H A shelved its plans for Valloire, and turned its interest to other areas. Martin resigned as mayor, and complementary elections were held in July 1964 to replace the councillors who had resigned and to elect a new mayor. Both the new council seats and the mayorship were filled by members of the *Syndicat de Défense*.

CATEGORIES OF PERSONNEL

In order to understand how Martin's behaviour appeared to the villagers and to analyse the strategies behind his actions and policy, it is necessary to look in some detail at the different categories of personnel involved in competition for the prizes of development. Valloire is very much a part of the wider economic and political system of the *département* and of France, and, as such, is superficially like thousands of other villages across that

F

74   *A Politician in Valloire*

country and even in Europe as a whole. However, in certain contexts villagers identify themselves as belonging to a special category of people. This category is most usefully described not in terms of geographical, institutional or market boundaries, but rather in terms of moral concepts, in terms of shared values. As members of a moral community, villagers see themselves as possessing a special set of normative values concerning equality, independence and kinship, a moral code different from the outside world. In most of everyday life these boundaries are latent and not readily perceivable. But in times of crisis the differences become manifest and take on a greater significance. At such moments, both sides suddenly realize that the other is a totally different species of animal. Each category sees itself to have a distinct code of values against which behaviour is measured, reputations made or broken, and according to which negative or positive sanctions may be brought into use.

Villagers see Valloire as a moral community composed of *gens du pays* (insiders), who live in the village and share a common set of values. The village community is contained within a wider social system and forms part of an environment made up of national and regional political, economic and moral structures, which affect the villagers and their values, but which are operated by *étrangers*, that is, outsiders, those who live outside the valley and appear to the villagers to act according to a different code of values.

Linking these two categories is a third, the local leadership category, which is both a product of, and mediator in, the opposition between the villagers and the outsiders. There is no local term for men in the leadership category, although sometimes they may be ironically referred to as *personalités du pays*. This label implies that they are men of the *pays*, while possessing some special distinguishing characteristic or ability. The lack of a more specific or commonly used label is significant, in that, according to the villager's code of values, everyone is equal.

VILLAGERS

The villager category consists of those who are believed to accept the values and attitudes that make up the *mentalité* of members of the moral community, the *gens du pays*. The most important concepts of the *mentalité* are those of *égalité* (equality), *indépendence* (independence) and *parenté* (kinship).

The three concepts are inter-related. In breaking the norms of one, the norms of the other two are likely to be broken. Essentially these are ideals. Everyday behaviour, played out according to the rules for obtaining these ideal ends, often demonstrates failure. The most frequently encountered attitudes are not those of independence, equality or trust between kinsmen, but those of envy, jealousy, and distrust that reflect a failure to achieve these ideals. Moreover, expectations concerning new opportunities are expressed in terms of ideal values. But this frame of reference does not offer clear pragmatic rules for action in a novel situation in which other competitors follow rules different from, or contradicting, those held by villagers.

The ethic of equality is confirmed in much of the villagers' behaviour. Positions of leadership and authority are played down according to the maxim *'Personne commande ici, nous sommes tous copains'* (No one gives any orders around here, we are all buddies). Equality is linked with kinship. Villagers claim that they are all related somehow. 'We are all *cousins or petits cousins.*' Most people know the kin networks of other villagers, just as they know the idiosyncrasies and reputation of every family. Those who do not have cars or modern domestic appliances, claim equal status with those who have, through their children who live in large towns and enjoy all these facilities. Everyone in the village owns land, and believes that one day they will be able to sell this at a high price for development. This theme is a potential basis for equality that cuts across present-day differences in income and occupation.

The norm of *indépendance* means that the family should be a self-contained unit of production and consumption. The ideal of peasant subsistence is to remain independent of external crises. However, in practice there is always a need for help from others, which implies dependence on them. Only kinsmen (who are by definition equal to one another) and those who conduct symmetrical arrangements of mutual aid (*rendre service*) can call on the services of others without appearing to be dependent on them.

Paradoxically, to achieve self-sufficiency is seen as a rejection of equality and a claim to superior status. Actual independence alienates a man from the community, he becomes *fier* (proud, hard) and an *égoiste* (egoist). *Indépendance* can thus become a term of abuse. In one sense *indépendant* is the opposite of *indetté* (indebted); in another it is the opposite of *brave* (fine, upstanding) and *gentil* (kind, someone like us). Applied to the individual it is a term of abuse; used of the group of which the speaker is a member, it is an expression of normative solidarity.

The third set of values are associated with *parenté* (kinship). *Parenté* makes a man one of the *gens du pays* and partly gives him his reputation. To know a man's family name is often sufficient to define a large part of his social reputation and network. The family links past, present and future. Kin connections, family characteristics and property are passed on from generation to generation. What a man inherits from his parents, he must hand on to his children. But particular units of land are not symbols of this continuity; rather it is the productive capacity of land which is valued. Land is not important because it has long been owned by a particular family, but because it is sufficient to feed that family. It represents a unit of production and a means of survival.

The family farm, or firm, should ideally provide work for the whole family, for this ensures its continuity. The emphasis is on continuity, and agriculture is not seen as the only way to achieve this. It is permissible and often necessary to *reconvertir*, to change one's basic means of livelihood in order to ensure survival. These fundamental ideas of continuity are carried over as organizational principles from the family to the level of the community as a whole. The survival of the community, its continuity and the need to find work and wives for the young men, are norms for the public community no less than for the private family.

In short, villagers have at the back of their minds a common set of rules for living. Young and old, rich and poor know that this is what they share as *gens du pays*. Those who need the support of the community, need to be careful not to seek personal rewards whose cost is the breaking of these norms. Those who reject the norms stand on their own and are vulnerable to the pressures that exist in times of crisis. With the collapse of the agricultural economy and the new opportunities offered in the tourist market, this is a moment of crisis for the villagers of Valloire. It is a time for both individual and community to *reconvertir*, in order to survive. But the decision involved, to sell land for money, requires a delicate re-interpretation of fundamental norms in the process of which it is easy to offend public opinion. It involves a new concept of money, rather than labour, as the resource to be capitalized. Most people recognize this, but deprecate it, saying 'In order to live before the war, one had a sum of work to do; now one must have a sum of money.'

OUTSIDERS AND LOCAL LEADERS

The *mentalité* of *étrangers* is not clearly defined by villagers except in that it is 'different' from that of the *gens du pays*. Outsiders are not seen as men in the round. They are beyond the moral community, and only some of their values are relevant, and these are the opposite of villager values. Outsiders want personal profit and put the individual before the group. Outsiders are not to be trusted; they behave with *puissance* (power) rather than *droit* (right). In a situation of crisis they form a background of uniform darkness which highlights the ideals and standards of the villagers.

Villagers recognize that particular individuals or groups of outsiders have different moral codes, some of which are more acceptable than others. The category *étrangers* can be divided into *gens comme nous* (people like us) and *les autres* (the others). However, in a crisis, all are beyond the boundaries of the moral community and pose a threat to its members' interests.

The *mentalité* of the local leaders is a mixture of villager and outsider norms. To be a local leader a man has to show that in addition to possessing the right pragmatic resources and abilities to negotiate successfully with outsiders, he has also the right moral qualities to represent and act for his fellow villagers. The successful leader is the one who achieves a balance between what people would like to see done and how they know it ought to be done.

In Valloire a distinction has to be made between formal and informal leaders. The latter holds no office and in his everyday relations with villagers takes great pains to conform to the norm of equality, even though it is known by everyone that he is richer or cleverer than them. He needs the support of the villagers as clients or employees, and with the former he must preserve particularly carefully the basic rules of mutual aid and *rendre service* (see Chapter 3). He thus controls what is essentially a moral team, unlike the elected official who depends upon transactional support. He is in a stronger position than the latter because he has a far greater bargaining power, which rests on a set of relationships at the same time more flexible and with a deeper legitimacy. He does not have to mobilize and maintain large-scale support; indeed direct personal ties with supporters impose a limit on the size of his effective following.

A formal leader is elected or appointed to an institutionalized office, such as that of mayor or councillor. But the office of mayor is not based upon villager norms nor is it institutionalized in terms of their values. It is, rather, an imposition of the external system, the national French government. As a result, the mayor is subjected to two levels of legitimization and sanction. Firstly, being part of the external political structure, the office is subject to the national legal system, and the sanctions of the external political arena. Secondly, the office is 'fitted' into the village value system, in as far as those who hold the office must be *gens du pays* and therefore must perform the duties of the office in accord with the norms of community morality. A mayor may thus be sanctioned by either side independently, or by both sides simultaneously.

The mayor depends for support on a transactional team of the majority of the electorate, strengthened to the best of his political ability by moral ties with strategically powerful and influential persons. However, dependence on the transactional support of the electorate is based upon a rather tenuous contract which is merely a commitment to help, an undertaking to find an answer to everyone's problems. This may be satisfactory for electioneering programmes but is inadequate for the pragmatic realities of administration. Once the mayor appears to the powerful few, or fickle many, to be no longer acting in the best interests of the commune, then he can be sanctioned. His authority is limited by the tight norms that control his actions. The solidarity that he needs for support is difficult to maintain and can easily be mobilized against him (by rivals), bringing official sanctions to bear upon him. For example, six councillors resigned in 1964, because they felt Martin had offended against village standards. He was thus left with a council smaller than the legal minimum size, and so forced to resign.

In Valloire, to be mayor is to be distrusted. Firstly, the mayor is a mediator between two moral systems, and so fully trusted by the members of neither. Secondly, he is both a person with special rights and a member of a community of equals. He is expected to negotiate with outsiders and to innovate, and he is thereby in constant danger of contravening the norms of equality and group solidarity. He is open to accusations of being proud, snobbish and egoistic; of behaving like an *étranger* rather than one of the *gens du pays*.

Different villagers see the role of mayor as fulfilling different ends. It may be regarded as a sufficient end in itself—giving respect and status in both the eyes of villagers and outsiders. In this case, the costs of office can be born provided a man has a solid moral reputation based on normatively integrated occupational and kin statuses. To others, the office of mayor in a tiny rural commune is no reward in itself; rather it serves as a means to gain greater and wider power. It is seen as a stepping-stone across the divide between the two social and political systems. The costs involved in playing a role in the local political structure are a worthwhile risk in the light of the rewards to be gained through interaction with, and participation in, the outside world.

MARTIN'S REPUTATION

A man's reputation is what is said about him. It is the overall response of people to both actor and role performance; an assessment not only of the results achieved but also of the manner in which they were achieved. There are certain individuals who have reputations fixed at the top or bottom of a scale, and not affected by performance in everyday life. However, most people have reputations that fluctuate according to context, criteria used, and the discussants' intentions.

What is said about a man by those whose support he needs, affects his behaviour by limiting the extent to which he can fulfil his aspirations. But it is also true that what is said about a man can serve to clarify and confirm both values and strategies among the discussants. People's inclinations to think or act may be strengthened or altered in relation to the example of one man's reputation.[11]

I shall now look at the assessment of Martin's reputation after the development crisis in the opinions of members of the three categories outlined above. I use accounts that villagers have given me to illustrate how Martin's reputation was assessed.[12]

VILLAGERS' OPINIONS

In 1959 Martin won the Municipal Election and was chosen as mayor: by 1964 his popularity had declined.

> Martin seemed an excellent choice as Mayor because he was *intelligent* (clever, bright) and had good contacts. At first he promised all sorts of advantages—he said that the last mayor had done nothing and he would change all that. However, all he then did was to try and profit himself. If he had been an *étranger*—someone like you—from outside the village—it would have been understandable. But he was one of us, born here, one of us *gens du pays*—it was like robbing your *parents* (kin) to get money . . .

> Martin made a lot of propaganda before the election, and spoke of all the things that he would do for the commune and the villagers. He was elected because his family was well known and *gentil* (decent). However, once he was in power he behaved like a monster, a scoundrel (*crapule*), a dishonourable man. Instead of benefitting the commune as he said he would, he behaved like a turn-coat and did exactly the opposite—trying to profit himself.
>
> For all the things he did he should have been put in prison. All the other communes in the valley considered that he should have been put in prison, but we did not want to do that because his family was *gentil*.

Martin appears to have been elected because he had the right qualities for the position and seemed to fit the needs of the moment. He possessed the necessary combination of qualities in being one of the *gens du pays*, and yet having acquired sufficient outsider characteristics to enable him to cope with *étrangers* on equal terms. The general promises made in his electioneering propaganda fitted a realized need, although they did not offer a definite policy.

It was only as events hardened and clarified into a programme of development that overt opposition mounted. Having established himself as mayor, he began to behave to the villagers like an outsider. He sought personal gain (they said), and at the expense of the villagers. Both texts mention the family. This serves to affirm his origin and his status; to condemn his actions and at the same time to limit the sanctions used against him.

Villagers saw Martin's behaviour as exploitation. He behaved with *puissance* not *droit*. The trust they had put in him had been betrayed, and he was accused of taking away people's livelihood.

> Martin tried to get land for nothing. He tried to get proprietors to sell their land near the village for only a minimal sum. Without this land farming in Valloire would really be finished. What would men of my age and older do? I am too young to retire and yet too old to work in a hotel. For the young men it is all right, they can learn specialized jobs, or even leave to go elsewhere if they do not like it.

Martin was also blamed for having tried to go too fast and do too much at once, while offering prices for land that were unacceptably low.

> What I object to is that Martin encouraged us proprietors to sell land, saying that we ought to accept ridiculously low prices, while he was hoping to resell at high ones. I would have sold, we all would have sold, if it had been a good price. If Martin had gone a bit slower and got better prices for the proprietors, he might have succeeded.

Martin failed to fit pragmatic actions into a normatively acceptable policy. He failed to handle land sales tactfully, and he had not created sufficient trust in himself with the villagers to carry him over the difficulties of an involved series of transactions with external authorities. Because the low prices appeared to be offered *by him*, people concluded that he was only concerned in making a profit for himself and not for the community as a whole.

> Proprietors would have sold if the price had been good. However, Martin was only offering 1.20 francs a square metre. When people began to complain, he started to talk about prices like 5 or 6 francs, but he did not mean them. It was posted up at 1.20 francs. I saw it in the Town Hall three or four times when I went in there—the secretary showed it to me. It was after Martin was forced to resign that he said 'Oh, people are mad. I have been offering five or six francs.' (Here informant adopted an outsider accent and manner.)

> Martin was out to line his own pocket. He was in with S C E T it was full of ex-officers. He was a paratrooper, and so he is hard like all that lot.[13]

> Another proof that Martin was out to profit himself was that while he was only prepared to offer 1.20 francs to us for our land, he himself sold off a piece of land to an outsider for 20 francs, that was scarcely even big enough to put a house up on.

Martin overplayed his outsider qualities. He appeared to have an egoistic concern for personal profit. He played the role of the smooth-talking official (notice the mimicry in the text above). The tough businessman approach is a necessary quality for local leadership in the present situation, but such tactics must only be used on outsiders and never on villagers.

Leaders are expected to line their pockets, but this must be done in deals with outsiders, not at the expense of villagers. A middleman is permitted to take his cut from 'them' but not from 'us'.

> Martin sold a lot of his own land and made a profit. All right—someone like a mayor is expected to profit from his position —he has a tough job and needs some rewards. Moreover, if he makes a bit of money out of deals with outsiders, he shows that he is *alerte*—wide awake and no fool.

Martin also adopted the wrong manner of treating villagers. He was *fier* (stand-offish) like an outsider.

> Martin walked up to me one day and said '*Madame*, are you the owner of that field over there, and this one here? The council has decided to buy them.' I was furious, but when I had told him what he could go and do with his council, he just said 'Oh, and what are *you* going to do with the fields—grow potatoes?' and stalked off.

> Another time I found his right-hand man daubing 'No Parking' signs in red on the newly painted front of my house. He ran the place like a bloody barracks. (This last phrase was in English.)

In short, people decided that Martin had tried to exploit the villagers in four main ways; taking away their livelihood; thinking too big and going too fast; offering too low a price for land; and behaving too much as an outsider. As a result:

Everyone was against Martin. The councillors had a meeting without telling him, and they decided to resign, leaving him with only three supporters on the council, so that he too was forced to resign. Martin was a Communist, though the mayor of Peron is a Communist and a good mayor all the same.[14] We wanted to change the mayor because then we thought it would all be different; but it is not. It is always the same system.

It was a pity that Martin tried to go too fast and his ideas were too big—otherwise he was a good man and had the right qualities for the position. He had good connections, spoke well, and was always travelling round seeing people in order to get things done. His trouble was that he tried to do too much for the tourists and visitors without properly understanding or providing for us locals.

OTHER LEADERS' OPINIONS

Discontent with and opposition to Martin were also building up amongst local leaders. Most of them were not against development; rather they opposed Martin because he represented to them exactly the wrong way of going about development in Valloire —the large scale, impersonal, outsider-backed approach.

Martin was dishonest (*malhonnête*)—he was just out to profit himself; all he wanted to do was to be Director of the resort. Therefore he wanted a big resort. He was just out for himself and offered no profit or even participation to the villagers. He did not even concern himself with them very much, leaving lower decisions to be made by the *garde champêtre*.[15]
The people of Valloire were not against the resort as such— that had to come, they understood that. When they voted against the plan, they voted against Martin as a man and not against the plan as an idea. He got everybody's back up. He tried to intimidate people—he even tried it on me and other *commerçants* (shop- and hotel-keepers). A good politician would not have done that, but would have realized that he must have people behind him, people on his side.

Martin acted with *puissance* not only to the villagers but to the other leaders. He did not communicate directly with the villagers, nor did he treat other local leaders as equals. Through failing to maintain solidarity he lost support and allowed opposition to form.

For some reason Martin would not explain to the village what his plans were. He preferred to keep them in the dark so that the first thing they knew about any new move was a demand to sell through the post. Not only had people a right to know what was going on, but with the people of Valloire it is a necessary tactic.

However, not only did he keep the village in the dark about his plans but he kept the council and even the *Syndicat Intercommunal* uninformed, making his decisions alone or with his *clique d'intimes* (cronies).

Martin's aloof and authoritarian manner did not help his reputation. But the criticism levelled against him was not entirely the result of either his manner or his actions, for there were inherent problems associated with the office of mayor.

Martin was put up for mayor by those who threw down the previous mayor. People here are like that. No mayor ever satisfies them, and having put him in power they soon find some reason to dislike him. So, the very men who campaigned to have him elected, try their hardest to get rid of him. The people here are sly *(méfiants)*—they say one thing to your face and another behind your back, and they are always squabbling amongst themselves.

So the leaders' opposition to Martin was more complex than that of the villagers. There were more fundamental reasons for opposition to him, than the simple charge of exploitation.

One of the shopkeepers called Emile, who played a prominent part in the *Syndicat de Défense*, sincerely held the villager norms as paramount while believing that those with ability could always make their own way successfully.

They talk as if everyone in the village will make his fortune with the resort, but that is just not facing up to reality. The people here think a resort is like a great umbrella under which everyone can find shelter. But it is not like that; most people are still going to be put in the cold—the ones who are badly off *(les malheureux)* now will be those who are badly off when the resort is built. There are no decent jobs; you can be a ski instructor or a *commerçant*. But to be the one you must be young, the other you must be born to. One can't change from a *paysan* (peasant) to a *commerçant* just like that. It is a matter of ability. If a man has the ability to start up a commerce, he will do it now and not wait until there is a resort. There are those who say 'Oh, Emile does not mind a resort at whatever cost to the village, because he will profit from it.' Well, in a way, they're right. I have no land worth speaking of and I have a going concern. So I would not *lose* if there was a resort but I would never be in favour of a *coup* like that of Martin's. I would not have it said of my sons and grandsons that their father had sold out the village to profit himself. Things like that are important in a village—I would never be able to stand on the bridge and chat with the men or play *boules* with them in the summer again. The large resorts change the spirit (*ésprit*) of everything. The tourists in them are *snob* and the attitude to commerce changes. Now, I am a *demi-paysan* (a part-time peasant)—I can afford to do things much as I please, and farm as a hobby. However, in a resort I would have to concentrate on my business and put all the money back into improvements in the shop rather than spend it on the farm. For the *commerçant* in the resort it is one continual round of borrowing in order to improve and expand. One's mind becomes set (*fixée*) on making money.

Emile sees himself as having commercial ability, which is not something everyone has—for that reason he is a leader. He is able to look after himself, come what may. A resort might enable him to profit from increased trade but would also destroy his relationship with the community. He would become isolated from the villagers, an outsider, a profit-seeker like Martin. Not only he, but his family would suffer through several generations. The resort would destroy both the community and the spirit of the village. Everything would revolve around the maximization of profit.

Another prominent member of the *Syndicat de Défense* was a local schoolteacher and Communist activist. Under normal conditions in Valloire Communists are not popular, nor for that matter is any party. But in the conditions of a time when 'it was the revolution', any reason for opposing Martin was adopted. The Communist propaganda played upon Martin's identification with outsider capital interests and his aim to exploit the village workers. In addition the party propaganda machine was efficient, far more so than Martin's. As Martin himself said to me:

The Communist party also came to the attack. I was accused of exploitation, of encouraging capitalist luxuries and investment, and of profiting from land sales. The resort was for the *gros riches*, there was no place in it for workers or *gens du pays*.

Now, I do not play that kind of politics. Anyway, they convinced people—they played on their fear of being exploited
and convinced them. The villagers were just stupid—slow to
realize their potential. For Valloire had great potential. It had
snow and sun, valuable things to the villagers, but they threw
their opportunities away at the persuasion of a few people
whose opinions they did not normally listen to. You could not
have found ten men in the whole of Valloire at that time who
were in favour of the plan. The present mayor and the *curé*
were against me. Emile ... Emile—do you know why he was
against me? He said that he already had as many clients as he
wanted. If there was a centre at Valloire he would neither be
able, nor want, to serve all the new clients ... but of course he
did not want to see any one else set up in competition against
him—all the *commerçants* were like that.

You see, there is the problem. You have a valley which has
had a steady emigration over the past two hundred years—
there is just not enough young men to be climbing guides and
ski instructors, not enough *commerçants* or even labourers.
You *have* to bring in people from outside—after all, repopulation is part of the scheme for making a valley viable. Yet the
locals see every man from outside as taking the bread out of
their mouths.

But not everyone was against the plan as Martin suggests.
Some distinguished the latter's reputation from the plan's utility.
One was another schoolteacher.

The members of the *Syndicat de Défense* asked me if I would
join them, but I refused. Firstly I felt myself to have been
personally involved in some of Martin's plans—though the
same reasons did not stop others, like the present mayor, from
joining. Secondly, I did not agree with the way that they were
going about things. If they wanted to get rid of Martin, right,
they should have got on with it, but there was no reason why
they should have jeopardized the whole future of Valloire
doing it. Development for tourism is the only future this valley
has, the only way our economy can survive. The *Syndicat de
Défense* tried to get rid of the mayor by using the evidence of
the plans against him—thereby destroying both the plans and
Martin. On the whole, people were not against development
as such but against Martin.

OUTSIDERS' OPINIONS

One departmental official who played an important part in both planning the resort and setting up S E D H A, had the following comments to make:

> A *pays* where there is already a bit of tourism, where there are already small *commerçants* established, is at once easier and at the same time more difficult to develop than one where there is nothing; easier because people have already taken the first steps (*prit le train*)—there is a basis of personnel and initiative with which to start. More difficult because everyone has the idea that they are sitting on a gold mine, and everyone is grasping and wanting ridiculous prices for their own little bits of land, and the *commerçants* are frightened of competition.
>
> I suppose that was part of the difference between Montbrison[16] and Valloire but it had more to do with the control and influence that the mayors had, than the degree of development already existing in the *pays*.
>
> At Montbrison they were agreed to develop and to sell. The mayor was well established. He had control over his council and they followed him. The mayor was a *paysan* but *intelligent*.
>
> At Valloire, Martin was a fine chap (*brave garçon*) . . . but he caused a lot of trouble. He treated people as though he was still an officer in the air force. He did not have an established position and the villagers did not follow him.
>
> One can develop where the people want to, but where they don't, there is nothing that you can do. It is not so much the price, but the *mentalité*.

This official put most of the blame for failure on Martin's handling of his role as mayor. He did not have the trust (*confiance*) of the villagers and their *mentalité* was wrong. The situation was made worse by his manner of behaving like an officer in charge of a manoeuvre instead of an equal amongst equals. The official did not think that price was so important as attitude, though villagers have said that it was an important reason in their decision to oppose Martin and the plan.

S E D H A's representative (five years later this was not the same man who dealt with the Valloire affair) said much the same thing as the official with an additional point about bringing in outside labour and capital, which is very similar to Martin's own view. They both recognize the problem: repopulation is contrary to the idea of maximization of labour.

Why did Valloire fail? The most important thing in development is the *psychologie*—if the people want to sell or not. Price is not so important—we have bought land elsewhere for 37 centimes the square metre. The prices offered in Valloire were the highest we were able to offer. Yes, we offered more for land at Montbrison but that was earlier . . . however, even there it was not money that made the sale easier, it was because the people wanted to sell. The mayor had the trust (*confiance*) of the villagers which the mayor of Valloire did not have. They wanted to develop there—and they believed that we were doing it for their own advantage.

However, there are again factors other than Martin's behaviour and reputation in the failure of the Valloire development project.

The pressures were too great. There was the opposition of the *gens du pays* themselves, which itself was partly fostered by the opposition of the other resorts who were afraid that Valloire would outshine them. They circulated propaganda and promoted political opposition. Then there was the conflict between S E D H A and S C E T, between S E D H A, S C E T and the *Service du Domaine*, between the administration's left hand and right hand.

Some people claim that external interests, opposed to the resort at Valloire, played on Martin's worsening reputation with the villagers by encouraging Communist agitation and propaganda against him. However, others say that his poor reputation showed that he was in fact a Communist (see note 14).

Thus, there was a variety of forces at work behind the overwhelming rejection of the plan for the centre at Valloire at the enquiry in April 1964. But even amongst the outsiders there was a strong feeling that Martin's manner and role performance gave him a reputation with the villagers that was an important factor in the failure of the project.

POWER AND SOLIDARITY

The difficulty that a leader has in maintaining his position and reputation while performing the role of an innovator, can be seen as the conflict between maintaining authority and pursuing a policy involving the exercise of personal power in order to achieve both public and private ambitions. The problem is for a leader to obtain legislation for actions which are the means to ends beyond, and contrary to, the norms on which his authority is based. Obviously, the weak leader is going to feel the costs of such a policy to a greater extent than a strong one, and Martin's position and performance suffered from both weaknesses and limitations.

Martin's assumption of a formal role as mayor meant from the start that his behaviour was limited by the sanctions defining the office. He did, in fact, declare that his best opening had been to stand for such a position. In the first place, he needed the office to establish an acceptable relationship with villagers; he would have found this difficult as an informal leader since he had lived for so long outside the village. Secondly, he expected his position as the formal representative of the commune to carry a greater weight with the external agencies from whom he proposed to seek financial backing for his development plans.

He had been able to achieve this formal authority through his *liste* gaining a majority in the 1959 elections for four main reasons. Firstly, he had the support and promotion of one or two powerful informal leaders. Secondly, there was a lack of strong competition. For thirdly, Martin, and he alone at that time, had the necessary combination of insider qualities and outside competence. Finally, he fitted the needs of the moment. The small teleski built in 1954 had shown people the potential that lay ahead in the development field. Their ambitions stimulated, they seized on Martin's ideas for development so that, though his policies were couched in the vaguest terms, his propaganda had a wide appeal during the election campaign. Martin appeared as the man who would achieve for them what they desired and this put him in a transactional relationship with the majority of the electorate on whose support he depended. Without realizing the full implications of it, he had implicitly undertaken to solve everyone's problems.

Villagers expected both to have their cake and eat it. They wanted innovation in accord with accepted values. In order to fulfil his heroic promise in the myth of development, Martin was required to achieve an impossible compromise. The extent to

G

which his role was, in any case, impossible was further complicated by the manner of his performance. His initial fears were
justified in that he found it difficult to establish any rapport with
the villagers. He failed to gain their trust and they increasingly
saw him to behave with *puissance* rather than *droit*.

Martin fitted the broad theme of the development myth, but
the charismatic boots were too big for him. He was never really
accepted or trusted by the villagers, but in the beginning they
did believe that he would deliver the goods. Disillusionment
came when it was realized that not only was he treading all over
everyone's toes, but he was not going to succeed in fulfilling their
ambitions. A variety of reasons then served to unite the majority
of people against him.

In the first place, Martin's office gave him inadequate control
over his political following in the village. The legitimacy of his
position in the villagers' eyes depended on his fulfilling the impossible bargain he had undertaken, to innovate a new economy
in accordance with the norms of the previous one.

In addition, Martin's personal manner and his inability to retain control over the course of the development programme
alienated the support of both the ordinary villagers and that of
the informal leaders who had initially backed him.

Martin attempted to reinforce his transactional hold on
authority by establishing normative personal relationships. This
would have given him a core following and consolidated his
position into that of a strong leader. Paradoxically, because of
the very nature of his office, any contacts that he did establish
were suspect since he and his partner were immediately thought
to be profiting themselves at the expense of the community.

Further, many of his strongest allies were those who carried
little weight with the villagers. His *clique* in the village were
either young and inexperienced, or men with poor reputations.
Many of his closest contacts were with mayors of surrounding
communes, gens comme nous but, in this context, rivals. Others
were ex-service contacts who were now local officials in the Departmental administration.

At the same time as he had inadequate control over his support and following in the village, Martin had inadequate influence with his external contacts, with *étrangers*. His attempts to
find private finance failed, just as his hope to form a co-operative

land agency in the village constituted a misunderstanding of villagers' norms and expectations.

When he failed to find private backers, Martin was obliged, as an official, to appeal for support and aid to those higher in the Departmental administration. In doing this he lost control over development policies, since the project was passed from local to central planning level, and national policies rode over local considerations. Just as Martin was unable to control S E D H A, so S E D H A had little influence over S C E T. He was too small a fish to take on the sharks in the oceans of the outside world.

His formal local role as mayor of a rural commune hampered his relationships with senior officials and his activities in the external business world; correspondingly his internal manoeuvres were hindered by the nature of his external connections. His position in both structures was inadequate in itself to achieve the ends he wanted and insufficient to give him the authority to act as he wished. He did not have the trust of the villagers, nor the respect of the *étrangers*. He found himself in the social no-man's land, the failed entrepreneur caught between two systems.

As the villagers saw things, Martin had dissociated himself from village morality. He had become identified in their eyes with the organizations and policies of S C E T and S E D H A. He appeared to be not so much negotiating with those bodies as actually in league with them against the villagers. He had become a total outsider, a suitable scapegoat for thwarted ambitions. All that had gone wrong, all the frustrations and failures could be blamed on him.

The outsiders also blamed the failure of the project on Martin's inept handling. They saw him as the 'wide-boy', the villager corrupted by the new opportunities of the external world, someone who was no longer a true *paysan—brave* and *intelligent*. He was the man out for himself who did not have the villagers' trust or confidence.

Martin had a near impossible role which he performed in a manner unacceptable to most people. His office gave him an inadequate role for the goals that he envisaged. He had never been entirely accepted by most villagers as an equal, and his apparent failure to fulfil his transactional bargain to their satisfaction led to a swift withdrawal of support. In the crisis of development competition, he became the mediator between two sides whom he failed to conciliate. Each rejected him, and yet without him they could not communicate. Immediately before and after the enquiry, the villagers and S E D H A had nothing left in common between them. When they met, they merely shouted abuse at one another. However, Martin represented something positive about change to each side. Reflecting on the experience of this crisis, both sides learned something about the other, changing and clarifying their conceptions and predispositions to action.

THE CHANGING INTERPRETATION OF VALUES

I have mentioned the myth of development. In some ways it resembles Burridge's idea of the myth dream.[17]

An innovator attempts to modify the existing set of normative constraints. Most times such men fail, but sometimes they succeed. When they are successful, they stand as examples to be followed by those who have the necessary conviction, ability or resources, and they stand as objects of envy or hate for those who do not have those beliefs, abilities or resources. But even if they fail, the example of their careers has some effect on the normative rules of the community, and on people's ideas and behaviour. Their example may encourage others to attempt different interpretations of, or may serve to affirm all the more strongly, existing norms.

I have outlined the career of one such innovator in this paper. He failed to bring about the changes which he had planned and did not satisfy those whose support he needed. However, he had, none the less, a profound effect on the values of the community.

Change is slow and cumulative and works itself out on several levels. In this paper I have considered the two levels of action and value. There emerges a kind of cyclical progression, with leaders rising briefly on the shoulders of their predecessors, before, in turn, falling away. Each one, however, has prepared the ground for, or at least made more obvious the pitfalls to be avoided by, his successors.

Burridge saw the myth dream in Tangu as a collation of peoples' inexpressible hopes and aspirations, only occasionally made articulate through the person and actions of a charismatic leader. So, in a sense, are the hopes and aspirations of development and the future in Valloire only made concrete and attainable by the ideas and efforts of individual innovators or leaders. Everyone has hopes and ambitions, and from time to time innovators appear and collate these aspirations and propose a policy of action. To begin with they are enthusiastically supported, their vague but comprehensive policies appearing to represent everyone's aspirations. But once the stage of policy implementation is reached it becomes clear that most people will be no better off than before. As a result, leaders or innovators become rejected—whether quickly or slowly depends on their ability to maintain support, project a favourable reputation and balance negative with positive sanctions. The successful innovator must convince others that his profit is theirs. This Martin failed to do.

But though they may fail in their stated and expected goals, they become incorporated into the myth of development. Their actions open up new opportunities, help to re-interpret old values or affirm new ones. They prepare the take-off points for new leaders and new policies.

Martin's career served to make clearer the values operating in the sale of land for development. In 1959 to sell any land to an outsider was to reject the norms of family and community. Martin's actions, directed towards reinterpreting these values, clearly showed the dangers of certain kinds of transactions, so that by 1967 a definite policy of land selling had emerged, which set out the categories of land that could be sold to certain people at certain prices under certain conditions.

Similarly, the events of 1959–64 clarified in people's minds the type of development they wanted. The dangers of large-scale development getting out of control had been shown to both ordinary villagers and other local entrepreneurs. The limitations of a formal position of leadership in this kind of situation had also been demonstrated. In addition to Martin's personal failure, the mayor and council that had succeeded him found themselves unable to go ahead with new development policies because S E D H A had already bought the key sites necessary for the development of a resort, and though they no longer envisaged developing the site for some time, they were only prepared to surrender their title for a price beyond the resources of any local official body.

Thus, present development is on a small scale, initiated by a number of informal entrepreneurial leaders operating as agents in land sales made by individual villagers. The relation between agent and villager is a moral contract based on accepted values of equality and mutual aid, and the local entrepreneur takes pains to show that he is taking his commission out of the pocket of his outsider-customer rather than of his co-villager client.

This book is about ideas of equality and inequality, independence and duty to community, and the way that these concepts affect political responses. In this chapter I have been concerned with a crisis situation in which such concepts were passionately employed and exaggerated in such a way that, in retrospect, the situation may be seen to have served to re-arrange the pattern of people's expectations and their predisposition to action. It is only after a crisis that people feel that both their moral perspectives and predispositions to action are clear for dealing with the kinds of decisions that have to be made in similar situations in the future. People tend to formulate some of the most important rules of the political game only through the post-mortem after each match has been played. Thus, informants' reconstructions of events at a personal and organizational level can prove a source of information about the process of normative reinterpretation and reconstruction that takes place at a structural level.

NOTES

1. I am grateful to all those who commented on an earlier draft of this paper, in particular Dr J. B. Loudon and Professor F. G. Bailey. The names of the village and all personal names are fictitious. The village is the same as that described in Chapter 3.
2. See *Franklin*.
3. I do not know the exact rank that Martin held. Accounts varied with the sympathies of informants, ranging from Wing-Commander (Lieutenant-Colonel) to paratrooper ('para'). He was generally referred to as having been simply an officer, and I conclude that probably he fell into the senior officer category, that is, the rank of major (or equivalent) and above.
4. *Syndicat Intercommunal pour le Developpement Touristique Hivernal de la Valloire et Ville* (Intercommunal Association for the development of winter tourism in the valley and village of Valloire). This was set up in September 1953 as an association between four of the communes in the valley to promote winter-sports developments there. The members were the mayors of the four communes concerned and two

representatives from each Municipal Council. Expenses were shared between the four communes, who also stood joint surety for loans. The Association's first project was to build a ski lift in the commune of Valloire which was opened in the winter of 1954–55.

5. A commune the size of Valloire has eleven elected Councillors, who after election vote amongst themselves to choose one of their number as mayor. Before each election, candidates for the mayorship draw up an official list (*liste*) containing the names of ten supporters who are offered as prospective Councillor candidates. These *listes* are used as election manifestoes and have a title setting out general policies. Martin's in 1959 bore the title '*Liste d'Action pour le Développement Agricole, Touristique et Sportif de la Valloire*'.

6. Sessional elections are held roughly every six years.

7. The French machinery for development and its control are complex, and my knowledge gathered, as it were, at the retail end of the process, is rudimentary, and imperfect. However, as far as I was able to understand it, S C E T (*La Société Centrale pour l'Equipment du Territoire*), is a central government body set up to initiate, control and finance tourist (and perhaps other forms of) development. This is done in practice through the setting up of local regional *Sociétés* wherever development is projected. Thus, in the Hautes Alpes, S E D H A *Société d'Equipement du Département des Hautes Alpes*) was set up. These local *sociétés* are *sociétés d'économie mixte*, which means that their composition, finance, profit margins and policy are rigidly controlled by law.

Plans made by officials in the local *Sociétés* have to be submitted to the central body for approval, which if satisfied, sends the plans on for final vetting by the *Service du Domaine*, a government department concerned with total land use and taxation. If the *Service du Domaine* is satisfied they finally cost the plan and grant the finance required. In the normal course of events, there is a long process of submission, amendment and resubmission before final approval is granted by the *Domaine* to a plan very different from that originally conceived at the local level.

8. These prices were based on an assessment of the land at an agricultural value on a national scale. On this assessment stoney mountain land, no longer even cultivated, ranked very low compared to that of the fertile lowlands.

9. The *Sociétés d'Equipement* were only *concessionnaires*, that is they developed on behalf of the communes and returned the developed area to the ownership of the commune after a period of time. Thus, a public enquiry had to be held before development could go ahead, to show that it was in the public interest. Exactly how such an enquiry established that opinion I do not know; that is, whether there was a show of hands at the meeting, a formal vote or a count of formal objections. Informants talked of 'votes', 'sending in forms' and 'signing their names'. All that is certain is that there was a delay between the enquiry in Valloire and a return of the answer from S C E T so it seems that some count or other interpretation was made.

10. The *Syndicate de Défense des Propriétaires et des Interêts Communaux* (Association for the defence of Proprietors and Communal interests) was a local association set up to organize opposition to the plan for a centre at Valloire.

11. For a discussion on this point see *Gluckman* (1) and *Paine* (1).
12. This analysis is based upon texts from my field notes collected during interviews with informants. Since these texts are translated and were not transcribed direct, they cannot be presented as actual speech, though I believe that the sense conveyed in them remains valid.
13. Whether he was or not I do not know (see note 3) but the implication here is obvious: paratroopers were considered to be utterly ruthless and brutal.
14. Whether Martin was a Communist or not is again unsure. As in note 3, informants' views varied with their sympathies, and this view may be compared with Martin's own view on page 85. Peron is the next commune up the valley; it has had the same mayor for twenty years and the Communist party has active support.
15. The *garde champêtre* (field guard) is an official whose duties are to oversee agricultural problems, such as irrigation and grazing rights, canal upkeep and boundary disputes. The holder of the office at this time was known as Martin's 'right-hand man'. When Martin's support was failing, this man became involved in a public scandal and resigned his office. Martin had tried to re-interpret the office as a kind of tourist guide, supervising campers and helping visitors. However, since the scandal in 1963, the office has remained vacant.
16. Montbrison was a resort in a valley to the south-east of Valloire. It was begun before Valloire in 1961 (hence Martin's wait of one year before S E D H A would help him) and was expanded after the Valloire project had fallen through.
17. *Burridge* (1).

5
Patterns of Informal Interaction in Pellaport

The village of Pellaport, with a population of about 250, is situated in the northern French Jura. It stands about 600 metres above sea-level, beneath one of the forested limestone scarps that traverse the area, breaking the land into a series of plateaux that run approximately from north to south. Essentially it is a farming community whose production economy is based on dairying. Cheese, a variety of Gruyère, is manufactured from milk brought twice-daily by each farmer to the village dairy. For almost six months of the year, from the beginning of November to the end of April, the cows are penned in the stable that runs parallel to the living quarters of each house. A limited quantity of cereals are cultivated, the grain being used to provide a concentrate that supplements the hay on which the cattle are fed during the winter. The dwellings are located within the village, the surrounding land being fragmented into blocks of parcelles, or strips. A farmer may exploit anything between 30 and 60 strips, representing a total area of 15 to 30 hectares (37 to 75 acres), his holding being scattered amongst those of his fellow villagers.

CO-OPERATION AND DISPUTE

Almost all of the routine tasks on the farm are carried out by members of the household.[1] Those events like the twice daily milking, the planting of root crops, the hay harvest and the birth of calves, which involve more than one person, are achieved by a team composed of husband and wife, father and son or parents and children.

Nevertheless, there are occasions when a man must seek help outside the household, particularly if his immediate family is limited in size, or if he is ill. Thus there were examples of men ploughing land for a first cousin, helping a brother-in-law plant potatoes, or a nephew capture heifers which could not be led back to the stable. Unrelated neighbours, too, would work together. One farmer brought his tractor to scatter the manure of another, whose machine was too small to power the device they had bought in partnership. When one man had a cow with a damaged hoof shoed, his neighbour helped to hold the beast still during the operation.

But if it is true that it is kin and neighbours who most often work together, it is also true that it is between these people that disputes most often develop: 'Quarrels usually occur within families' was one comment.

One of the characteristics of the unsociable is that 'you do not feel at ease in their company' and the one dispute which I witnessed directly centred around such an accusation. One housewife was accustomed to calling on her neighbour to talk with her, but the neighbour refused ever to make a return visit. Eventually Joelle had written a note to Marie, enquiring why she insisted on behaving like that, and received the reply: '*Je ne suis pas de bon coeur chez toi.*' Joelle had been upset by this, and called on a friend to mediate. The latter, however, maintained that the best thing to do was simply to wait until the ill-feeling had subsided. It was, she commented afterwards, a very stupid quarrel, and speaking for herself she preferred men to women, because men were not so easily upset.

Two first cousins living opposite each other in the rue de la Rivière quarrelled over the construction of a bunker for their manure. Eventually they built two, side by side, but without using a common wall in the centre. This visible evidence of non-co-operation was generally observed. One of the anecdotes related about a now deceased farmer, known throughout the village as 'the Seigneur', was that he often quarrelled with his brother, and once went into the latter's house to strike him with an iron bar.

The most spectacular breakdown in social relations in recent years must have been that generally attributed to Eduard Maitrugue. Eduard spent most of his working life as baker in the neighbouring village of Vaux, and only returned to his natal village on retirement. He does not seem to think of himself as a full member of the community. It was a constant theme of his (in contrast to the general opinion) that I had done badly in choosing to work in Pellaport, a village which he maintained was twenty years behind its neighbours. During 1966 he became seized with what the villagers diagnosed as '*la rancune*' (malice, spite). First, he quarrelled with his brother César; then with his brother-in-law, Claude Bavarel. Inspecting some of his pasture one day, the latter discovered that an old stone pipe, which he was using to carry water to a cattle trough, had been smashed with a sledge-hammer. Eduard was strongly suspected. Soon afterwards Claude's second cousin the *Maire* (Mayor), a fourth inhabitant of that corner of the village, discovered that during the night the tyres of his trailer had been slashed with an axe. Eduard was again thought to be responsible. Finally, Nicolas Jouffroy whose stable stands opposite the *Maire*'s house, suffered a number of deaths among his cattle, as a result of which he lost the certificate declaring his stable to be free from tuberculosis. Someone had seen a figure going into Nicolas's stable during the night, and (suspecting poison might deliberately have been planted) passed the information on to him with the cryptic message, 'What went into your stable came out of it again.'

Despite all this, however, Eduard was co-operating regularly both with his brother and Claude Bavarel throughout the time I was in the village. Nevertheless, when I commented on the fact to Claude's son the latter confessed that his father still 'had a tooth in his head' about Eduard's past activities.

The general conclusion seems simply to be that *the most intense social relationships*, both positive and negative, develop between kin and neighbours.

This essay is about the ways in which the villagers evaluate each other's worth as members of the same community: the significance they attach to various forms of behaviour, and the terminology used to describe the 'good' and the 'bad' person. Essentially, it is concerned with the relationships that emerge as a result of transactions between individuals.

For Blau, such transactions are the most important aspect of social life. He starts the introduction to *Exchange and Power* with a quotation from Georg Simmel which includes the phrase: 'all contacts among men rest on the schema of giving and returning the equivalence'. Nevertheless, Blau himself points out that a study of the properties inherent in such relationships cannot explain the whole of a social structure and ideology. In the first place, the study of values is excluded. It may be that, within the limits that norms of fair play impose, an individual is free to select those relationships that he believes will be most rewarding to him. Nevertheless, it is the community's values that will determine how an individual and his transactions are regarded by those with whom he comes into contact, dictating whether he is subject to approval or criticism. Even if all communities engage in social transactions, they certainly do not all evaluate them in the same way. In the second place, the forms of social organization that emerge implicitly, as a result of the processes of competition and exchange, can be distinguished from those that are established explicitly, with formal rules to co-ordinate activity towards the achievement of specific objectives.[2]

What I am here concerned with, then, is microstructures, not macrostructures. Macrostructures are composed of elements that are also social structures, while microstructures are composed of interacting individuals (Blau, 1964: 24). There are two levels of interaction in the village, the formal and the informal. The macrostructures of Pellaport are the agricultural co-operatives (controlling dairy and village bull) and the communal administrative structure. These are composed of an electorate, a council and a president or *Maire*. Even if posts such as that of *Maire* are occupied only by one man at a time, he does so as a *person* fulfilling an institutionalized *role*, not (ideally) as a total individual.

The essential features of social exchange are characterized by Blau as follows. An individual for whom a service has been performed is expected to return the service on another occasion. If he does, then the other is encouraged to offer further services, and a bond is established between the two. If the first does not reciprocate then he is labelled as 'ungrateful': the failure to reciprocate involves a loss of credit and loss of trust until eventually (as his reputation spreads) the offending individual is excluded from further exchanges. A person who is unable to return services on which he depends places himself in a position of subordination to the other who provides the needed resources. One who has the resources, but declines to reciprocate, demonstrates a refusal to acknowledge the other as his equal. The two general functions of social exchange are, then, to establish bonds of friendship, or to establish superordination over others.

In Pellaport, if one sought help, one looked first among the members of one's household; failing that one would ask a close relative or a neighbour. The way in which some of the villagers viewed the situations analysed by Blau can be seen in the following remarks.

One farmer stated that when you helped others it was most often those who were *de la même parenté* (kinsmen). You might help neighbours from time to time, but he himself would only help his cousins: despite the fact that it was essentially a question of *reciprocité* once you started working for others they might ask too much, and he himself didn't have enough free time for that. Claude Bavarel (who will be one of the central figures discussed here) took a rather more liberal view, commenting that although you would first ask a kinsman should you want help, you might in the second place go to an unrelated neighbour. When I enquired if in the latter case you were particularly obliged to return the service he replied, 'No; to *rendre service* is to *rendre service quand-même*,' and went on to give an example. When Felix Viennet's unmarried uncle was ill, Claude had mown thirty acres of hay for him, and he had expected nothing in return. 'In any case,' said he, 'he's dead now.' I suggested that Felix might have inherited his uncle's debts, but M. Bavarel retorted that he'd helped the nephew as well. Two years ago Felix had had an operation, and the whole village had helped with his harvest. M. Bavarel cut two *parcelles*. But, he added, the Viennets were not very *courageux*; the first to help, if a man is ill, should be his wife and children.

A third farmer, expressing what seemed to be a common response, said that one might work with either kin or unrelated neighbours, but that most often one found brothers or brothers-in-law co-operating. The important thing, he said, was that there should be *une bonne entente* (a good understanding) between the people in question.

Sometimes informal co-operation may take place on a wide scale. In the summer of 1968 one of the elder farmers fell from a ladder while repairing his roof and broke his leg in several places. The 'whole village' turned out to help with his harvest (he and his wife have no children and his father died in 1948). Then, at the beginning of the winter, when Pierre Bavarel was rebuilding his stable he demolished a large part of one wall and left the remainder standing unsupported. When snow began to build up against what remained it collapsed, leaving him with half of his farm in ruins. Again the 'whole village' turned out to help; some farmers came down from the neighbouring hamlet of Montoiseau, and Pierre's wife's brother travelled over from St. Gabriel (4 km. away). Mme Bavarel provided meals for everyone while work was in progress.

The basic distinction between social and purely economic exchange is, according to Blau, that social exchange creates *unspecified* obligations. Since there is no way to ensure an appropriate return for a favour, social exchange requires trusting others to discharge their obligations. The benefits involved in social exchange do not have an exact price in terms of a single quantitative medium of exchange. This means that those involved cannot precisely specify the worth of approval or help in the absence of a money price (93–95). This characterization was echoed in the villagers' comments. Co-operation at an informal level is not carried out for money, nor should a precise check be kept of debt or credit in terms of hours of work performed. But although the obligation to return services may not be stated explicitly, it is certainly felt in a diffuse way. 'Are you obliged to work in return for those who helped you?' I asked one farmer. 'No,' he replied, 'you are not *obliged*, but *en principe* you do so, although there is no question either of money changing hands or of a precise count of work done being kept. Nevertheless,' he added, 'there are one or two in the village who do not return the work you do for them.' Sometimes people implied that all was not well when the 'whole village' had to help someone. The one who fell from his roof 'liked to have others working around [i.e. beneath] him'. Felix Viennet's family were 'not plucky'; Pierre Bavarel should have had more sense than to leave his wall unsupported. But with the possible exception of the first these people were not proud, but in one way or another *foolish*. Felix seems at times to occupy that status of something like the village fool: '*il est un peu fou, lui; sa tête n'est pas trop solide*' (his head is not all that firm). His habit of constantly singing a song that began '*Aline dans son jardin fleuri*' led to his acquiring the nickname, Aline; a man with the name of a woman. While this attitude doesn't seem to deter others from helping him, it may well exempt him from the conventional requirements of community life. The various implications of the label '*fou*' are discussed below. Nevertheless, one can certainly go too far: beyond a point the diffuse sanctions of exclusion from the pattern of informal interaction will be brought into operation. For some villagers, Maurice Genre, a neighbour of Felix, had reached this point; largely due to the activities of his aunt (mother's sister), a member of the same household, who was notably antisocial. When one elderly man listed for me the people whom he had assisted recently he included Maurice, but added: 'Never again, after what the old woman said to me.' Having discussed the topic he suggested other people I might ask, and when his wife put in '. . . and Maurice Genre', he retorted: 'No, not them; *ils sont fous là.*'

GOSSIP AND SCANDAL

Much of this information, both that about quarrels and that about the lack of social spirit in such people as Maurice Genre and Felix Viennet, was transmitted by means of *gossip*. It is gossip which is primarily responsible for bringing interpersonal relationships into the field of public affairs.

The debate between Gluckman and Paine on the analysis of gossip brought out several useful distinctions. It is possible for gossip to play a useful part in preserving the harmony of life in the community. Cliques and aspiring individuals can be kept in their place, and leaders selected on an informal basis, without disputes being brought into the open, and hence threatening the unity of the group. In measuring the performance of others against the norms, gossip ensures that these norms will repeatedly be underlined. Nevertheless, if the group *is* breaking up, gossip and scandal may only provoke the process of disintegration. It was Paine who put this point most clearly: 'There is no *a priori* assumption,' he argued, 'that gossip of itself either avoids conflict or exacerbates it . . . gossip is a catalyst of social process.'[3] In accusing opponents of not conforming to the norms, the gossip

or scandalmonger may simply be using one of the stratagems of
Stratagems and Spoils.[4] It seems also to be important to distinguish between the kind of private conversation that is primarily
intended to obtain information about absent people and their
activities, and that which is primarily designed as a covert
attack upon one's rivals. For Paine the first was to be labelled
gossip, the second scandal. Gluckman preferred to exclude the
first from consideration, and confine the term gossip to 'idle
talk . . . which is largely (about) the evaluation of morals and
skills'.[5] I myself would prefer to use the terms in a way similar
to Paine, since it seems difficult to separate informative from
evaluative talk. The specific utilitarian purposes of an exchange
may be vitally concerned with an evaluation: whether or not, for
example, a person such as Felix Viennet is a trustworthy partner
for social exchange. This, however, is a subject on which many
villagers would agree, and it should, I think, be distinguished
analytically from purely selfish attempts to discredit a rival. One
of the definitions given for scandal by the Shorter Oxford English
Dictionary is 'the utterance of disgraceful imputations, defamatory
talk'. Since, however, the word *scandal* is often used to refer to an
outrageous *event*, it might perhaps be more exact to label the two
forms of conversation, informative gossip and scandal*izing* gossip.

Before going on to describe the meanings attributed to the key
words in the evaluation of personality in Pellaport I will therefore consider one notable example of a long-established antipathy between two men and their respective families: those of
Claude Bavarel and Augustin Jouffroy, who live opposite each
other on the main street of the village. Those remarks of M.
Bavarel's described here illustrate how the principles of evaluation may be used in scandalizing gossip.

Firstly the Jouffrois are *proud* (*fiers*). When the father married,
he chose a girl from a village some kilometres from Pellaport
'because there were no families rich enough for him here'.
Nevertheless he made a bad choice: his wife never does any work
around the house. She has no self-respect, in fact she is a little
crazy: you can tell by the way she wanders through the garden
whistling silently to herself. When he was on the way to the
wedding Augustin stopped for a drink in a café beside the main
road. In the bar he met an old friend whom he hadn't seen for
some time:

'Where are you going today, dressed so smartly?' enquired the friend.

'Oh,' Augustin replied, 'I'm going to get married.'

The friend had shaken his head: 'Turn back before it's too late,' he warned. But Augustin thought *he had no need of anyone's advice* (*il croyait qu'il n'avait pas besoin d'avis des autres*) and went on to the wedding.

Secondly, their behaviour does not bear out their claims to high status. For years Augustin kept his manure heap in front of the house, beside the road ('Where he now has those old tractor tyres filled with sand, so that his grand-daughter can play there'). No-one who claims to be better than his neighbours could do a thing like that: it's *living like pigs*.

Thirdly, the son—Nicolas himself—is a bit *crazy*. While he was building his new stable and barn he drove a tractor into the barn before nailing down the floorboards: the planks slipped and the rear wheels of the tractor fell through the gaps. 'Happily' no-one was hurt, but it was typical of him that he should have been so foolish. It had taken a considerable amount of effort to lift the tractor out again. It was Claude Bavarel who once dismissed Nicolas's frequent purchase of new machinery with the expression: *'Oui, il y a des oiseaux comme ça'* (Yes, there are featherbrains like him).

CULTURAL CONSTRUCTS FOR THE EVALUATION
OF PERSONALITY

In talking about 'informal' patterns of behaviour, I have been using the word not to describe patterns that are acted on implicitly while remaining unformulated by the actors, but to denote behaviour patterns for which no precise procedures are laid down and which are not subject to organized sanctions.[6] There is a very well-formulated scheme according to which such behaviour is evaluated. Having described some of the informal relationships (both positive and negative) within the community, I will now go on to consider the system of values according to which individuals are weighed up by their fellow villagers.

The key words in this evaluation are, *gentil, fier* and *fou*. In conversation *gentil* and *fier* are used in structural opposition, denoting respectively social and anti-social behaviour. At a

H

more detailed level, however, this opposition is not maintained, and *fier* becomes a term that extends across the social/anti-social dichotomy. It is this ambiguity that seems to make it so useful a reference in scandalizing gossip.

Gentil was generally regarded as a word whose meaning was self-evident: it had few synonyms. When I enquired what it was to be *gentil*, the usual reply was *'Mai c'est la gentillesse, quoi?'* Most people , however, went on to elaborate on this statement, and in doing so showed that there was not, apparently, complete agreement about what it implied. To some, graciousness was a very Christian quality and they described actions that had obvious biblical referents: to be *gentil* meant to love one's enemies, to help a stranger who was ill by the roadside. You don't have to be rich to give pleasure, said the *Curé*, who, as you might expect, was one of the main exponents of this interpretation, but when you are weighed down with cares it costs something to wear a smile. Others were a little less idealistic in their requirements. For many people, to be *gentil* meant simply to show good-will and readiness to participate in equal social relationships: to be polite, to be willing to help when help was required, not to provoke quarrels with your neighbours.

While in casual conversation the word *fier* had always been used as though it were the contrary of *gentil*, when I enquired what exactly were the connotations of the word, it was universally agreed that it was *not* so: *gentillesse* and *fierté* might well be found in the same person. You should be proud of your appearance, of your work, of your house: 'Mme. Bavarel must be proud to be as gracious as she is,' said the wife of another farmer. 'Those who are not proud of their work live like pigs,' was an expression used more than once; the pig was often singled out as a symbol of asocial habits. Both Augustin's keeping manure in front of the house, and his wife's reluctance to do housework, marked them out for M. Bavarel as people who lacked such self-respect.

The opposite of graciousness was conveyed in a number of words: different people suggested *orgueilleux* (arrogant), *méchant* (malicious) or *hargneux* (surly). In the past, villagers who exhibited these characteristics were mocked by the others by means of derogatory nicknames such as 'The Customs Official', 'The Seigneur', 'The Pasha'. These were the people who were proud without justification; they were *rien du tout*. They tried unreasonably to assert themselves at others' expense. 'It is the pride of one against another that is bad,' was one explanation offered. Such people imagine they can do without the help or advice of others, as did Augustin when he paid no attention to his friend's warning on the way to the wedding.

Sometimes people were accused of exhibiting *jalousie*. It forms a kind of counterpart to pride. If one person accused another of being unreasonably proud, the latter could retaliate by accusing the first of jealousy. The two terms form the poles around which quarrels between unequals develop: villagers recognized that inequality in the number of machines or cattle owned was a likely source of tension, the important thing being not to draw attention to such differences (see below).

If one is *fou, on ne répond plus à ses actes* (one is no longer responsible for one's acts). This might be because you were madly in love, consumed with jealousy, drunk, or so obsessed with work that you never stopped to rest. Alternatively it might mean no more than that you were a little simple: it was in this sense that villagers applied the term to Felix Viennet, and Claude Bavarel to Mme. Jouffroy when he described her whistling in the garden. However, it became clear fairly soon that the word *fou* was often being applied rather loosely, and in a way that made it available as a label in scandalizing gossip. Some of the villagers pointed this out. One explained: 'We use the expression to describe anyone who behaves in a bizarre fashion; if you saw someone doing something that was unreasonable you would dismiss it by saying: "Oh, he's crazy." But,' the speaker continued, 'you should not confuse this kind of action with the *folie* of a madman.' Another, having described how one might appear crazy through drink or passion, went on to say that there were certain people in the village who were crazy because they behaved in a fashion that was *tout au contraire des autres* (entirely contrary to the rest). I think this (in this case) apparently innocent comment indicates just how important the concept may be in a situation of change. This is a topic which I will consider again below.

Some were more tolerant of idiosyncrasies than others. One farmer, to illustrate what the word *fou* implied, described how he had once watched Felix Viennet wheel his water tank down the hill to the village square, fill it from the pump and push it back to the farm without, apparently, thinking of connecting it to the tractor. Having said this, however, he dismissed it with the comment: '*Mais chacun a sa manière!*' (Everyone has his own style.)

It seems to me that the way in which these terms are interrelated corresponds very closely to what George Kelly thought of as the structure of personal constructs. The aim of personal construct theory (*Kelly; Bannister and Mair*) is to discover how people represent to themselves the events of their environment. The individual is supposed to establish a series of related concepts in order to predict the outcome of future events, and these constructs are strengthened, revised or abandoned as the events take place. Personal constructs are said to be based on similarity and contrast: the individual opposes good to bad, black to white. They differ from the constructs of conventional logic in that the latter would oppose *black* to *not black*, including in the latter category both the contrasting and the irrelevant. Personal constructs, however, have a specified range of applicability: excluding certain things as irrelevant. It is meaningful to say that one's shoes are not white; not to say this of the time of day. Nevertheless, some constructs have a wider application than others. Kelly describes two ways in which one construct may subsume another. It may do so by extending the cleavage implied in the other: *good* may include all that is *intelligent*, and more, while *bad* would include all things that were *stupid* and other things besides. Otherwise, the more general construct may cut across the other's cleavage: *evaluative—descriptive* might thus be designed to cut across *intelligent—stupid*, making both evaluative and contrasting this dichotomy with, for example, that between *light* and *dark*. Diagrammatically, the situation could be represented as follows:

	evaluation		description	
decreasing range of applicability	good	bad	light	dark
	intelligence	stupidity		

Each individual has his own construct system. Similar constructs may be concealed in the use of different words, or different constructs implied despite the use of similar words (cf. the way in which *fier* has different meanings at different levels of analysis). Thus, two people may attribute the same terms to a different range of meaning, one making *black—white* purely descriptive, the other extending the dichotomy so that it also had an evaluative sense. Another source of individual variation lies in the variety of terms that may make up the negative pole of constructs in which a common label is used for the positive aspect: *kind* may be opposed to *cruel, tough* or *critical*, each of which would place *kind* in a particular light. It was in just this way that different people opposed *gentil* to *orgueilleux, méchant* and *harngnux*, and so too that some interpreted *gentil* more idealistically than others.

The most important point, however, must be that a comparison of the villagers' various explanations of the terms shows not only that there was a degree of individual variation, but also that there was to a large extent consensus as to what they implied. Kelly argued that the potential diversity of personal constructs is limited by a common cultural background. While, he said, stimulus-response theory would see people grouped together on the basis of similarities in upbringing and in environment, a sociological approach—such as Kelly would prefer—emphasizes the similarities between what members of a group *expect* of one another. That makes the psychology of personal constructs an anticipatory theory of behaviour, not only in terms of personal outlook but also in terms of what the individual anticipates others will do and, in turn, what he thinks they are expecting him to do. People belong to the same cultural group not merely because they behave alike, nor because they expect the same things of others, but especially because they construe their experience the same way. (Condensed from *Kelly*, p. 94.) As long, in fact, as people act according to a shared set of expectancies, their behaviour will validate continued use of the existing constructs.

The terms *gentil, fier* and *fou* are used in order to define a cultural construct in which, broadly speaking, *gentillesse* refers to the willingness to participate in the reciprocity of social relationships between equals, and *fierté* to the deliberate refusal to do so. The range of applicability of this construct is, I would argue, wilful behaviour: it excludes those who, because they are *fou*, cannot be held responsible for their acts. The constructs formed by, for example, the opposition between simple ill-will and the malicious spitefulness of *la rancune*, or that between self-respect and the priding of oneself over others, are, I think, subordinate constructs: they have a more limited range of applicability, and may be used to make a more detailed analysis once the person discussed has been placed in the correct super-ordinate category. A diagram similar to that given above to illustrate Kelly's examples might look like this:

	la gentillesse	*la fierté*	
decreasing range of applicability	*fierté de soi-même*	*fierté d'un contre l'autre*	
		la méchanceté	*la rancune*

One way of looking at these terms is to see them as the labels for the values shared by members of the community: the norms which define whether or not fair rates of exchange are being maintained in the transactions that take place between individuals. Just as each individual may have his own personal construct system, so different communities may have different sets of norms: even if all are concerned to conceptualize the properties inherent in social exchange. The dichotomy of *confidenza—riguardo* described by John Martin for his Italian village,[7] while equally having as its subject-matter the evaluation of transactions between individuals, implies a rather different analysis of the situation. Firstly, the words refer to the relationships that are established rather than the attitudes of those entering into them. A relationship of *confidenza* is one in which there is trust and intimacy; *riguardo* denotes the wariness which goes with the fear of becoming too greatly indebted to someone who would otherwise be one's equal in status. Secondly, the relationship feared by those who show *riguardo* is one in which they themselves would become dependent through their inability to make returns for needed services: while *fierté* describes the attitude of those who refuse to reciprocate despite possession of the needed resources. This suggests that at least part of the explanation for these cultural differences may lie in the relative wealth of the French over the Italian community.

SIGNALS AS EVIDENCE OF A PERSON'S DISPOSITION

A second way of looking at the terms is to see them as though they were a language which gives meaning to the many individual transactions that occur between members of the community. Each transaction could be thought of as a statement about the relative status of those involved, deriving its significance from the way in which the terms used to describe the attitudes of those participating are structurally related. What is particularly important is that the key words refer to states of mind, and states of mind are in themselves unknowable; they reveal themselves only in outward behaviour: in *pragmatic transaction* and *symbolic communication.*

So far in this essay I have been concerned with the first aspect: transaction. What I will now go on to discuss is the second: symbolic communication.

When asked to define *gentil, fier,* etc., the villagers did so not only in terms of how such values were expressed in patterns of co-operation, or in refusal or inability to recognize one's obligations towards other members of the society. They referred also to patterns of symbolic behaviour on which, in practice, they rely to a great extent to obtain evidence of others' attitudes. Each of the major personality traits is associated with a set of *signals,* which are taken as much to *predict* how a person would behave in an exchange relationship as how he acts in those already established. A person signals his attitude many more times than he engages in an actual transaction.

The signals of graciousness are those of sociability: you do not sit in your house all day brooding over your own affairs, but go out and greet people in the street. The simplest way to do so is to say '*bonjour*' and to shake hands on meeting and on parting; although sometimes this might be felt a little too formal: 'How many people are there in this village?' someone once demanded rhetorically. 'You can't say "*bonjour*" to the same person ten times in a morning!'

One of the younger farmers gave quite a long exposition on the subject of showing one's sociability. The correct thing to do, said he, was to make *une boutade* (a witticism) *pour détendre* (to ease the situation). Often, he explained, you would make some comment on the work in progress. Certain comments, however, had been so over-used that it was no longer *une affaire d'esprit* (wit) to produce them. The three brothers over the road were for ever demanding, if you were loading a trailer of manure: *ça charge?*; or if you were cutting wood: *ça coupe?* and that irritated him. One such overworked expression was to say, if you saw someone picking apples in a tree, 'It'll be fine tomorrow!' and when the other enquired why, you replied: 'Because the monkeys are climbing!' The *Maire*, apparently, had suffered this exchange so often while changing bulbs in the street lamps that he was wont to reply: 'No, it'll rain because the street below me is crawling with frogs.'

To stay in your house all day, to walk down the street without greeting those whom you pass, shows a lack of graciousness, and like the more positive signs of boasting or presuming to instruct others, indicates a lack of social spirit. 'I may have good cattle, and I may be proud of the fact, but if I mention it too often to others they will accuse me of being conceited,' said Claude Bavarel once. Another, when he attempted to explain to some of the younger farmers what they should do to capture an escaped cow, was eventually silenced with the remark: 'My God, he lectures like St. Paul!'

During the cereal harvest Nicholas Jouffroy arrived one afternoon in the corner of the valley that was being cut, in his *deux chevaux* (a small car). Those already present were sittting on a trailer in the sun, drinking beer and wine. Nicolas stopped some metres from the group. His small daughter was with him in the car, and when someone held up a bottle, asking if he would join them, he retorted by producing a bottle of lemonade; saying that he and 'Liddie' would drink that. One man expressed the vague air of resentment among the group by demanding: 'What's that, whey?' This was not, I think, simply meant to imply that wine was a rather more powerful drink than lemonade. The whey left over from cheese manufacturing in the village dairy is used as pig food, and I suspect that (perhaps just implicitly) there was a suggestion in the comment that Nicolas was not coming up to expected standards of sociability; that he was 'living like a pig'.

One of the most striking things about the interpretation of signals is that there is a far greater degree of misunderstanding possible than there is in the realm of the exchange of goods and services. In principle the villagers recognized the distinction between a state of mind and the signals that expressed it, as did those of Goffman's Shetland Island community. Someone made the classic comment: 'There are many here who are polite to your face, but jealous behind your back.' Another maintained that you could be jealous of your neighbour's having twenty cows when you only had ten yourself, but continue to behave in a gracious fashion for all that, greeting him when you passed in the street and inviting him in for a drink: 'Some people show their jealousy,' said he, 'and others keep it to themselves.' Goffman's book *The Presentation of Self* was primarily concerned with the ways in which people deliberately attempt to mislead others by signalling an attitude to which they do not in fact subscribe. I think, however, that there is another aspect that is equally interesting; namely that if people assume, or demand, that behaviour be mutually predictable and equivalent—that everyone should speak the same cultural 'language'—there may be misunderstanding over others' values. The unintentional presentation of inappropriate signals could have a great impact on social relationships.

Thus Claude Bavarel himself was often mentioned as being not particularly gracious, but in a way that people apparently found a little difficult to pin down. He was unfortunate, since his wife was notably *gentille*, and he suffered more than he might otherwise have done in the comparison. One couple offered the following explanation. It was not that he was unco-operative, since he was always ready to help others when asked, but he was *distant* (aloof). It was his *allure*, his demeanour. He walked to the dairy and back twice a day without looking to right or left, and not saying a word to anyone. I suggested to the couple who were speaking that perhaps he was failing to give the right signs. The wife agreed that this could be so, and commented that one could even appear proud through timidity, although whether or not that was true of him she didn't know. Here, then, is someone who is apparently gracious enough, but who was unfortunately failing to give the right signals, and hence being labelled as antisocial. There were two men, an uncle and nephew, between whom social relations seemed to have broken down. On different occasions they both explained to me that the rift had formed ten years ago, when the other had inexplicably ceased to call out a greeting as he passed.

DEVIANCE

So far I have treated the community as though it were largely homogeneous, but this is in fact not entirely so. Pellaport has been undergoing relatively rapid change, both economic and political, since the Second World War, and as different people have followed different courses of action or advocated different policies, so heterogeneity has been introduced. As more choices of action become available, so there is more scope for diversity in behaviour patterns. But this, from the point of view of those who remain close to the norms, means that more people will be behaving in apparently bizarre fashions. This is particularly true of innovators, but it also applies to those who persist too long with traditional methods.

Those who are attracted to each other, Blau writes, generally agree about basic issues if an associate insists on holding a contrary opinion the others will try to dissuade him, and if this fails they will reject him: 'he is defined as a Red, and his arguments no longer have to be taken seriously' (p. 71). Kelly makes a similar point within the framework of personal construct theory, and suggests what the result may be. Those living in the same community tend to behave alike because they share a set of cultural constructs, defining expectations of how they and others are likely to behave. If in such a situation a person fails to behave according to his neighbours' expectations, they respond as though he had threatened them; and indeed he *has* threatened them. 'Now he may start to fancy himself as an unpredictable person —unpredictable that is for other people. In that case he may go right on shocking the neighbours. His conceptualization of him-self, at the same time, is markedly affected. In order to maintain his pose he may have to construe himself as a "shocking" person' (p. 177). So, when standing with a group in the village square Felix Viennet would live up to his role as the Fool by pretending to strike the others on the back of the head with a sledge hammer, and Nicolas Jouffroy, the wayward innovator, would sit at general meetings of the agricultural co-operatives with his hands in his pockets and his feet on the bench in front.

What I am concerned with here is the way in which departure from the norms affects the others' perception of the deviant as an individual. Leslie Wilkins, in a study of *Social Deviance*, claimed that there were two respects in which a village community differed from an urban one. The first was that members of a village culture have far greater experience of each other as total personalities, and that for this reason they are better able to tolerate inherently deviant individuals. While a town dweller can reject the *role* of mental subnormality, for villagers this would be to reject the *person*, Jack, 'who is part of the total culture' (p. 63). 'Maybe he drools, but he is also known to be harmless, and his father was a good workman' (p. 68).

I think, however, that this rather benevolent view of village life should be qualified in two ways. Firstly, material such as Elizabeth Bott's shows that close-knit communities are not confined to villages. While presenting the village as the type of such a group, *Bott* argues that they might be found in any area with an occupationally-homogeneous population, where migration to and from the district was low (p. 104). The converse of this is that in any community where the population is heterogeneous, accurate knowledge of others is likely to be reduced. Wilkins does in fact modify information; suggesting it is not size, but the rate at which information about deviants is obtainable, that is the crucial factor; but he maintains that in general as the size of the community increases, so the amount of information about the system available to its members declines. A second reason for qualifying Wilkins's picture of tolerance towards deviant individuals in the village community can be seen in Susan Hutson's material on change in Valloire.[8] She shows that knowledge about a person's background may be used just as much to pull aspiring individuals *down* into the body of the community as to lift deficient ones into it.

The second contrast that Wilkins sees between village and urban culture is in fact very much related to this point. It is that knowledge of individuals in all their aspects means that each particular person is allowed far less latitude around his allotted role than would be so in the anonymity of a town. In the village 'the blacksmith may not behave like a banker even in his spare time'. In an argument similar to that of Kelly, Wilkins suggests that the rejection of a deviant sub-group has the effect of a self-fulfilling prophecy: as the deviants see themselves to be rejected, so they will tend to establish their own subculture. This in turn will further decrease the ability of either deviants or parent culture to obtain information about each other: crime generates intolerance, and intolerance generates further crime (p. 90).

Deviance has led to the increasing isolation of some farmers in Pellaport. The most striking example is that of Maurice Genre's refusal to hire the combine harvester. Once everyone else had adopted this new technique he was ridiculed by the remainder, and as he withdrew from the community so this reduced his chances of learning just how efficient the most recent combines are.

Those at the other end of the scale, who innovate, are in something of a similar position. First, they are likely to be dismissed as 'crazy'. In behaving in a fashion that is 'entirely contrary to the rest' they are unavoidably giving off signals of abnormality, however rational their motives. This exposes them not only to genuine misunderstanding, but also to the malicious gossip of their rivals. In Blau's terms, they become 'Reds'. The point at which the innovator ceases to be off-course, is that at which the body of the village also change and conform to the new pattern: a pragmatic rule becomes a normative one. Past innovators often vindicated themselves or were vindicated by their friends, with the comment: but x, y, z (their critics) soon started to do the same themselves. Despite this, however, people continued in their refusal to learn from the subsequent justification of past departures.

The innovator's second problem is that if he attempts to persuade others to accept his judgement (something that may be crucial in the field of political innovation), he runs a strong risk of being labelled 'too proud'. Certainly Nicolas Jouffroy suffers this problem now. Despite the fact that many of the other young farmers admire him, Nicolas was well aware that some villagers did not approve of his activities. He seemed to accept this a little defiantly: 'What if they do say I'm proud?' he once demanded —'Everyone has a right to be proud of their efforts.' It was rumoured that he had ambitions to become *Maire* when the present one retired, but several of the older villagers were preparing to resist this threat: 'He will want to run everything himself; he won't listen to others' advice,' I was told. Evidence for this is found not only in his own behaviour but also in that of Augustin, his father, a former *Maire*, whose meetings were boycotted by the contemporary council because (according to Claude Bavarel) 'he refused to listen to them'. Notice, however, that Nicolas justified his ambitions by appealing to the principle of legitimacy, by referring to the normative framework: 'Everyone has a right to be proud of their efforts.' An ally of his among the younger farmers once made the same point, contrasting Nicolas's thoroughness with Felix Viennet's behaviour: the latter was incapable of ploughing a field properly and had no idea how to use machinery.

CONCLUSIONS

Kinship plays an extremely important part in the field of informal social relationships. In this area of activity (as distinct from that of inheritance) the kinship system can be thought of as bilateral: no practical distinction is made between one's mother's and one's father's relatives, and often a man will have close ties with his relatives by marriage as well. What results is a whole collection of ties between brothers, brothers-in-law, uncles and nephews . . . people who help each other, share machinery, drink together in the bar. Equally important are the ties between friends or neighbours; often, in fact, kin and neighbours are the same persons. It was constantly stressed, when talking about such relationships, that with kin and friends you worked without precisely counting the hours performed by one person for another, and without dealing in terms of money. The overall pattern is of a network that extends from one end of the village to the other. 'In an organized group the component individuals make up a larger social whole with common aims, inter-dependent roles, and a distinctive sub-culture. In network formation, on the other hand, only some, not all, of the component individuals have social relationships with one another.' (*Bott*, p. 58.)

Sometimes relatively large groups assemble informally: for specific tasks such as refencing the communal pasture and moving the heifers to and from the pasture during spring and autumn, or, on a more long-term basis, for the joint purchase of farm machinery. But there are no rules to say precisely who should associate with whom, or on what conditions, and in general the only associations that form on the basis of interpersonal ties are small and impermanent. It is important to note that the kind of person with whom one co-operates is exactly the kind of person with whom one most often quarrels, and that people may even co-operate with those with whom they have recently quarrelled. The values that govern such relationships are those expressed in the concepts of *gentillesse, fierté,* etc.; ideas which conceptualize the degree of another's sociability. They are not associated with organized sanctions, but simply with the diffuse ones of ridicule, ostracism or public disapproval. As much as they provide a relatively objective scheme for judging another's sociability, moreover, the terms also form a framework for the kind of covert evaluation and one-upmanship on which scandalizing gossip is built.

The general picture of community life at this level is, then, not one of the organic solidarity that appears in the realm of formal association (that of the agricultural co-operatives and municipal council), but one of the solidarity that is created by a multiplicity of overlapping allegiances and the temporary divisions of passing conflict.

NOTES

1. In the past, the farming household might have included several adult siblings. This is no longer so, but with one exception each household contains the minimum of a married couple. Sometimes members of three generations are represented.
2. Despite his emphasis on the importance of the properties inherent in social exchange, *Blau* does take both these qualifications into account (pp. 18, 147–55, 199).
3. *Paine* (1), p. 283.
4. *Bailey* (4), p. 102.
5. *Gluckman* (2), p. 34.
6. The first sense is that in which it is used in *Firth* (2), p. 4.
7. Unpublished field report, University of Sussex.
8. See Chapter 3.

6

Rendre service and Jalousie

The commune, which I here call Auguste, was the chef lieu *(county town) of the canton of Auguste in the west of Ariège in the French Pyrenees. The commune has a permanent population (that is, people who remain in the commune for the winter) of about 320, of whom 200 live in the main village of Auguste at 500 metres altitude. A further 120 live in the eleven scattered farms and hamlets that perch in the hills above the river valleys (at between 600 and 800 metres).*

Auguste, and her nearest neighbour and rival village, Sept, stand at the junction of two river valleys and two roads. These two roads, and, therefore, two valleys, are now joined to open a ski-ing area, but none of the roads provide a route through into Spain. The roads that lead into the canton terminate there. This fact accounts for the long isolation of the area and the late (in relation to other areas of the Pyrenees) attempts at development and change.

The economic base of Auguste is peasant agriculture. Apart from a small (100 hectare) rich plain at the confluence of the two rivers, the rough hilly terrain inhibits arable farming. The peasants have milch-cows and raise sheep. The main crops are for fodder—hay, maize, wheat, beets and potatoes—and fruit and vegetables for domestic use. However, few full-time culti-vators are left in the commune.

At the beginning of this century the population of Auguste was over 1000. But poverty, especially in the hamlets, forced migration. As the peasant population declined the artisans and commercial people who depended upon the peasant market, left too. In the twentieth century the rate of depopulation rose, and took most of the young people from the commune. Now sixty per cent of the permanent population are over sixty. Most of these supplement their pensions with some farming. There are only four active young peasant households and they claim that circumstances forced them to stay. Like everyone else in the commune, they do not want their children to have to work the land. The cultivators and retired people talk of their commune as 'dead alive', a 'lost corner'. They find it peaceful and calm, a good place for holidays, but a sad empty village.

The main part of the population is aged, living on their pensions and in some cases involved with agriculture. It is primarily with these people that this essay is concerned. However, there are some younger families in the commercial sector of the commune. There are six shopkeepers or café owners, a tailor, a decorator and a man who keeps a garage. The commune also has three road workers, some members of the national police force, three wives who are teachers, two electricity board employees and a youth leader living in the village. One man, now the village's mayor, lives in the village but commutes weekly to work in another department.

While the old people think of their commune as a sad place, depopulated and lacking youth and vitality, the new mayor, with the tacit support of his municipal council, is trying to bring development to the commune. He wants to develop the resources of the area, promote tourism, increase commerce and enlarge the population. To understand the problems facing a village leader attempting change it is necessary to know how the people make meaning out of action, and how they understand others.

'JALOUSIE'

I was told by the people that I would understand nothing until I knew about the *mentalité*. 'It is a bad *mentalité*: we are all *jaloux*.' 'The people around here are individualists and quite independent.' 'Here the villagers are greedy and cunning. Each one is out for himself.'

The most commonly used word to describe *mentalité* and the behaviour of others was *jalousie*.

> We went and asked if he [a migrant living away from the village] would sell us land to consolidate our field. We offered a good price, but he refused. He was *jaloux*.

In this context the English word 'jealousy' would not be appropriate. Indeed, when I heard the word I asked 'jealous of what?' My informants simply repeated what they had already said. By looking at other examples the meaning becomes plain.

> Every household is *jalouse*. I am not building myself up, but just look at machinery. I buy a machine and the others follow. Frank is always next. People want to be as good as one another, so they buy the same machine. There is no co-operation in this approach.

Here *jalousie* is explained in terms of its results. 'They buy the same machines.' 'There is no co-operation.' They also talk of motives. 'People want to be as good as one another.' *Jalousie* evidently has the sense of 'pride'. It is the protection of one's own interest or status. This statement is clearly about competition. The speaker was at pains to say that he was not building himself up. Yet it can be read as follows: One man buys a machine: this looks good and may be taken as a bid for community respect: to protect one's own reputation vis-à-vis the first man, one does the same. The action is one of self-protection.

In this context, 'status' means the reputation of a man in a community. The reputation that any man has will depend upon the values of the community. In Auguste this would involve many factors: the way he fulfils his role as head of the household, as father and husband; the way he behaves towards his neighbours; his family history and so on. But it is also influenced by material possessions and life-style. *Jalousie* can be understood as the protection of one's own rights or status against a perceived challenge.

In the example below, Frank's wife is talking about Paul, whose comment on buying machinery is given above:

> Their hay-baler ran out of string. I had string. They did not ask me for any, and I did not offer. They are *jaloux*.

Here the word connotes pride. In *patois* the exclamation '*que jalouso*' is common, and *jalouso* means pride, protective jealousy.

> Everyone makes comparisons. If one person buys something new the others want it as well. People have more money, they want more and spend more. They are *jaloux*; it was not like that before.

I

Money has made everyone *jaloux*. Before it was more fraternal, people helped one another, one could ask for help. The commercial families made hay like the peasants.

The village is full of *jalousie*. It's the old age pension that did it. Everyone has more money so they are *jaloux*. Before people cared for their parents, now it is not the same, everything has changed.

These three statements blame money for an increase in *jalousie*. Money has made people competitive. Competition exists because everyone wants to defend their own status. Money not only means increased buying power; it also provides more areas of comparison between households and more areas of competition. To protect one's own interests and status is harder than in the past.

The people of Auguste believe that men are motivated by jealousy and pride. This belief not only explains the behaviour of others but also prescribes action. In order to protect oneself from the self-interest of others, wariness (*méfiance*) is necessary. People claim with vigour: 'I owe nothing to anyone.' 'We never buy on credit.' 'We were born independent.'

Jalousie means that people act in their personal interest. They act for their own gain and may exploit others to this end. It is necessary to be wary of others. To protect oneself one must not only be wary, but pursue one's own best interest, as others do, or risk being exploited. People should help their neighbours and should be kind and considerate to others. But one should be careful in giving or accepting help.

The outcome of his set of beliefs is that independence is highly valued and tenaciously guarded.

GOSSIP AND SLANDER

Jalousie is both expressed and activated through gossip. Gossip, like *jalousie* is expected.

Although *jalousie* prescribes a studied lack of concern in the affairs of others and the people are quick to condemn some forms of gossip, they think that some talk is only natural in a small community. Good, 'natural' gossip is called *bavarder*, which means idle chatter. The people say that where everyone knows everyone else general news-passing is inevitable. But it is not always considered harmless. *Mauvaise langue* is indisputably bad. It is slander, the passing on of defamatory information about others.

Gluckman (1963) writes that the function of gossip is to express group values. This is the sense in which *bavarder* is said to be natural. But he also says that the fear of gossip may be seen as a product of the lack of privacy. The ambivalence about *bavarder* may be understood in this way. It threatens privacy.

But gossip is ambivalently regarded for another reason. Seeing other people talking, it is not possible to tell if they are merely chatting or spreading defamatory information. As everyone is out for themselves it may well be the latter. *Mauvaise langue* can be understood (*Paine*, (i), p. 283) as protection of one's own interests. However, it may also be seen as status competition, as a way of lowering another person while boosting oneself. The scandal spreader may try to present another man as less honest, good, attractive or morally worthy. By so doing he can assert his own worth.

Radcliffe-Brown suggests that manifestations of social distance (like reserve or respect) will be pronounced where social relations seem ambivalent. Here I have presented chatter as a matter of ambivalent judgement. Indeed, fear of being thought a scandal spreader makes some members of the community avoid speaking to others for any length of time in public. Old women are especially prone to *mauvaise langue*, and they are sufficiently sensitive to avoid being seen in public *tête-à-tête*. But the fear of getting a reputation as a gossip, as a woman with a *mauvaise langue*, does not prevent social intercourse between people anymore than fear of *jalousie* keeps neighbours apart. Ambiguous situations must be confronted and problems faced. A person who avoids contact with others will not only be seen as *jaloux* but as *sauvage*. *Sauvage* is used to criticize people. It means not only timid, but also uncivilized and incapable of dealing with others. Although the dividing line between *bavarder* and *mauvaise langue* is narrow, and although *jalousie* necessitates caution in social contacts, one cannot gain community respect by avoiding others.

Fear for one's own reputation presents the people of the commune with a problem in social interaction. The problem is keeping a balance between avoidance and sociability. For although *jalousie* describes how people are, it is not how they ought to be. People 'ought' to act out of *bonne volonté*. *Bonne volonté* is goodwill, community spirit and openness. These qualities are valued and gain communal approval. The appeal for *bonne volonté* can and does provide a moral imperative which legitimizes an appeal for action. I have heard both mayor and priest appeal for *bonne volonté* in pursuing some project, a new road, land reform or tourist housing. But although the villagers accept that *bonne volonté* is good, and what everyone should have, they do not think that others act out of community spirit, or that they themselves, should. If the world was perfect everyone would manifest *bonne volonté*. In fact one sees *jalousie* everywhere.

Because the actual world of people is a world of proud, jealous others, people in the community who are acknowledged to be men of *bonne volonté* are also thought to be rather odd. They are not normal. Therefore, to be a man of *bonne volonté* does not necessarily give community respect.

EXPLOITATION

Evidently there is a problem in the balance between avoidance and concern, between independence and community spirit.

The people here are like all the people of the Midi; they cannot join together. If you hold a meeting they may come and applaud, but they will not come to another meeting. They always have other things to do. If you organize an association you end up doing all the work.

In the North people can weld together; here they cannot. Here they are not disciplined. They do not have confidence in their neighbours. They suspect their neighbour of trying to eat them, and this is because they are trying to eat their neighbour. Here we cannot amalgamate or unionize. The basic reason is the lack of confidence in neighbours.

We were born independent; it is in our blood. The Arabs ruled here for over a hundred years before they were packed off to Spain. They left their mark on the people. The people of this area are 200 per cent individualists. We were born independent. Yet, if you ask a man to do you a favour (*rendre service*) he will do it fourfold. Otherwise, he will let you get on with it alone.

The same spirit rules relationships between communities:

Auguste and the neighbouring commune do not co-operate, because they are *jaloux*. It is the same with neighbours in the village. Everyone is afraid that the other will eat him up. They are *jaloux* and so they do not co-operate.

In fact, the world is a dangerous place:

There will always be injustice. Big fish always eat little fish. As long as there is a world it will be like that. People cheat others. It is worse now than before. . . . The priest may talk of changing the *mentalité*, but that is his job . . . he talks to make money. Money is needed for everything. . . . To get money you need the help of the Deputy. Some men are stronger than others. One doesn't get money just because of need; one has to be in the right party as well. It is always like that. Everywhere one is cheated. If you buy things you cannot know if it is good or not . . . (cf. *Wright*, p. 189).

These three quotations use the same metaphor to describe relationships between neighbours. The 'bigger' 'stronger' or more powerful will try to take over or 'to eat' the weaker. Neighbours are both hostile and exploitative. Wariness is necessary. Reserve offers protection.

But more than reserve or wariness are made necessary by this view of the world. If any man is stronger than another the lesser will be exploited. It is necessary, therefore, to try and maintain equality and always to avoid being in a weak position.

RECIPROCITY

The need for extreme caution co-exists with a positive value put upon being a good neighbour, of looking to the needs of others, and of showing the elusive *bonne volonté*. Yet, even in helping others it is necessary to keep a balance between giving and receiving. A man who makes his help too obvious and refuses return will be suspected of trying to become stronger. He may arouse fear, and so not gain a good reputation.

The villagers' word for co-operation and giving service (*rendre service*) implies an exchange. As far as possible the people avoid asking or receiving help in situations where exchange of the same type of resources is not possible. The absolute shortage of labour in the commune, and the fact that some households lack sufficient flat arable land means that co-operation and exchange are necessary. By keeping a balance in the exchange people try to maintain their independence.

The attitudes of the people may be understood in the following way:

Independence is opposed to dependence.
Independence is positively valued: dependence is negative.

Individualism is opposed to co-operation.
Co-operation is positively valued.

Individualism is NOT independence and is negatively valued.

Individualism is the avoidance of contact with others: 'I have no need of you.' Independence is the ability to co-operate but to avoid being regularly in a receiving position and so becoming indebted. Hence it is the *reciprocity in co-operation which maintains independence.* Extremes of pride and individualism force people apart and would destroy any sense of community. Balanced reciprocity binds people together.

The highly valued independence and co-operation are united in reciprocity, through which the gap between what is (*jalousie*) and what ought to be (*bonne volonté*) is bridged. Co-operation and mutual aid involve balancing dependence and independence. This balance is possible in the relationships of mutual assistance. A man must reciprocate to maintain his independence, pride and reputation.

Mutual aid is called *rendre service*. This means, literally, to return someone a service. *Rendre*, used alone, means 'repay' and therefore implies exchange and it closes the gap between *jalousie* and *bonne volonté*.

Informants insisted that if one gave a *service* there was no legal obligation to repay. There was, however, a moral obligation. To *rendre service* was to do someone a favour. If one accepted a favour, one felt obligated. *Rendre service* did not apply in situations where duty was involved. Thus, a father would not *rendre service* to his son, nor a son to his father. The two were duty-bound to assist one another. Between neighbours help was not a duty in the same way, neither was repayment. *Rendre service* is assistance done as a favour.

The favour need not be immediately reciprocated, although repayment is expected. A man should not offer to *rendre service* to another because those words imply a favour that will be repaid. Rather one should offer to give a helping hand, *un coup de main*. By so doing the sense of a return being expected is kept in the background. It is then up to the recipient to judge what return, if any, need be made.

Rendre service is commonly used in the community to describe the help that neighbours give to one another, mainly in agricultural work. The services involved are ploughing, cutting wood, harvesting or offering the use of grazing land. Exchange is between equals.

In these instances the same sort of goods or services are exchanged. The return for ploughing a field is visible and tangible. The importance of this point will emerge when we look at the alternative form of *rendre service*. The first form of exchange is symmetrical, in the sense that both partners should take care to treat each other as equals. Of the farmers who would be capable of working a field for an elderly widow (that is those who have a tractor or strong cows) she will ask the assistance of a man with whom she feels she could enter into a reciprocal relationship. Her choice will be such as to minimize her own possible indebtedness, and one where the exchange need not be instantly balanced. In practice, for most people, there is one farmer whom they know best, who is a friend, and it is from him that they ask for labour services.

Giving and receiving in the agricultural sector is largely carried out in the idiom of friendship. Although the friendships in the village are instrumental to some extent, so long as an emotional component is identified in the relationship, neither partner need fear being exploited or 'being eaten' by a stronger neighbour.

Rendre service is also used to describe an exchange of a different form. If a man in a factory went to the boss and asked for a job, and the boss found him one, this would be an example of someone giving service. The man who got the job could never repay the boss, but he could show him respect, or perhaps give him symbolic gifts of garden produce. If a gift demands a return, and no tangible return is possible, the repayment will be through support or esteem. This is asymmetrical reciprocity. This kind of *rendre service* describes a patron/client exchange. The patron has access to specialized services or resources. He makes these available to another man. The recipient has no control over these specialized services. To repay his debt he gives esteem or political support.

In Auguste people value giving service to one another. Such services should be in the idiom of friendship. The balancing of returns should never be obvious. The asymmetrical form should not take place between neighbours. For this reason people are wary in co-operation.

If one cannot repay a service, and the relationship between partners is not cordial, then the recipient feels indebted. There are two ways of overcoming this, either of which may jeopardize the reputation of the recipient. He may offer esteem to his creditor and thus suggest that they are no longer equals. Alternatively he can cut off contact entirely and risk not only getting a reputation for ingratitude but also finding no one else willing to help him.

AGRICULTURAL EXCHANGE

The formalization of exchange in *rendre service* is one way of giving help with minimal risk of misunderstanding. It allows for independence and co-operation. It is more than a utilitarian exchange and never purely monetary or momentary (*Sahlins*, p. 39). It is part of a continuous personal relationship where, within certain spheres, each gives and receives according to his needs and ability. Neither gives more than the relationship can sustain; but the relationship should be able to sustain periodic imbalances.

Gina, the wife of one of the village's youngest cultivators, Jo, said that she did not like this 'rendre service business'. She was upset when people felt obliged to make immediate repayment.

Her husband, Jo, had helped a couple of ageing peasants who could no longer manage the heavy work themselves. When he married and she came to the house the old people resented her presence and the fact that her husband's first interest was very firmly in his own land and family. On one occasion Gina had a row with the old woman who threatened to tell Jo what a terrible woman he had married. Gina was furious at their behaviour and no longer talks to the old woman.

Gina said that whenever her husband helped this couple the old woman came rushing round offering to do things which were totally unnecessary. Gina felt that the woman merely wanted to pay off a debt, and did not offer to help in a spirit of friendship. In *rendre service* there should be a balancing of giving and receiving, but this balancing should not be made obvious. Gina's disapproval of the old woman who returned services hastily was similar to the distaste which the Trobiand islanders have for a man who makes *kula* like a trade barter (*Malinowski*, pp. 189–190). *Rendre service* should be help in the cordial spirit of friendship. Repayment is never immediate, and the amount repaid is left to the debtor. Services are given where there is a relationship of trust. However, Gina and her husband continued to help the old couple. Their *rendre service* arrangement would have been hard to break without severing all links between the two households. It would be seen as a sign that the families were *fachées*. As *Mauss* (p. 11) says: 'To refuse to give, or the failure to invite is like refusing to accept—the equivalent of a declaration of war; it is a refusal of friendship and intercourse.'

In the example of Gina's family, the younger man gave service to the old. Many of the *rendre service* exchanges in Auguste are of this form, since the young farmers have tractors and the older peasants have land but lack machinery. But there must also be trust. In this case the old couple knew Gina's husband well enough not to fear that he would make capital out of the relationship and force them to feel subservient.

In agriculture relationships of *rendre service* exist mainly between old landowners and younger peasant farmers. The landowner gives a field. The younger man ploughs and works other fields and the two households work together in weeding and harvesting. The old couple give land and labour; the younger man provides heavy labour. Families who *rendre service* are drawn closer by the exercise of the relationship.

The exchange of services in the community, and the fear of *jalousie* and gossip have much to do with status considerations. But, in addition, decisions about how to run the farm owe more to considerations of status, indebtedness and the desire to feel independent, than to calculations about maximal returns on units of labour or capital.

A striking feature of agriculture in Auguste is the small size of the fields. This is partly the result of the inheritance laws which require, roughly speaking, equal division of the land between children. The fields are often too small for mechanization and yet, within the village itself, there are not only three tractors but separate sets of attachments to go with each tractor.

The cultivators each buy their own equipment. Yet, as an earlier quotation shows, they realize that this number of machines is not necessary. If they had not realized this themselves, visiting agricultural advisers have made it clear. Nevertheless, machinery is still duplicated and no thought has been given to the manner in which it could be shared. This too is an aspect of the *mentalité*, of the desire to be independent.

Each farmer wants a motor scythe, since scythes are needed at the same time of year. Sharing would be difficult. Tractors also, although not efficiently used, are in great demand in certain seasons and sharing them would require careful organization. However, the attachments which go with the tractor, and which are expensive (the maize-sower, muck spreader, harrows and balers) could be shared. This equipment is not used all the year round and I have never seen any two of these in the fields at the same time. Such equipment could be communally owned and each man could borrow the machine for the necessary time. Even in the village, where the three tractor owners lived and worked near to one another, each bought his own appliances.

They are reluctant to share equipment. While Paul was making hay, the engine of his baler spluttered and died. Rain threatened and there was still a lot of hay to get in. Frank's machine was lying idle some fifty yards away and its owner was not far away. Paul left his machine and went to the garage in the village, a quarter of a mile away, to get a mechanic to mend his hay-baler. When I asked why he did not finish the work with Frank's machine he said: 'I would not like to. What if something happened to it? No, we never borrow.'

Paul never borrows and he was proud of the fact. He never bought on credit and he did not ask for the help of the agricultural adviser. He was independent. Frank's wife knew this and attributed it to jealousy: he did not want to be indebted to others and wished to be independent.

On the other hand, neither Frank nor his wife offered either baler or string. Their failure to offer must be understood in terms of not wanting to threaten Paul's independence by making him feel indebted. Another example will make this clear.

Paul bought a secondhand maize-sower. It was the first maize-sower in the commune. When Jo, the third young village culti-vator, heard about this he burst out: 'The bastard! Why did he have to do that? If he had told us first we could have bought one together.' Frank said of Paul's machine: 'If he'd told us we could have got one together; a new one with a muck spreader as well. That would have been better.'

Jo and Frank were friends. They had an active *rendre service* relationship and enjoyed working together. They trusted one an-other. Their relationship was both emotional and instrumental. However, they owned no equipment in common and neither of them repeated comments of this kind to Paul.

Paul insisted that, if anyone asked, they could borrow the machine. He was not boastful about its efficiency; indeed he seemed most hesitant about it. He claimed that he would be happy for anyone to use it.

In the event, Frank, who grew more maize than anyone else in the commune, sowed all his maize by hand, as usual. He did not ask to borrow the machine. Paul did not offer. Other villagers saw this as an example of *jalousie*. Frank could manage, as he had other years, without the new machine. He had plenty of labour in his household. Although the work would have been done quicker, and would have been less arduous with the machine, it was not worth the risk of being refused, or of being accepted and feeling indebted to Paul. The relationship between the two men was not sufficiently warm for an imbalance to be easily supported. Paul, on the other hand, could not offer. This would have seemed to draw attention to his new possession and looked as if he wished to gain respect, both by lending the machine, and by owning something which Frank valued but did not possess.

If Paul had offered the machine to Frank he could have, on another occasion, asked for some string for the baler. The two men could have developed a mutual aid relationship with their machines. But, as I have shown, giving and receiving were not small matters in the community. Exchange followed social relations. To have extended their exchange relationship to include machines would have been more than their emotional friendship could sustain. Friendship would have been too openly instrumental and independence threatened.

The relationship with Jo is different. He now works the land part-time. He has another job as a lorrydriver in the town. He co-operates with Frank for much of his work and the two households visit frequently. The mutual respect between the two men is such that they do not fear indebtedness. They know not only that each will receive as well as give, but that neither would try to exploit the other or make him appear dependent.

Frank does not have this confidence in Paul. Furthermore, Frank does worry about the way the villagers assess relationships and allocate respect. He did not wish to risk looking indebted to Paul.

Jo is Paul's cousin. The two families are not very close because of a dispute between their parents over the inheritance. But Jo had sufficient self-confidence to ask for the loan of the machine. His request was not refused. Jo was delighted with getting the work of sowing done so quickly and effortlessly. Paul was pleased that Jo spoke so well of the performance of his sower.

Jo's action in borrowing the machine where social links between the two households were so weak, seems hard to understand in view of what was said earlier about independence and fear of indebtedness. However, the explanation of Jo's action reflects a change in the *mentalité*. Jo and his wife were young and had adopted many modern views. The most important of these was that they had confidence in their own value and worth. In a sense they had made their own reputation. They were not afraid of being thought indebted to Paul. They were relatively unconcerned with the community's judgements.

There is a partial lack of co-operation between the three younger farmers. However, co-operation does exist between each of these three young farmers and older peasants. Evidently, it is easier for an old, retired person to enter into an exchange relationship with a younger person than for two young people to co-operate. There seems only one way of understanding this. Young people are expected to be independent and to be capable of managing all farm work alone. The older people are respected for their age, and they are not expected to be able to do heavy work alone. An old man's reputation is not at risk if he accepts services from a younger man. A young man who accepts services from an equal risks appearing dependent.

POLITICAL EXCHANGE

Rendre service may also describe relationships of inequality. The superior partners in Auguste were, in the past, the *notables*. These were the leading old families, doctor, lawyer and merchants, who combined wealth with education and had political power. Now these men have gone from the community and it is politicians who act as patrons.

In Ariège politicians of all political parties frequently employ the phrase *rendre service*. Evidence of having given services to people, or of ability to *rendre service* forms an important part of election propaganda. Because *rendre service* implies a moral obligation to repay, the politician can use this to gain support and esteem.

The mayor of Auguste uses his capacity to give service and help people in order to win political support. In France one needs the signature of the mayor on many forms, especially for starting a business or for building. People also seek the mayor's advice before filling in pension or social security forms. In rural areas, like Auguste, where many of the old people are illiterate and unsure of their rights, this gives great scope for a mayor. I was told by many informants that a mayor could claim that he was doing the people a favour, and so win their esteem and respect, when in fact he was only doing his duty as mayor. One man described this as follows:

> When the old people go to the mayor with a form, he would look at the form and then pause with his hand over the paper. Looking at the peasant he would say that he would *rendre service* to them; he would *rendre service* and fill in the form.

The informant who presented this scene said that with a person who knew the law and their own rights the mayor would not pretend to be doing them a favour, he would just sign, as was his duty. (Cf. *Whyte*, p. 241.)

The mayor not only wins esteem and possibly votes by claiming to *rendre service*, he may also use past services as a means of persuading a man to support his schemes. On one occasion I went with the mayor on a visit to persuade a landowner to sign over land for a new road. The landowner was out, but his wife refused because they did not like the direction that the road was to take. As part of the appeal to the family, the mayor mentioned how he, as mayor, had done them a favour. Water had been piped to the cowshed at communal expense. This was not their right; the mayor had authorized it as a favour. The moral force of this appeal failed because the landowner's wife claimed that they had a right to water in their barn and refused to agree that they had received a favour. As the mayor left with his business still unsettled he offered to do the family another favour. He suggested that their son could get leave from national service to help with the harvest and that if he came to see the mayor this would be arranged. The following day the landowner walked to the village, and signed the forms.

Any would-be leader or political representative will try not only to *rendre service* to people, but to get them to acknowledge that he has done so. *Rendre service* and the obligation to repay only exists where a service is a favour, where duty is uninvolved. Where people are still often ignorant of their rights, and the mayor's duties, he may win support from those who feel indebted to him for some political service. However, some people in the community do not acknowledge any debt to the mayor. They are aware of their rights, and his duties. This does not make political patronage impossible but it does mean that a mayor now needs more than his status in the commune to win supporters. He needs also to be able to perform services which fall outside his responsibilities as mayor.

Where a person has received a service which the giver was not obliged to give, the receiver feels indebted. If he received the service from a village-equal, he may cancel the 'debt' by returning the service in some way. If the relationship between giver and receiver is asymmetrical then the recipient can only offer his support or esteem. Political practice of many years has taught the people to be wary of asymmetrical relationships. Stories of how the old patrons took the people's money and land still circulate. Present political practices are well known. The manipulation by politicians of the values of independence in part explains the wariness the cultivators show of any outside experts. As an example I describe briefly some of the attitudes towards agricultural advisers.

THE MODERNIZATION OF AGRICULTURE

In the market town to which the cultivators of Auguste go about once a fortnight to sell animals, there is a *Foyer du Progrès Agricole*. There are many such *Foyers* in rural France. They are staffed by nationally recruited experts, paid by the government, who can advise cultivators on the most rational way of exploiting their land. The services of the centre are free to cultivators and form part of the national effort to bring agricultural production into line with national needs. This is to be done, broadly, by modernizing agricultural techniques and discouraging small-scale subsistence farming.

The working of the *Foyer* was also intended to bring cultivators into contact with one another, as well as with advisers, and to encourage some form of collective effort to find solutions to local agricultural problems.

The agricultural adviser appointed to the commune of Auguste tried to organize the farmers into a group to experiment with new fertilizers and new strains of seed. This group was called a *Groupement de Vulgarisation Agricole* (G V A). A meeting was called and it was well attended. Each farmer was given a free sack of fertilizer. The second meeting was well attended. One man had prepared a report on how he had used the fertilizer and the results. No new gifts were given out. At the third meeting only four cultivators were present. It was said that it had all been a trick; they were expected to report on the seeds but farmers did not have time to do that. The G V A would give them nothing and only asked them to work for it.

The four men who continued to attend the meetings were three of the youngest cultivators in the commune and a returned migrant (from America) who had married a local girl. They continued to attend the meetings and the adviser visited their farms. The only man to give reports and experiment with crops was the ex-migrant. The other three reported not finding the adviser very valuable. One of them explained it like this:

I know I have a problem with my farm. We are always running backward and forward and I need the help of all the children to get the work done. But, I do not know what question to ask him. I don't know what's wrong; I just feel it must be wrong.

This farmer knew that on the plains and in other regions two people could run a larger farm than his. He also clearly felt that much too much time was spent at work. He once said 'If we counted all the hours we work and our families, us cultivators would never make a living wage.' However, the cultivators did not keep accounts, and they worked every hour they could. The only way they knew of saving time and energy, of modernizing, was to buy machines. The adviser could have answered special technical problems, but the cultivators were not capable of formulating such problems.

Communication was imperfect between the adviser and the cultivators whom he visited. Furthermore other peasants resented both the help the expert might have been giving, and the expert himself. He was described to me as a city man who looked as if he never muddied his shoes, let alone understood the problems of mountain farming. He was an outsider and could not know what local life was like.

The cultivators criticized those who used the adviser. One man said: 'There is an adviser. He goes to some of the others. He gives them grain and fertilizer for nothing. They were supposed to report back to the rest of us, but they do nothing. You see the *mentalité*? The adviser has never come to us. We did not ask him. We owe nothing to anybody.'

This man had not tried to rationalize his farm by using the free advice of an expert. He took this as a virtue. 'We owe nothing to anybody.' By doing so he was valuing his reputation for being independent above reduced work and increased yields.

On the other side the ex-migrant clearly enjoyed discussing farming with an expert and was keen to try new methods. Everyone in the commune considered that he had only come to the commune because he was so rich that he did not need to work, and he farmed to amuse himself. But the other three were young farmers who had families to support and not rich amateurs. Why did they risk the criticism of others?

It could be that they did value rational economic procedures and an increased income above the criticism of their neighbours.

If they had gained higher prices for their sheep they would have won a certain praise from local farmers. Possibly they hoped for this. But it is also worth noting that all three were members of the village council, and sensitive to the appeals of the village mayor. Thus, if the G V A and the adviser had been presented to them as a good thing, something worth following up, they would have done so as much out of a sense of duty to the mayor (who had done many services for each of them) as for their own economic gain.

CONCLUSION

I presented the *mentalité* of the people of Auguste by considering the words used to describe it and their meaning and then discussing the effects of attitudes upon exchange relationships. It is clear that villagers are deeply concerned about their reputation in the community. People want to be thought good neighbours and men of goodwill; yet they do not want to be thought to be trying to win a fine reputation. They want to be independent without struggling for it, and to be helpful neighbours without seeming to thrust help upon others.

Depopulation and education have intensified wariness by making people seem less equal and extending the areas of comparison. But there are also some people in the community who no longer give importance to old people's values. They do not fear being thought indebted by their neighbours because they have other values by which to assess themselves.

Change is not towards increased community spirit, greater *bonne volonté*. The mayor appeals for *bonne volonté*, especially from the older villagers who are the land owners. The younger supporters of the mayor acknowledge a moral force behind this appeal. The priest calls for *bonne volonté*; the agricultural advisers tried to create goodwill and co-operation. But the people are still mainly concerned to protect their own interests and their own reputation against others. As soon as any man acts, mayor and priest included, they are assumed to have acted for their own gain.

Independence and jealousy explain the lack of community-wide co-operation, and account for wariness in relation with outsiders. These values do not, however, preclude co-operation

K

between households, when in the form of *rendre service* and perhaps these values could be manipulated to bring about change and development. But *bonne volonté,* as community-wide co-operation, is accepted only as an ideal; it is not seen as a practical possibility.

7
Reputation, Criticism and Information in an Austrian Village

Sankt Martin is a mountain farming community. It is situated at the head of a long, narrow valley which runs into the south-facing slopes of the Austrian Tyrol. It has a population of 1020. Most inhabitants live in farmhouses scattered in groups of between two and four on the mountain slopes, within an area of about three square miles and at an altitude of between 1300 and 1750 m. Only since the Second World War has there arisen a small nucleated settlement around the church on the valley floor. Each landholder owns scattered parcels of forest, meadow, arable land and mountain pasture; there is also a small degree of joint ownership of certain areas of land. Agriculture is chiefly subsistence; any cash income comes through the sale of cattle and timber, although a few farmers gain supplementary incomes from non-agricultural sources. In the last 5–10 years, local demand for unskilled labour and greater ease of transportation has led to an increase in the non-farming element of the population (Arbeiter). *Tourism is at a minimum and restricted to a short two-month summer season.*

Administration is centred in the Gemeinderat (*council*) *which consists of ten local men elected by the villagers. These remain in office for periods of six years and are headed by the* Bürgermeister (*Mayor*) *whom members of the council elect from among their number every three years. The* Gemeinderat *also acts as an intermediary between the village and the regional government. Also living in the village are four customs officials with their families and two members of the* Gendarmerie (*Police*). *These men, apart from the priest and schoolteachers, are the only temporary residents in the community.*

In this chapter I am concerned with the traditional value system, the image which the individual presents on the basis of this value system and the ways in which internal criticism defines and maintains the system.

CONFORMITY

Gabers Moidl, who manages the household and farm of her dead brother, has for years been an eccentric with little regard for the social niceties of community life. She is termed 'Original' (different) with something like affectionate pride. Her eccentricity in no way threatens the village and its traditional values.

Anton is a small landowner with a large family. He is forced to supplement his income with occasional labouring jobs. An informant described him as a good Christian, an upstanding family man and a thrifty farmer who is well thought of in the community. This same informant on another occasion had other things to say. The discussion concerned Anton's ability to send three of his children to grammar schools on his supposedly minimal income. He is one of a handful of family heads who consider it worth doing. The priority he places on education was condemned as stupidity and ambition. He was accused of stinting the rest of his family to pursue the exaggerated ambitions he has for the three talented children (one of whom is a girl, which makes it worse in the eyes of the village). He is said to lie and cheat and beg for charity, in order to gain enough money. Finally, he is considered a hypocrite since he uses a good name gained from apparent adherence to the traditional values as a cover for his nefarious activities. The informant had helped Anton financially at one time and received nothing (according to him) in return. Qualities which he had originally praised he used in the second instance to support adverse criticism.

The case of David provides a similar example, but with a difference. He and his wife have a farm of the same small size as Anton's, but of better quality and situation. They have one son who is now a priest and missionary. On account of the sacrifices they have made to give this son an education and because —in doing so—they have robbed themselves of both son and heir, they hold considerable prestige in the community. This is so, although David is really only a small-holder and holds little influence in the village otherwise. But in supporting their son to the priesthood, they have given the village the honour of being able to sport a young missionary priest. This is something of which the whole village can be proud. However, if the son's education had led to anywhere but the priesthood, it is likely that they would have received the same criticism as Anton. A son's place is on the home farm and as perpetuator of the family line. The only higher calling is that of the priesthood. Anton's two sons have little intention of becoming priests. The benefits accruing from their education will belong to them alone, and thus do not justify the expense. Such educational advancement is really a form of conspicuous consumption as damaging to the ethos of equality as other material signs of wealth (such as car ownership, modern dress, use of leisure time for entertainment) are considered to be. Anton is also considered to be acting stupidly in delaying the chances of his children of earning money and thus relieving him of a financial burden which takes a toll from the rest of the family. Both the end towards which he aims and the means which he employs are condemned. He is making use of the obligations owing to him as a community member by his neighbours and kinsmen, in order to further his own personal ambitions for his children. David's personal religious ambitions happen to have coincided with those of his community, even if they clashed with his interests as a father and a farmer.

THE CONTRADICTION

Every villager sees himself in two separate and sometimes opposed contexts. He is a member of a geographically and socially distinct community. He is also an individual who must interact with other individuals. As a community member, he is constrained and motivated in his actions by loyalties and obligations which belong to him as a member of a recognized whole. These loyalties are broadly based. He finds that he is obliged to adhere to a single set of rules which regulate the various sides of his life— economic, political, social and religious. Transgressions are met with sanctions, which are feared. The interrelatedness of various activities renders a man, say, caught in a disregard of the codes of economic behaviour, vulnerable also in his social life. He may lose his equal right to common resources and forfeit the support which he otherwise expects as a member of kinship and neighbourhood groups in the village.

As an individual, a man's position is different. He is concerned with keeping open his access to as many resources as he can, even at the expense of his neighbours. Nevertheless, one important element in this self-protection will be the goodwill of his neighbours. He will need to guard his reputation. This reputation will, however, rest upon an intimate knowledge of him by the others with whom he interacts. He will be known to them in all his roles. He must therefore be careful that his behaviour in each role corresponds to the image which he wishes to project.

But it is unlikely that a man's personal interests are entirely consistent with his obligations as a community member. He is therefore faced with a contradiction. His reputation in the eyes of other members of the community will reflect his success in so behaving as to protect his image. This may involve subterfuge; a display of conformity in one area to disguise a breaking of the rules in another.

The contradiction facing a man in the village is recurrently exemplified in the way that people view themselves as a community and as individuals. 'We are all equals here. No one tries to make out that he is more important than another.' This declaration of equality is balanced in behaviour. There is little evidence of deferential behaviour in speech or action, except on ceremonial occasions when orders of precedence, based on office, sex and age are followed: these are not continued into everyday life. Categories which the villagers themselves make do not reflect stratification into distinct social classes.

This emphasis on quality of community members (plus consensus on the relative inferiority of other communities) is countered by extensive criticism of individuals and groups or categories inside the village. This criticism is voiced in both public and private, although it is often criticism by implication rather than direct reference. A group may be directly criticized for its actions and failure to measure up to a required standard, without the naming of individuals. An individual is more likely to face implied criticism through the spreading of gossip in which the accompanying value judgements are not actually voiced.

The contradiction between equality and one-upmanship-through-criticism is not openly admitted by the villagers. Equality is an ideal, just as the role of a man as simply a cog in the community wheel, is an ideal. It is asserted in order to deflect the threat to cohesion which would arise from public doubts about the reality of this ideal. The interdependency existing among all the villagers makes this seem a real enough danger. For the community member, the emphasis is on co-operation and sacrifice for the good of the whole. The benefits accruing from this will probably come to him indirectly and will benefit his neighbours and kinsmen also. For the individual the notion of co-operation and mutual working to the common good is irrational since it may not be to his direct advantage. He is unwilling to help his neighbours and kinsmen; he may lose thereby. His own brother—as a potential competitor—is untrustworthy, unless his interests happen to lie in the same direction.

The contradiction is covertly recognized. But open acknowledgement would be dangerous and proclamations that all villagers feel, and are, equal bolsters the ideal. Criticisms of individuals also supports the ideal by showing up the deviants. The criticism itself (or fear of it) acts as a sanction against their deviance. Criticism of the community as a whole by outsiders is also made to support the ideal. Outsiders pick upon such characteristics as narrowness, backwardness, greed, too great an individualism and religious fanaticism. The villagers agree that these are negative attributes. But they are acknowledged by a sleight of hand by which they become positive attributes in excess: narrowness becomes traditionalism, backwardness is caution, greed becomes thrift, and independence and piety replace self-centredness and fanaticism. In ascribing these noble attributes to the entire community, there is a further emphasis on the unity which is said to exist.

THE DISTRIBUTION OF WEALTH

There is as yet no recognized inequality between those villagers who are fully *'eingebürgert'*, whom I shall call the 'insiders'.

Past economic instability and total emphasis on subsistence agriculture have hindered the growth of a permanent class system based on attributes such as wealth and occupation. Birth is still largely seen as into a family and into the village, not into any particular stratum of the village population. There have been no criteria on hand on which to base any long-lasting distinctions. Certainly, prestige is to be gained through ownership of land, buildings and cattle and the larger land-holder would gain more respect than the small-holder. However, the fortunes of the average farming family have histories of such instability, and bankruptcy (until the end of the Second World War) was so common, that even today's richer farmers have had no chance to cement themselves into a distinct class, nor to build up any sort of endogamy or separate kin groups. Nor are differences in wealth great enough to have made any sort of classification easy. Wealth was never considered to be unaccompanied by insecurity and impermanence. A man with land, the ability to work that land successfully, a large family to minimize labour costs or wealth enough to employ labourers and housemaids, was assured of prestige in the community. But this balance could be upset by one bad year or by one short period of bad management. Bankruptcies forced sale of land, and mortgages were frequent. Holdings were decimated through selling off of separate parcels, a process disallowed in 1900 when some holdings were already too small to be economically viable.

Survival often depended upon co-operation. Dependence was both on the community as a whole in the form of financial relief, and on neighbours and relatives for help with labour etc. in times of need. The effect was that of a seesaw. One gave help when necessary because one never knew when it would be needed by oneself.

State help and improved economic conditions are now minimizing the need for this type of mutual exchange. But although economic pressures may be less, social repercussions of this earlier pattern of dependence are not so easily lost. Certainly these customs are neither so stable nor rigidly imposed as previously. In the case of house-building, the residents of a man's neighbourhood were until recently obliged to contribute building materials and labour (and/or provisions for the builders) until the house was completed. This was done on the basis of a future return. Now a house-builder finds difficulty in obtaining help other than on a cash-return basis. The old system of *roboten* is no longer considered acceptable: at the same time its passing is attributed to the financial greed of individuals.

It could be supposed that with the greater present security in agriculture and continued emphasis on the value of land and other traditional values, the climate would be right for the emergence of class distinctions. Thus farmers have a firmer hold on their land. They could in theory form a more consistent status group above labourers, craftsmen, shopkeepers or forest workers. But they still do not possess enough capital and suitable land to turn more towards cash production for an outside market. Household needs and labour difficulties (fixed prices for labour now virtually exclude all but familial employment) keep down the numbers of cattle which could be offered for sale. Cash returns which do not immediately have to be ploughed back into the holding are relatively small.

New ways of making a living, not involving the ownership of land, are now becoming more common. These are jobs which pay wages. As the community becomes more consumption-orientated, it is the wage-earners who have the cash to fulfil expectations of living standards which have changed considerably since the war. Non-*Bauer* (non-farmer) families, with resources to compete for prestige, have emerged, being no longer disqualified by their landless state. Such people can now set up separate households and gain a greater say in the life of the village. In earlier years, they had the alternative of staying as labourers on their fathers' farms or leaving the valley permanently, or of being trained as craftsmen to meet the needs of the farmers (which put them at once in a slightly subservient position). Few of them were able to become independent through the purchase or inheritance of a village holding.

Thus, the *Bauern* have met with a threat, not to their position as landowners, but in an arena in which they have less means to compete. Both *Bauer* and non-*Bauer* have achieved certain degrees of security: *Bauer* through subsidy, machinery and better working; non-*Bauer* through a regular wage packet (though not necessarily job security). Thereby non-*Bauern* have gained some of the independence previously reserved for *Bauern* alone. The old system of prestige based on traditional values of moral and material authority, which provided relatively established status positions but *not* permanent occupation of these positions, is gradually giving way to a changed system. What is the nature and extent of this change?

One effect is the greater emphasis placed on the role of the individual. Earlier, a man's status could be considered to be more or less indistinguishable from that of his family. A migrant placed himself outside the arena. A labourer was dependent upon his father and/or elder brother. Marriage to an inheriting daughter or direct inheritance from a childless relative merely extended the network within which both obligations and reputation of the individual was that of the group. A member of such a family possessed greater potential support than had the inheritor of a smallholding, whose non-inheriting relations had probably been forced out of the valley to seek work, leaving him and successive generations of his progeny isolated. Now that younger sons (and increasingly, the daughters too) of farming households are discovering financial and residential independence, they find that they also have to establish and protect their own statuses. The degree to which this is necessary depends upon the extent to which a man is still identified with a family group in social and economic terms. Marriage and the setting up of a separate household generally means that a man is considered responsible for his own behaviour (although this in turn may still affect the standing of his family of origin). So, in a way, there are many more people who have entered the field of play in their own right. Nevertheless, some of these extended families continue to be considered in certain contexts as corporate groups and to have a group reputation.

Material attributes may not be used to claim higher status and thus deny one's equality with other villagers. Even positions of authority held by insiders are short-term and elective. The only permanent positions of authority in the community are those to which outsiders are appointed. This makes it difficult for an individual to exercise power outside his immediate family circle without being toppled by criticism. In fact claims to distinction may actually lower a man. An instance of this: education entitles the individual to respect, higher than he would normally receive. But the very process of gaining a higher education removes him from close contact with the villagers. As there is no use for the skills of the educated within the village, he invariably becomes a permanent migrant, and as such is admired from afar. But anyone who has an education and yet tries to claim equality in the community on the same basis as the other villagers, is derided for not going elsewhere to make use of his qualifications. His education will in fact help to lower his prestige. Peter returned to the village after taking the *Matura* (Higher Certificate Exam). Although he worked on his father's farm, he tried to use his superior intelligence to gain influence. He was for a time partially successful, but also tended to be used as a scapegoat in crises and be given greater responsibility on account of his supposedly superior powers. He was criticized at the same time for using his education to boost his status in circumstances in which it had no place. He was eventually expelled from all committees on which he had played a role, and openly ridiculed as '*der Misthaufenprofessor*' (professor of the dung-heap).

In short there is no possibility within the community as yet of becoming socially mobile through the acquisition of resources (or loss of them) which might raise (or lower) an individual or family according to any internal stratification. Social mobility continues to mean movement out of the valley. Once out of the valley, a man remains part of the community only on the strength of his kin connections.

Nevertheless, the community member feels threatened by these changes. He sees in them the break-up of the community. This in turn will affect his position in the traditional structure, introducing greater competitiveness—hence insecurity. His reaction to this is even greater emphasis of unity in the face of the non-conformity (of others). This means a re-emphasis of the old value system. There is vehement condemnation of those attributes which imply any sort of claim to difference. A man is criticized for being '*herrisch*' (domineering), '*stolz*' (proud), '*eigensinnig*' (self-willed). A greater condemnation is to be labelled '*stadtisch*' (literally 'town-like'). This is a recently-arisen colloquialism, applied to both appearance and behaviour. Although outside the village, the word implies admiration for a modern outlook, within the village its application is consistently derogatory.

KINSMEN AND NEIGHBOURS

Since there are no firm class distinctions, patterns of kinship and marriage tend to be limited not by social but by practical barriers, which, however, are by no means rigid. A man may marry his neighbour's daughter merely because he finds it simpler to meet her, rather than anyone else, without his intentions being made clear to the entire community. Similarly, a *Bauernsohn* with inheritance expectations is unlikely to marry an *Arbeiter*'s daughter who is considered neither mentally nor physically fitted to the hard task of becoming a farmer's wife. Certainly the older *Bauern* members do not consider *Arbeiter* as decently marriageable fodder. However, this bias is countered in two ways: the proportion of marriageable girls to marriage-minded men in the valley is still too high to allow the women much pick; also a girl is no longer so much governed by her parents in her choice of a husband. In this way, the lack of any marked endogamous group leaves the field open for the establishment of community-wide networks.

Formal associations within the village are too few and too limited in membership (apart from those traditional associations connected with agricultural production and exchange) to provide a setting within which interaction could conform to a set pattern uninfluenced by informal contact. Those associations which provide for leisure activities are too recent in origin, are largely run by those who belong to the semi-outsider category, and thus do not greatly affect interpersonal behaviour. Individuals are reluctant to play roles in communities which give them positions of command or obedience (however temporary) in relationships which, on the informal level, it is in their interests to keep on a basis of reciprocity. It is impossible to play out roles on an entirely formal basis even in formal situations. For instance, some members of the *Gemeinderat* (village council) feel that the importance of the business they are involved in should be enhanced by the use of High German. But as soon as they find themselves opposed they will switch to dialect so as to be more persuasive. Never is the equality and friendship implied in the use of the intimate second person form abandoned.

In informal contact, individuals are careful to keep the balance between friendship and imposition. In chance meetings, greetings are always exchanged. In terms of address, the only discrimination is that made between young and old. The older generation will be accorded the respect implied in the dialect '*Dös*' ('you', 2nd person plural); otherwise the singular '*Du*' form is used. Uncertainty as to status and lack of knowledge, which would otherwise afford greater formality, is lacking between villagers. Chance meetings are typified by exchange of information concerning the weather, state of agriculture, the health and occupation of various members of the households in question, but seldom are personal opinions aired on such occasions, particularly those which might cause controversy.

Contact, outside the boundaries of day-to-day work, is considered as strictly a leisure occupation. But leisure activities are seldom legitimate except when work is forbidden—that is, on Sundays and Feastdays. For this reason, the traditional visiting patterns are still important. Kin or neighbourhood relationship is a sufficient recommendation for the giving of hospitality since the close connection presupposes early potential return. In such a situation, one's debt to a kinsman is not as great as that to an acquaintance, who will invariably—when offered hospitality—bring a small 'present' in exchange. When one becomes too indebted to an individual or household (in terms rather of behavioural exchange than cash exchange), one's pride in independence is lowered and bonds of obligation may be formed (in the case of non-kinsmen). Thus, when it is a case of long-term obligation, a man will prefer to ask his kinsman for help—and failing that—the community in general via the *Gemeinderat*. Only when it is a case of short-term aid—possibly a short loan or seasonal labour—will he ask a non-kinsman, and then preferably a neighbour with whom such reciprocal aid has been practice in the past. Since maintaining equality in reciprocity is difficult, strategies are frequently adopted to disguise any outstanding imbalance. The creditor is shown to be actually under obligation to his debtor in previous exchange, or the two may be related affinally through some long-distant marriage, both of which constructions minimize the inequality otherwise demonstrated by the dependence of the one on the other.

Similarly, because of the strong positive evaluation placed on hard work, and the classification of social intercourse as a leisure occupation (particularly for the women), visiting seldom seems to be totally divorced from duty. Visiting relatives is taken to be a maintenance of relations which would otherwise fall into abeyance, through lack of contact. Visiting non-relatives must come into the categories of business transactions, *Kranken-besuche* (obligations to play the part of Job's comforters by sick beds), the offering of sympathy for a death etc. Otherwise, people leave themselves open to criticisms of work-shirking and scandal-mongering, as well as that of sponging, all of which lower their prestige.

Emphasis on reciprocity and equality intensifies dislike of indebtedness. Even an agreed cash exchange for services rendered or for goods bought, must be supplemented by the offering of hospitality, to cover up, as it were, the bare bones of the trans-action and lessen its impersonality. Otherwise the payment of cash implies an impersonal relationship, similar to that entered into by strangers and hints at an asymmetrical transaction (em-ployer and employee) and therefore not acceptable between two villagers. This attitude however is lessening as cash exchange becomes more important. Thanks are also offered as if in pay-ment, but they are disguised as far as possible to absolve the giver from indebtedness. Effusive thanks are received with em-barrassment as the thanker puts himself into an inferior position. Since a service is performed in the knowledge, either that it will be returned some time in the future, or that it rests on an obliga-tion (such as that attached to kinship) and does not involve in-debtedness, thanks are considered superfluous. In fact, they are dangerous since no amount of thanks can cancel a debt, but on the contrary increase it and thus the amount which must later be paid back in kind. Into the same category comes apology which is made as little as possible since admitting to being in the wrong is tantamount to admitting (however temporarily) to an inferior status by recognizing a defect in one's own be-haviour.

One outcome of this refusal (publicly at least) to grade people into superior and inferior status positions is a desire to avoid situations in which inequality must be displayed, and to disguise as far as possible those in which the relationship and its apparent asymmetry are unavoidable.

Both avoidance and disguise are favoured by the geographical lay-out of the valley settlement. The farms are widely scattered. Since work for both the man and wife is largely confined to the house and the land connected with it, there are few opportunities for chance meetings except for those with neighbours, and dur-ing a shopping expedition, church attendance, or in visiting the inn. Ideally the woman's place is in the home. Her meetings with others are therefore more tightly circumscribed than are those of her husband who can spend some of his time in the inn. Since the valley settlements are generally groups or hamlets of from two to six houses, the possession of good neighbours is of utmost importance. Neighbours are regarded as honorary kin. Blood kinship may in some instances be recognized only by the barest civilities demanded by the relationship, which will not be utilized for any closer contact. Neighbours however, will not only be given allotted places in most of the ceremonials affecting a household, but are depended upon for economic aid and for sociability. In fact, neighbours are the only persons for whom avoidance is an impossibility. In reciprocity, repayment must be at least potential if not actual. Thus partners in an exchange will be those for whom expectation of repayment is real—that is, kinsmen and neighbours. Then interaction on a social level will be undamaged by temporary failure to repay on economic level. An exchange relationship may be set up between households who see in it mutual benefit in spite of being connected neither by kin nor neighbourhood. However, without these ties, the relationship will be viewed as unnatural and likely to lead to the deprivation of others.

Neighbours are obvious partners with whom relations of reciprocal aid are set up, practically because of their proximity, and socially because of the greater chance to keep the exact nature of the relationship a secret from other people. But neighbours are also a danger. Of necessity a neighbour is likely to know more of his next-door household than would a kinsman who lives at an hour's walking distance away. Neighbours are called upon in times of trouble: but they possess a lot of potentially dangerous information, and they are not inhibited in the use of this information to the same degree as kinsmen. Neighbours are thus a present help and a potential danger.

One further factor which increases the importance of neighbours is the relative lack of non-instrumental friendships beyond the schoolroom level. There is no word in the local language to describe emotive friendship. Mutual liking is merely a welcome accessory to a relationship more instrumental in origin. '*Gut bekannt*' (well known) may describe a relationship based on long periods of mutual help or exchange (sometimes continuing from one generation to the next between households) in which custom and trust have lessened the demands for strict fulfilment of obligation. *'Gefreundet'* (a local version of the usual *'befreundet'* —friendly relations) replaces the High German *'verwandt'* (related) to describe blood or affinal relationships and could be translated more correctly as 'alliance' than 'friendship'.

Through the frequency of interaction and greater interdependence between their members, there is a *'Nachbarschaft'* (neighbourhood), which is community consciousness below the level of the village community. Officially, administrative divisions of the village area are *'Fraktionen'* which roughly correspond to the informal *Nachbarschaften*, within which the bonds of reciprocity are strongest. In the village centre, where since the last war there has grown up some sort of nucleation, it is easier to choose the neighbours upon which to rely. On the mountainside, one is stuck with those at hand. Nevertheless there are loyalties entailed which can impel a man to change his stance and to be viewed differently by others according to context: as an individual he is on his own; as identified with his family, his loyalties are to his own particular household; as part of a neighbourhood, he can criticize or deride members of another neighbourhood en bloc and rank them according to his own (useful since it avoids the risk of picking out individuals for criticism who are likely to be related in some way to members of one's audience); on the community-wide basis he can speak and behave in terms of equality to all other villagers. But it is on the neighbourhood basis where he must reach the best compromise between the series of contradictions with which he is otherwise faced in his interpersonal contacts. He must be friendly and yet avoid gossip, sociable and yet modest, independent and yet co-operate, reserved and yet not proud. By dependence upon his neighbours, he can choose his associates beyond the neighbourhood boundary without running the risk of forfeiting his right to aid when he needs it. The nature of this aid has a greater chance of being kept secret if it is limited to the neighbourhood, just as he has a better chance of being able to provide some sort of return at a later date. He knows, that if he tries to practice avoidance within his own neighbourhood, he will be isolated and find it more difficult to get people to co-operate with him. Avoidance beyond the neighbourhood boundary will not be so much to his disadvantage.

The recent stabilizing of the village economy has loosened dependence of each man on his fellow and on the community as a whole. This affects neighbourhood relations as it does community relations. Stability has come in the form of aid which has the effect of maintaining the *status quo*. One effect of this has been to make more apparent the possibility of asymmetry. In other words, the fluctuating fortunes of most householders made it a real possibility in earlier times for a farmer in need one year to be in a position to make repayment the next year for help received. Now it is less likely that he could. He will therefore be less ready to either ask for help or to offer it. This loosening of the economic tie disturbs his social relationships with neighbours: there is a growth of independence. This of course is accentuated by the widening of occupational categories. By residence pattern and work routine, members of these categories are altering the form of the *Nachbarschaften* and providing them with elements which cannot become components in the traditional modes of interaction.

REPUTATIONS AND THE RULES FOR GOSSIP

I have described, in general terms, the background against which villagers assess those whom they consider to be their own kind. The basis for behaviour and assessment is the ideal of equality. The assessor, by criticism of another, implies his own conformity. Thus the ideal is constantly reinforced. Moreover criticism is both a weapon in competition and a means of self-protection.

The reputation accorded a man arises from a mixture of two kinds of information. These are either direct contact or gossip. His characteristics will be observed originally and abstracted from transactional conduct by a few people who interact closely with him, who refine and consolidate their impressions into something transmittable, and thus provide the ingredients for a reputation. So, although a man may actually interact frequently with only a few people in his immediate neighbourhood and kin group, upon his behaviour with these few will depend the reputation which is sifted through to others in the village.

Criticism is legitimate only when the speaker is believed to have access to relevant information on which to base his judge-

L

ment. Networks of kin and contact throughout the valley do not spread information evenly. Disseminating false information is thought to be malicious; so is criticism unsupported by examples. It is dangerous to criticize without sufficient evidence for this exposes the speaker's malice. From this comes a noticeable eagerness within the community to endorse an opinion known to be widely held, and a reluctance to voice a criticism arising from purely personal opinion.

Despite the reluctance to voice personal opinions, a substitute may be found under cover of information exchange, providing the speaker manages to keep the right side of the thin line drawn between *'plaudern'* (chatter) and *'tratschen'* (gossip with malicious undertones). Opinion is voiced by implication. The audience is left to draw moral inferences. The man who can gain a reputation for *'gut erzählen'* ('story-telling') without being also suspected as a scandalmonger is a man to be respected. The inferences to be drawn from his speech are considered to be the work of his audience and therefore the blame for them is not laid at his door. Nevertheless, he must always keep the composition of his audience in mind. For instance, careless use of a derogatory nickname (usually never uttered in the presence of its owner or his immediate circle) leads at once to the assumption that the speaker talks with unfair bias.

In a community as scattered as is Sankt Martin, the information channels (by word of mouth) are far more important than direct observation. Correspondingly, those known to be collectors and storers of information are feared as much for the information which they can give others on which adverse judgement may be based, as for the criticisms they themselves construct and voice. Also a greater emphasis is placed on those nodes of the information network (e.g. shops, inn, church) where news, information and gossip is gathered and disseminated.

There are right and wrong ways of handling information. Frieda has low prestige because she seems oblivious to the demand that one should at least have some sort of cover for the passing of information. The frequency with which anyone is seen to come into the village centre is calculated against the geographical distance of shops, church and inn from the farmhouse. Too great a frequency (unjustified by necessity) by those from outlying farms gives them quickly a reputation for work-shirking and gossip-mongering. Thus the common covers of church attendance, shopping, Sunday drinking and visiting (most of which are based on normal obligations) are necessary. For instance, non-members of the *Frauenrunde* (women's group attached to the church) unanimously condemn the group as a hot-bed of gossip, in which no-one in his right mind should involve himself.

These generalizations can be illustrated by the case of Cilli. She originally worked with her sister in the village inn (one of the hubs of information exchange in the main part of the village). She was in her late thirties when about ten years ago she married. She stopped working and now lives not very far from the village centre, but in a position where she cannot learn much about village affairs merely from observation. Nevertheless, she goes into the village as little as possible. During the week she goes out to attend church and to collect milk in the early morning. On her way, she occasionally visits relatives in the inn and farms (one of which is well-known as an *'Informationenquelle'*—'the spring of news'). She avoids being seen on the street talking for more than a few minutes, and leaves all the shopping to her husband (unusual in that it is considered woman's work). For the remainder of her time, she stays at home, where, however, she welcomes visitors. Her reason for avoiding contact with people— even to the extent (as she admits) of being very bored at home— is the wickedness of the villagers: they have nothing better to do than to speak ill of one another. In the village, one learns nothing new but merely bad gossip passed from one to the other.

Her behaviour in the privacy of her own home is different. Her first question to visitors is always: 'What news have you brought from the village?' She milks them not only of information about their own households but of what the villagers are talking about in general. When asked to give her information and opinions in turn, she prefaces nearly every remark with the equivalent of: 'between you, me and the gatepost'. She speaks freely in condemning violation of generally accepted norms, so long as she is not called upon to identify persons. Then she usually becomes noticeably non-committal.

But there are exceptions to this rule. Her eldest brother inherited their father's possessions—a small farm and an inn. She criticizes this brother for his refusal to keep an eye on the main chance, for being too set in traditional ways of the village, for his obstinacy in refusing to co-operate in a scheme to aid non-farming villagers—a scheme which would have cost him nothing but his consent. In him, she says, are many of the bad characteristics which prevent change of attitudes and development in the community.

The second criticism which stands out from her repertoire is that of a family whose relative wealth and enterprise mark them out from the majority of villagers. It is this quality of separateness that she condemns: 'What reason have they for thinking themselves above everyone? They may have more money than most people, but that is no excuse for using it to set themselves apart. They are too proud and have too much their own way. Everything they do is done ostentatiously.' In contrast to her relationship with her brother with whom she is fairly close, she has very little to do with this second family. She is neither related nor a neighbour. However, in the past this family has had a history of hostility with some of Cilli's close relations.

As far as access to information is concerned, there are contained in the two above instances various assumptions about the code according to which Cilli works: (i) that casual chatter most probably consists of idle gossip; (ii) to be seen too often indulging in it in public is to invite criticism as a scandalmonger, also to be imputed with laziness (since the woman's place is in the home and trips outside the home should be seen to be necessary); thus (iii) activities such as church-going, kin visiting, milk collection, etc. may provide sufficient cover for information exchange. Shopping however may not be sufficient cover since the exchange of information—being in front of an unregulated audience—would obviously be more public and therefore dangerous. Also, in this context, the gaining of information might demand more of a return in the giving of it than in a more private exchange.

Cilli is unfortunate in her degree of access to information, since (besides those mentioned above) she does not have any reasons for going regularly to the village centre. Neither does she possess a husband who frequents the inn or who comes into contact with other men for the imparting of information. Thus: (a) she feels the need to gather information in order not to become isolated, but (b) must cover up her tracks in doing so—particularly since she does not have many opportunities in the ordinary course of events to learn about village activities (e.g. through observation).

Her attitude of self-protection extends into the degree of freedom she feels in expressing her own opinions. Her occasional expressions of personal criticism seem inconsistent in two ways when placed in relation to her usual lack of condemnatory words: firstly, while it is natural that she should criticize a family to whom she would be expected to have no feelings of obligation or loyalty, she also criticizes her own brother, to whom she should have the highest loyalty. Secondly, the criticism which she voices in these two cases seem to be directly contradictory. In her brother she complains about characteristics the opposite to those she finds in the other family.

I think the explanation here is twofold. Firstly, in a quarrel, the means of support on which a man almost invariably can count is his family. In the absence of any strongly supported formal associations and the frequent common interest of a family in an economic enterprise, this is only practical. The loyalties existing between two siblings are so much taken for granted that they cannot be damaged by criticism by one or the other in front of a third party, *unless* there is known to be long-standing feelings of hostility existing between them. In other words, an individual feels less vulnerable in criticizing close relatives than he does when his criticism is of less narrowly defined relations. Furthermore, in this case, the criticism offered was of a general kind, not based on particular scandals.

At the other extreme, Cilli was speaking of persons whose distance from her in kinship and everyday interaction minimized the repercussions her criticism could have had on herself. Secondly, she was uttering a generally voiced criticism which could not have been traced to her alone. In speaking of her brother, she spoke with the authority of having maximum information. At the same time, she had the protection which the brother and sister tie gave to her and which prevented her words from damaging the reputation of the brother. In the second case, she was echoing the commonly held opinion which constituted the reputation of this family among all those with less than close relations with them. Because of her lack of contact with this family, she felt safe in identifying herself with this opinion.

The content of assessment and criticism revolves around the one main theme. From Cilli's words, it seems that use of wealth and its display (but not necessarily mere possession of it), is taken to constitute claims for higher status. Display of wealth is seen as a denial of equality and a refusal of co-operation. Signs of wealth displayed in dress, ownership of cars, obvious expenditure on entertainment or travel, extravagant house-building or furnishing, are seen to be the open acknowledgements of personal gain at the expense of the community and thus a failure to abide by the local value system. Indeed, most forms of conspicuous consumption (even possibly investment in farm machinery where it is not considered absolutely necessary) are said to reflect the modern '*städtisch*' way of life. The safest use of wealth thus would seem to be to let it stagnate. Cilli's criticism of her brother appears to contradict this, but in fact does not. Cilli is not wanting her brother to depart from accepted ways but merely to show more initiative within them, and to co-operate more with others. Certainly she is not calling for more ostentation from him.

The quality of the family criticized which both gives the criticism force and enables Cilli to utter it without compunction is their 'out-of-ordinariness'. This is itself a crime against the norms. True or not, these accusations are believed and the family is to some extent excluded from the village. This is the more easily done since they live relatively isolated from all but one close neighbour. This exclusion can never become as complete as in the case of true outsiders. The activities of the family are contained in the village. They have lived there for generations, and they still fall into the category of '*Bauern*'. Besides which, they have a large network of kin spread throughout the valley. Nevertheless, those not obligated by near or more distant kin ties, take advantage of the economic independence which this family has built up, to accord it a certain amount of distrust, and to have as little to do with it as possible.

The situation of this family suggests something else: those least likely to suffer from exclusion are those least likely to conform. They do not need a cloak of self-protection like that which Cilli assumes. Social and economic independence *is* a form of self-protection and an alternative to avoidance or ingratiation. To see this more clearly, one must examine a range of people who are wholly or partially outsiders. But first I summarize.

The foregoing suggests the following points concerning the techniques of assessment-making and the use and effect of gossip and criticism:

(a) The standard continually used in construction of a reputation is that based on an ideal state of equality among all
villagers. Equality presupposes conformity to local values.
Use of resources not generally available in the community is
only justified if it does not create imbalance in the village
structure.

(b) Assessment and criticism will depend on geographical and
kinship distances, since these affect the strength and frequency
of interaction and therefore the information available to the
asssesor.

(c) Assessment should not usually be direct, but implied in
the process of passing information through which medium
the speaker absolves himself of responsibility for an adverse
judgement.

(d) Criticism will depend upon sufficiency of knowledge.
Where information is sparse, the individual will be especially
wary of offering personal opinions. Similarly, where information about an individual or household is scarce and cannot be
easily gained through gossip, the people concerned tend to
be excluded to some degree.

THE POSITION OF OUTSIDERS

Anyone who is in some way considered an outsider will not be
judged on the same basis as others. Insiders all have an equal
right to judge and be judged: outsiders do not. The boundary
between mere local residence, and full membership of the moral
community lies between two modes of assessment. Particularistic
assessment, made in the context of interaction, implies local birth,
membership of village-based kin groups, and close connections
with land-owning householders in the community. The greater
the possession of these components which give community membership and identification with the traditional value system, the
greater freedom will a person have in the manipulation of transactions without the danger of sanctions being applied against him.

An outsider cannot achieve acceptance into the community
(although he may attempt to claim it). But he is not absolved
from conformity to the local moral values and if he disregards
them openly, direct means (complaints to police or priest or

council) or indirect means (the spreading of gossip) may be used to expel him. I consider first partial outsiders and the solutions which they find for their problems.

The relative positions of insider and outsider can be seen in the contrast between two women married in the village. Frieda lived most of her life on her brother's farm as a spinster. About twelve years ago at the age of forty she married the brother of the then *Bürgermeister*. He retired early through injury from his position as head man in the local sawmill. They live in a newly built house near the middle of the village. Neither of them have much to do with their time and have built up reputations as sources of information and gossip. Frieda is criticized for not staying at home, where a woman's place is, but spending her days going from house to house in the vicinity of the village centre, keeping other women from their work and collecting and spreading any gossip she can find. Her husband, known as '*Fürwitz*' (inquisitiveness) is said to stand at suitable vantage points with binoculars, collecting information which he later disseminates to his cronies in the inn. Despite their unfavourable reputations and the care with which people view any association with them, they are accepted. Frieda gains entry into the houses she visits because on the basis of neighbourhood and kin ties, she has a right to entry. Although her hostesses may grumble, she does also provide them with a good source of information, and the gossip which she has a hand in spreading does contain considerable sanctioning power.

In contrast there is Maria, coming from a village about eight miles away and married to a locally born and bred lorry driver. In appearance and way of dress and in the way she brings up her children, she distinguishes herself from the other local women. In this she is criticized. She herself complains of the unfriendliness of her neighbours, talking of her efforts soon after her marriage (now nineteen years ago) to become part of the village. Now she has given up and keeps herself entirely to herself since she has discovered that unless someone sees a profit in helping her, they are more likely to cheat her or leave her alone. In conversation she is called '*Du*' but seldom spoken to in dialect. This has the effect of denying her any sort of higher status which use of the '*Sie*' form gives to some others of the outsider women; at the same time she is excluded from participation on an equal basis with the other villagers. Communication in dialect would reflect some sort of acceptance, even if it were purely 'honorary'. Because of this, she is also shut off from sources of information which would enable her to interact more fully with others. She is visited by no-one and herself never goes to other houses. When asked why the villagers left Maria so isolated, an informant said it was because they did not know her well enough and that she was considered a spreader of lying gossip.

As an outsider, Maria is not considered to have enough information about others on which to base direct criticism or that implied in gossip. Equally, the villagers do not possess enough knowledge of her to classify her as a full community member. Her marriage to a local man is her one claim to community membership. It does not give her the ability to gain and retain acceptance in the same way that Frieda can, despite her reputation as a bad gossip.

There are different ways of reacting to the exclusion forced on to outsiders. Rosa, now an old woman, was born to a family which moved away from the valley shortly before her birth. She inherited a house in the village and has spent her entire life, since her late twenties, in the community. But she has no near relatives there, and as an unmarried woman is an exception to the general rule in that she is of independent means. She herself says that she has never been truly accepted by the villagers, and that it was some considerable time before they showed her any friendliness. Her reaction to this situation has been to act a neutral role in her dealings with anyone else. She visits only near neighbours—and then only when it is necessary. She is loath to do even the necessary shopping for her household. To be seen outside the house without some purpose would damage her reputation since she would be thought to have gone gossiping. What information she does acquire, she gathers from neighbours from whom she collects milk and from listening-in during her infrequent visits to the shops. When forced into conversation, she plays a yes-man role, seldom venturing an opinion and never advancing any information of her own before absolving herself of all responsibility for the content. The only visitors she receives who come purely for a chat come from outside the *Gemeinde*. On Sundays, she occasionally entertains some old men on their way to or from church. They come more to meet each other, on the one day of the week when they are not separated by work and distance, than to see her. They are given food and drink for which they offer gifts in exchange, and they talk among themselves of village affairs. Rosa is present but seldom takes part.

Rosa has therefore accepted the exclusion granted to her. Although she misses the social contact which greater interaction with other villagers would give her, she is convinced that to guard her own seclusion was the only way in which she could make life bearable for herself in the community, and she is proud of the reputation she has of being discreet and a person of high moral standards (which reputation does not, however, make her an integral part of the moral community, as far as her audience is concerned).

Ludwig has found a different solution. He is locally born but was for some time absent from the village and he married an outsider. He both welcomes and reinforces the seclusion in which he and his family are left. He interacts with the villagers on an official basis and emphasizes this part of his role in the community, dealing with individuals in his capacity as postmaster, and with groups in that he is member of the council and organizes many of the formal associations. In these roles he tries to make himself indispensable, but on a basis which rules out competition. He emphasizes the inequality of the relationships he strikes up. Through superior knowledge and expertise, he can offer advice to the villagers for which he receives respect (though not necessarily support in his political manoeuvres). He is addressed in the polite '*Sie*' form or the intermediary '*Dös*' of the dialect, although only a few of the older generation would talk to him in dialect. The attempts of Emmerich, a boy in his early twenties, to initiate a '*Du*' relationship with Ludwig was taken as an insult; 'Not only did he start calling me "*Du*" without my permission, but he thinks that because he is about to become secretary to the *Gemeinde*, he can establish himself on terms of equality with me. To do so, he is lacking in respect since he is no intimate friend of mine.' Even some of the older people who used to call Ludwig '*Du*', now address him as '*Sie*' and call him 'Herr Bachmann' and 'Herr Postmeister'. The result of this is that in his private life, he is left severely alone, making no visits and receiving no visitors except on business. This is in contrast to his younger brother—the baker—whose relationships with his customers are enacted on a purely informal basis.

Ludwig therefore does something not possible for others—he projects an image almost entirely upon a public front. He bypasses informal social contact, from which he is excluded both by people's attitudes to him and by his own initiative. He is regarded with suspicion because he is an advocate of tourist development and change in the *Gemeinde*. Even so, he makes his public role effective since he presents himself as the only disinterested councillor, working only for the good of the village. He claims that he is not working for personal ends and sees himself as the strengthener of the traditional values which are being transgressed by full community members. When asked why he should wield any influence in the village when he is regarded as an outsider and appears to have little support apart from that of his personality, an informant said that it was because Ludwig was prepared to work slowly and along traditional channels and therefore could not be found wanting according to the accepted moral base.

Because the role in which he interacts with the villagers tends always to be his official one and because he makes himself generally useful in this role, Ludwig is one of the few people whose claims to higher status are accepted in the community. He has put himself at a point of distance from the community members which they are willing to countenance because he does not insist on interaction on all levels (in other words on complete membership of the moral community). Ludwig has been able to make a fairly rigid separation between his public and private life because he remains a semi-outsider and his services in the public sphere are needed by the village.

Ludwig and Rosa are half-outsiders. The full outsiders are people who are in the village for a specific purpose. Their residence is generally temporary and they interact with the villagers only so far as their official positions demand. These include the schoolteachers, customs officers, police, and the priest. They are part of the group in so far that their local residence obliges them to conform to the broader-based codes of behaviour—at least outwardly. They must, for instance, go to church regularly, show friendliness and interest in village affairs, balanced by discretion and not too great a degree of intimacy. Beyond this point, their activities are of little interest to the villagers. They are in no position to compete with the villagers, nor do they offer a threat to the community cohesion since they are not considered to be a part of the moral community; and their personal interests are unlikely to involve interaction with the locals. Nevertheless, if they involve themselves too much in village activities either within or outside their official roles, they are placed under the same sanctions of control that the villagers use upon one another. These sanctions are if anything more effective in the case of outsiders since they have poor sources of local support.

This is well shown in a recent case in which the head of the local school (from outside) was thought to have transgressed the commonly held values. This case demonstrates the instrumentality of most relationships of outsiders with the villagers, and the power which group sanctions can have.

In an attempt to break down the gulf existing between master and pupils in the valley, the school head established relationships on a social level with a few of the young people who had recently left school or were just about to. These he invited to his flat in the school for evenings of talk and entertainment which included music and dancing. This in itself was an exception. Not only was he treating and talking to the young people as equals and giving them access to his private life, but he was also doing it on a Saturday night—a time generally disapproved of for any sort of celebration as it jeopardized chances of getting to church early enough on the Sunday morning. He made the occasions as loud as he could in order to annoy the priest who lives across the street—and with whom he is ideally supposed to work hand-in-glove. Gossip began to be spread by the relatives of the young people he invited: he was said to be reducing his own authority, at the expense of the respect young people should bear towards their elders. He was bringing the young people of both sexes together for sexual orgies and introducing them to all sorts of perversions —at the same time inciting them to rebellion against their elders and against the moral values which they had been taught by their parents. Specific details (quite false) were given of the ways he was doing this, and condemnation was supported by discussion of his unorthodoxy in other ways, which until then had been ignored. Parents of the other children in the school became alarmed and as a body they laid a formal complaint with the local police inspector. The only course open to the teacher was to lay an official complaint against them for defamation of character. This was successful and the business officially closed. However, he had to pay the price of now total isolation and lack of support in any of the improvements which he had begun to make in the school. The people remain suspicious of him and ostracize him. This treatment comes even from the young people with whom he made friends because the greater loyalties they have been taught to feel towards their parents and towards the community prevent them from open opposition. Because these young people are associated with him only by emotional bonds—which relationship carries with it the least of obligations—and not on the ascriptive ties of kinship, in a crisis such as this he is left alone. I was told that the strength of the gossip against him was a product of the 'Angst' which the villagers felt in the face of his attempts to reform the school structure and alter the attitudes of the children to their parents. A common comment at the time was: 'As far as I am concerned, he may be doing good, but most of the people cannot see it because they automatically suspect changes. Anyway, he is an outsider.' Secondly, the gossip went unrestricted. The teacher had no natural supporting group; no villager had therefore to be careful about where he spread the rumours. They were circulated openly in the guest-house and the women's religious discussion group. The success of the campaign was accelerated by the silence of the priest whose intervention could have halted its progress.

This is not an instance of an attempt to increase prestige. The teacher knew that he was accorded respect consistent with his role but that as an outsider he could not hope for more. So long as he kept within the bounds of his job, according to what was thought proper, his presence was tolerated even though he did not possess much freedom within it, and lived, as it were, on the fringe of the community. But as soon as his activities seemed to be *threatening* the community, it resulted in his ostracism. Through his influence with the younger children, he seemed to be trying to change the value basis on which the community identifies itself. In doing this, he was entering into competition with the parents. In a way, he was trying to move further into the system by influencing the young people *outside* the accepted roles of master/pupil. The answer to this was to expel him from it, since he—as an outsider and partially unknown quantity —was vulnerable and a legitimate prey.

To conclude, anyone who seems thoroughly to disturb the local values, is subject to the severe sanctions which corporate action—aroused through gossip—can impose. This is because to attack (verbally) or to flout (behaviourally) tradition is tantamount to personal attack on the upholders of that tradition. Their security seems to be threatened. And this is countered by a community-organized threat to the non-conformer. In this sense, a man's reputation (especially as it rests on moral values) is of interest to those villagers both near and far in interactional distance from him. In as far as his behaviour threatens the corner-stones of village values, he becomes the victim of the sanctioning power of gossip.

8

Public and Private Interests in Hogar[1]

Hogar is one of a line of villages which lie in the south-facing valleys of the Spanish Pyrenees at an altitude of between 800 and 900 metres. The economy is based upon stockraising. Fields on the valley floor are privately owned but the pasture on the elevated slopes of the mountains belongs to the community. Timber resources are also exploited collectively and just under one-fifth of the working population are employed in the saw mill or cutting the trees. The area of common land which is under the control of the municipio *(town) is seventeen times greater than the total amount of privately owned land. The two types of public property together are known as the* termino. *The town itself contains 200 houses of which 150 are lived in permanently. These are divided into 180* viviendas *or separate family apartments, with a population of 825 people.*

There is no through road into France from the valley and consequently all contact is with the south, including marketing, power supplies and distribution points. There is, however, an unmade road which runs parallel with the frontier and which connects to similar villages in their individual valleys. In the past Hogar with its termino *was largely self-sufficient. Until recently it produced nearly all its own requirements, and its only export was surplus population.*

'The people have no kind of understanding of the meaning of association; they feel only suspicion, envy, and mistrust between themselves; therefore individualism reigns supreme, although they understand that this system does them harm.' (*Los vecinos no tienen nada de espiritu de asociación, pues sienten recelos,*

envidias y sospechas entre ellos, y por lo tanto, impera total-
mente el individualismo, aunque comprendan que este sistema les
perjudice.) That was written by a man in Hogar. If he is right,
people there value individualism even when it gets in the way of
co-operation. At the same time envy and mistrust, which prevent
co-operation, are deplored. People would like to curb individualism, but have no idea how to do it.

THE INDIVIDUAL

One stereotype of the man from Hogar is the shepherd or herds-
man. He has to trust his own opinion and judgement; he is quite
alone for many months of the year (except, perhaps, for a son),
his home is the lonely *borda* or mountain cabin which also shelters
the animals. To the people of the plains such a man is *cerrado*
(closed), *reservado* (reserved), and *antipático* (unsociable). He
not only keeps his own counsel but mistrusts the opinion of
others; not unnaturally, since practical knowledge is shared
equally between everybody. No one ever interferes with a man,
his herd, or his family, and there could only be friendship so
long as the privacy of these domains was respected.

But such a stereotype does not explain why anyone should co-
operate at all, nor, if people were so isolated, why leaders arose
equipped with power, wealth, and prestige, greater than the
average. The answer lies in the *casa*. A man, his herd, his family,
his house, and his labour all come under the same name—such
and such a 'house' (*casa*). The house belongs clearly in the town
and it is here that co-operation and competition take place.
Successful management of a house, together with careful manipulation of its relationships with other houses, qualify a man to
compete for control over public property (the *termino*). Thus
there are, in effect, three parts or phases in building the kind of
reputation which leads to and maintains public power.

A *casa* (house) is a group of people, closely related to the household head, and living under the same roof. It may be divided
into several domestic units but it usually involves only one *work
unit*, organized and directed by the household head—*la cabeza
de la familia*. He is the only adult entitled to vote and he speaks
for the house; the rest of the family are morally committed to
support and obey him.

House resources are not equal. The efficiency of the labour goes up and down as time passes. The patrimony of privately owned fields varies in size from house to house, and the house herd or flock also varies independently, since a large herd does not require a larger amount of private land. But the relative size of these resources is not taken directly into account when assessing reputations; rather it is the manner in which the work unit is organized which calls for moral judgements. The first phase of a man's reputation concerns his ability to control his labour and manage his land and stock efficiently.

Internal house unity is fostered through an *espiritu de clan*, which means *una confianza en su mismo* (a confidence in themselves) and a respect for the family head. A house which manages to keep several sons until well into their maturity, combining this with an expanding patrimony, is known as a *casa fuerte* —a strong house. A man who cannot keep some kind of unity in his own house has little chance of establishing a dominant reputation.

The *casa* is in open competition with other houses, and the skill displayed in this competition amasses credit in the form of prestige, which can in turn be used to help maintain internal order. Part of the game is to build up the image of one's own house and denigrate that of others. Therefore other houses are said to contain *mal trabajadores* (bad workers), their women are *sin verguenza* (without shame), and they all *hablan mal* (gossip) too much about others. What is clan spirit in one is *presumido* (vain, conceited) in another, internal confidence becomes external *sospechas* (suspicions), and looking after one's own by seizing the main chance is *impudente* (barefaced, shameless) to those whose bid failed. People serve their own *casa* against others and expect the rest to do the same. They do not envisage altruistic service of the community. Houses may suffer from internal dissensions. When a man loses his reputation, for example, by being labelled *un borracho* (a drunk), this reflects upon the *casa* more severely than a *casa* benefits when a man gains prestige. They believe that when one loses they all lose, but when one gains he will try to limit the advantages to himself. The solidarity of the house may be at stake. This is because a man can never hope to establish his own house reputation without first building an individual one, and if he already has a household, he has no

M

interest in sharing possible economic gains with other members of the work unit who have no children to feed.

Women, who are also the main purveyors of gossip, play an important part in keeping a house united. A wife must look after the immediate interests of her own family, defend the reputation of the house into which she has married, and also, to a lesser extent, safeguard the interests of the *casa* in which she was born. It would take more skill than most women have to win this game all the time, and other females are quick to point out the way she favours one house over another. If there is a complete breakdown of relations between kin, whether inside or outside the house, a person may *hacer la risa* (become a laughing-stock) and so lose all prestige. Women fear the tongues of *la risa* more than the men as the latter are away from the town each day, while women stay at home.

'VECINDARIO' (neighbourliness)

There are no class discriminations in Hogar and there is no tradition of a landed aristocracy. Standards are set by whatever family happens to be the richest, or best educated, at the time, and there is no certainty that it will continue to be top in the succeeding generation. Hogar is a part society in a larger culture and most of these resources are now acquired from outside. Initially they are always scarce resources over which certain families have a near monopoly, and they can be 'traded' for material benefit or reputation.

Houses with wealth or education or both appear to create a network of reciprocity with other houses. There are two ways of judging such a performance. The normative intention is reciprocity, that is, a relationship of equality; but the pragmatic effect is to rank households on a prestige scale precisely because resources are seen not to be equal. Relationships between *casas* are initiated or maintained through transactions, and these transactions are used to build up the strength of individual houses. The need for each generation in a *casa* to establish its own transactions and achieve its own prestige and credit helps to keep the system going, and this also explains why when one set of standards is absorbed by the majority, others are continually being sought in order to re-establish scarcity. Thus the same system safeguards the prosperity of a house, redistributes wealth and expert knowledge and services, spreads the risk against economic disaster, and builds up a dominant ranking position for certain families—all at one and the same time.

All men are thought of as being morally equal, normatively as good as each other (*somos todos iguales aqui*). Visible differences become the subject of gossip and envy. Gossip is one medium of exchange in the competition for prestige between houses. It is more diffuse than *envidia* and it involves the constant reappraisal of individual and house reputations. Envy involves *la mala cara* (malice: *lit.* the bad face) and it is directed against a specific person or *casa* usually by a small group of people who feel wronged in some way. The intention is to harm more than the reputation; if possible all transactions will be terminated, social relations cut to a minimum, and even efforts made to ruin the *casa's* prosperity. Thus *envidia* is stronger than the English 'envy'; it suggests also bad blood, spite, mistrust, suspicion, calumny and other forms of hostile action.

It might seem that a man would be well advised to look after his own house affairs and forget about gaining a reputation by manipulating relations with other houses. But in reality, in spite of the risks, no one can ignore his neighbours, and besides, no house is so secure that it does not need help from time to time. No house can do without a cushion against the risk of economic failure; it may need to combine forces against outside threats or demands, or to make use of certain specialized services which only certain houses can supply. Prestige is acquired according to the ability to offer help or the willingness to be helpful, and high reputations in this regard are a kind of insurance against difficulties in the future. But to give a service is to expect one in return and those who cannot keep up the exchanges become the moral debtors of those who can. As Pitt-Rivers has written:

Poverty implies no inferiority in other spheres than the economic, and only the inability to respond to generosity places a person in a position of humiliation, for it exposes him to the accusation of being grasping. That is to say, it is only where economic inferiority is translatable into moral inferiority that it involves loss of prestige. *It is precisely where all men are conceptually equal that this translation is able to be made* [my italics]—because no subordination is recognized which might exonerate one man for returning the favour of another.

Pitt-Rivers (3), p. 60

From the results of a survey which ranked houses according to economic resources about twenty *casas* were considered richer than the others. Of these, apart from the acknowledged *casa fuerte*, four were shop owners, four had small businesses, three were professional men, and one was a returned emigrant with a fortune. The shop owners and craftsmen are clearly in a position to offer credit which their clients are unable to repay at once. Such services cannot be settled easily in kind as the shop owners are also small farmers who produce enough for their own requirements. The gain in prestige that helpful businessmen enjoy has to be weighed against the loss of business and a careful balance maintained between both sides.

The point is that the community positively values credit (and those who give it) as a means by which a farmer or stockraiser can exist until the next harvest or sale of stock. But the same system is open to the idea of a house head getting whatever he can 'free' by putting off payment as long as possible and enjoying the benefits at once. In this way he benefits his own house at the expense of other houses or the community at large. If the debt is too large it rebounds back upon the debtor and his house would have lost independence; if the credit is too short the shopkeeper will lose his goodwill; if it is too long he will eventually go out of business.

Professional people increase their prestige by offering expert knowledge derived from their superior education. They are expected to write difficult letters on behalf of others, act as middlemen in protracted personal negotiations with the outside world, and put local people in touch with useful contacts in faraway places. Such services and resources cannot be matched by local men and they give the title of *Don* or *Dona* to all educated people as a special sign of respect. Small gifts are given to professionals as they do not usually farm themselves. Such a gift does not repay the service, but allows the recipient to bestow further services and the debtor to ask for them. In this way, usually only the richer men proceed beyond the second phase of reputation building. The third stage is that of community

direct control of the common lands. This responsibility is normatively entrusted to such men as the community 'officially' believes
might administer common resources fairly on behalf of all (*el
termino es de todos*). There are also sectional interests to consider
such as the saw mill, the tourists, and the sportsmen, as well as
the pastoralists. Nevertheless, it is expected that houses will try
to get what they can for themselves from the common land, as
van todos a pilla y pillo (everybody plunders).

Only richer men customarily become deeply embroiled in
community politics, since only they have sufficient reputation
and following. But, since quite small differences in wealth count,
medium-sized houses may also involve themselves in the hope of
spoils. In such a situation a high reputation with a medium
patrimony may bring success. As each *casa* is out to further its
own ends it is possible that, in Bailey's words, 'Equality comes
about through the mutual cancellation of supposed efforts to be
unequal,' and thus in effect the result is the same as the normative
ideal of equality through co-operation. *Lison* has written the
proposition the other way round; community norms are limited
by the 'competitive spirit which is a driving force behind all
aspects of the social system' (p. 351). But the paradox is still the
same: the intention is to serve one's own interest while appearing
to serve the interests of others, to put family before community
while appearing to do the reverse, and to verbalize equality
while striving for unequal advantages. With such a pattern of
expectations, leaders are open to suspicion in spite of the higher
prestige that their position affords.

The purpose of moral superiority is believed to be the possibility of converting it into economic advantages. But to be seen
to make this conversion tarnishes one's reputation. Consequently
leaders present as many actions as possible in terms of the public
good even though the real objective may be quite the reverse.
As Bailey has written:

> Honour or prestige or wealth or ritual purity are goals cul-
> turally understood and accepted by the peasant. Dedicated
> service to the public weal is not, and when used as an appeal
> seems like hypocrisy.
>
> *Bailey* (4), p. 148

On the other hand:

> They believe that competition for material and political prizes should remain within bounds. . . . No matter what goes on in reality, the public life of a peasant community is ideally conducted in the idiom of co-operation.
>
> *Bailey* (4), p. 148

One must compete from behind the façade of a non-competitor in order to convey the impression that community values are being respected. Reputations are preserved intact by the skill displayed in manipulating pragmatic inequality within the normative framework of equality. Economic rewards are denied the man who cannot lead while preserving his reputation as one who considers himself no higher than anyone else.

REPUTATION AND PROFIT

The individual Hogareno attains economic independence at the head of his house by combining the resources of the house patrimony with the family herd. Using this as a base he can increase his wealth by careful management of the natural increase of the herd and the adroit use of human labour. But such methods are slow even by the standards of a peasant time scale, and consequently other ways are sought to achieve the same ends. Within the valley the only means that can be so used are either the resources of other *casas*, or of the common land, and these resources are equally open to every other house head. Therefore, the resourceful peasant seeks to attract the help of cheap labour, or he tries to acquire new fields, or he tries to ensure that he obtains a bigger share of the common pasture and timber than everybody else. As every other house is bent on the same tactic it is hardly surprising that there is a strong suspicion of so-called altruistic motives. Only the man with the highest reputation can expect to withstand the accusing mistrust of his neighbours, when he tries to exert an effective leadership role.

The costs and benefits of this process are such that a man can withdraw from the arena whenever he has had enough. Some will remain only active within the house; others will be content with mutual respect between houses; and a few will try for the biggest prize and become mayor of the town. Each stage requires a bigger following but promises larger rewards, and the following is achieved by maintaining a high reputation in spite of economic success. Hence high profits are attained in inverse proportion to high prestige, at least during the process of acquiring a good reputation. As the Hogareno widens the extent of his prestige so he has a greater possibility of controlling the available resources to produce a higher economic return. But at the same time this will involve him in a power struggle which invites counter-sanctions. The greater the power the higher the risk of possible reprisals. The community can grant a high enough reputation to the man who serves it so that he may be able to control a large part of the common resources—but always in the name of the *pueblo* as a whole. So long as he can maintain this normative image of himself, he can pragmatically exploit public resources for the benefit of his own house. This is principally why, at one and the same time, high reputation linked to public service results eventually in open scepticism, and why public servants are subjected to virulent personal criticism. As one informant wrote:

> But this ideology demonstrated in the common good, is strongly opposed to the ideology of the individual. To that collective ideology is directed the accusation of being hypocritical and insincere.
>
> (*Pero esta ideología patentizada en la colectividad es muy opuesta a la ideología individualmente considerada. A esa ideología colectivizada es a la que hay que acusar de ser hipocrita y falsa.*)

Inevitably those with little reputation and power are cynical. But at the same time, so long as the common lands exist there must be some kind of public organization to run them.

Envidia is the word which describes attempts to discredit a house head, reduce his prestige, diminish the power he has and lower his chances of attaining power in the future. Envy is avoided if individual power can be presented as selfless service to the people. Normatively the mayor and councillors stand for co-operation through consensus, and real authority is therefore based upon the degree of consensus obtained by an individual towards the idea that he is really serving the community.

But once again the position is delicate because people believe that it is possible to turn this normative authority into personal power. Any commands, whether given normatively by the mayor on behalf of the community, or pragmatically by an individual in his own personal interest, meet with disapproval and resistance. People tend, however, to make the pragmatic interpretation and the mayor is often attacked for behaving as an individual rather than as a member of a council. But there is yet another level of complexity for people also believe that a man does right when he looks after the interests of his own house. In short, the norms contradict.

It seems that 'house norms' have the edge. The point of ranking and the power which it causes the community to grant, is the opportunity for the individual to cut short the slow processes to prosperity and security. This does not mean that all office holders will be seeking personal advantages all of the time; but all are aware that the manifest possession of prestige or authority is accompanied by the latent opportunity to gain wealth and power. Of course, it is quite possible to pursue these goals without seeking to present them as community service, and an expanding patrimony earns a certain respect however it is acquired. But the man who can afford to ignore the critical gaze of his neighbours is rare in a face-to-face community and service to the common weal is one way to avoid it. *Wolf* outlined the problem when he asked the question, 'How can a given peasant household best survive in the face of such differential and differentiating pressures?' The answer lay in two contradictory directions:

(1) By developing mechanisms for sharing resources in times of need.

or

(2) To let the selective pressures fall where they may, to maximize the success of the successful, and to eliminate those who cannot make the grade.

(pp. 78–80)

He says that most peasant societies 'fall somewhere in between these two extremes', but, as we have seen, the value system will clearly reflect the two ideologies. In simple economic terms the first solution may threaten the success of the *casa*, while the second allows no security through spreading the risk. In Hogar the common land exemplifies the first solution: individual houses and their patrimonies lean towards the second; but neither of these interests are allowed to trespass to the point of excluding the other.

MICRO-POLITICS AND INDIVIDUALISM

When existing irrigation channels were surveyed after the introduction of the common irrigation scheme in 1968, the Council decided that an old water course which was now used as a path should cease to be an irrigation channel and a new way would have to be found. The opportunity was taken to construct a new canal around the side of the hill at a higher altitude than the old system and thus include several hitherto dry fields. A work gang was formed by the farmers who stood to gain and the new channel was cut by them, extending for one kilometre around the hillside. The new route was pegged and excavated before the ditch was due to be connected up to the main concrete conduit, and here the problem arose. One man with two fields between the ditch and the conduit refused to allow a ditch to be dug across his land on the grounds that it would detract from its value. He suggested either burying the pipe underground or taking a longer route around his fields along a wall belonging to another man. This the latter refused and anyway the cost would have been much higher. As no one can cut a channel across a field without the owner's permission, there the matter rested, neither owner giving way and each convinced that he was right.

The elements of this situation are the following: (a) The Council decided to make the initial change. (b) Some farmers decided to use the opportunity to alter the old irrigation line and reach more fields. (c) They worked collectively to complete the new channel. (d) This collective effort was halted by two individual farmers not directly involved. (e) A confrontation developed between these two farmers, both refusing to back down. (f) There was no means of imposing a solution: the others tried to mediate and persuade but failed.

Up to the present collective aims have been thwarted by Hogareno norms of family independence and personal pride and the result has been complete stalemate. Neither the council as a body, nor the mayor as an individual, have any powers of arbitration and hence one cannot go to 'higher' authority. Any attempt to institute such powers locally would invite strong opposition on the grounds of family independence and mutual equality and reciprocity. It is likely in this dispute that some sort of compromise will eventually be reached, but in the meantime the farmers have lost the extra irrigation and the ditch is falling in. The difficulty is to find a means of arbitration which does not infringe family independence, especially as family self-help is the one norm that everybody is agreed should be retained both normatively and pragmatically.

During a financial crisis experienced by the saw mill in 1968 these feelings of hopelessness about communal projects became very apparent. One man wrote:

> Taking the *Mancomunidad* as a public body, it is clear that it does not care a hang if the Forestry department and, naturally, the saw mill finds itself in a difficult situation: the community is completely indifferent as to what can happen; we can say therefore that psychologically the community in this matter is highly negative and pessimistic.
> (*Consideramos a la Mancomunidad como un ente colectiva y veremos que le importa un rábano, si la Explotación Forestal y, como es natural, la Empresa, se encuentra en una difícil situación; para la comunidad le es completamente indiferente lo que pueda occurrir; podemos decir por tanto que psicologicamente la comunidad es en esta ocasion altamente negativa y nefasta*).

The solution to this situation in his opinion was to strengthen the 'ideology of the community' so that its influence could be felt powerfully by individuals, while at the same time accommodating their point of view. Steps must be taken to 'demonstrate clearly the superordination of general interests over particular ones', and the way to do this was to distribute ample information and consult all opinion equally. In other words try to involve the individual more completely in the process of decision-making, rather than extending the powers of the administration to take decisions on behalf of the *vecinos*.

When the Council decided to establish the saw mill in 1952, a problem arose as to the exact nature of the rights held in the *termino*. If these rights to common resources were *derechos propios* then they were held in the name of the Council on behalf of the *vecinos*, but if they were *derechos communales* then they were held by the *vecinos* and simply administered by the Council. Nobody worried about such an academic distinction until such large capital schemes were envisaged which necessitated exclusive economic control. Clearly if anybody could cut wood according to his own choice, for his own exclusive use, the saw mill would not be able to rationalize its own production or safeguard the future supply. Unfortunately the ancient archives were destroyed by the French in 1808 and it was not possible to settle the matter beyond question, although the Council won a *de facto* right to control the wood resources. People still argue the ins and outs of the affair and the mere fact that the Council could not prove absolute authority is taken as an indication of *casa* authority being the ultimate arbiter in the past concerning the use of common land. That is, consensus between houses was the means of decision-taking and since all were involved, all had an interest in seeing that the decision was respected.

Nowadays, according to the *Donaciones Reales* (1962) the Council is '*el competente para regular y distribuir el aprovechamiento de los communales*' (the competent body to regulate and distribute the management of common land) (1962: 14). When the attitude to collective management is so pessimistic, however, then as long as insufficient consensus is obtained, the result will be a desire to look after one's own family and ensure that '*mas perderan otros*' (others will lose more).

The practical difficulties of combining group consensus with large scale enterprises is sufficient reason for the loss of confidence. Since in practice full consultation is impossible, mistrust increases. It is as if the scale of economic operations has outstripped, at least for the time being, the value system of the community. Peasants cannot transform their economy without a willingness to concede authority to the representatives of larger corporate groups than the family.

As pesonal reputation gives access to economic opportunity, it is logical to suppose that the latter cannot change without profoundly affecting the former. There is some indication of this in the desire to alter 'family warfare' so that the community can benefit, but as houses are the locus of most of the values there is inadequate support given to community bodies. The fact that the Council is also a tool of outside authority does not recommend it to the community. In the past the Council was more preoccupied with balancing 'the supposed efforts to be unequal' than it was in leading families towards *el espiritu de asociación* (co-operation). Now it has to take a more positive role and this has, if anything, increased the amount of character assassination without creating stronger moral support for the community at large.

In this situation future developments can take one of two possible courses; one is the adaptation of family life to a wider range of activities and the possible elimination of the common land, and the other is the incorporation of independent families into co-operative units to work the resources on a group basis. Apart from the various economic merits of either solution, the possibility of realizing individual prestige in one or the other, will be an important factor in determining which one comes out on top. If individualism and independence are to be overwhelmed by co-operation and association then some kind of personal prestige must be made available inside the associations.

CONCLUSION

Reputation is something which has to be achieved by all adult members of the community. This involves ranking on a prestige scale that has three distinct stages, the individual, his house, and the community. People judge a man's performance as a leader through each successive stage, and his following depends upon his ability to combine private prosperity with an image of public magnanimity. This in turn enables a house head to maintain internal *casa* solidarity, to manipulate external labour and physical resources for personal advantages, and to influence the course of events in the valley. The competition between houses and the extreme individualism of the people creates a picture of mistrust, suspicion, and pronounced independence, which only a high personal reputation can hope to overcome, and such a reputation is the only means of uniting the community for co-operative actions.

The opportunity afforded to local leaders to increase their private wealth is a strong incentive to seek leadership roles. Hence the more powerful the man the more virulent the attempt to see that he does not convert common resources to his own use, and the more certain the expectation that he is bound to try to do just that. Thus everybody wants to see an equal distribution of income from the common lands, few are prepared to undertake the task unless there is something in it for themselves, and owing to the presentation of self-seeking disguised as community service, nobody believes that any Hogareno is really dividing the profits equitably.

The present unrest over this situation has been accentuated by the growing size of the organizations which now control part of the common resources. *Casa* rivalry has become occupational competition between sawmill workers, lorry drivers, stock raisers, caterers to the tourists, etc. But no one has any real authority to settle disputes and ill feeling persists. Only a man who has remained completely dedicated to the common good and whose prestige is equal to his sagacity, can satisfy his potential critics. But while the community may benefit from his leadership his own *casa* is likely to become impoverished unless he has a close relative who is working for a contrary end. As one Hogareno put it:

> One of the most pronounced characteristics of the inhabitants of these valleys is individualism—perhaps the principal cause that so many societies here collapse after being constituted generally with good ideas and being well founded.
> (*Una de las características mas acusadas de los habitantes de estos valles es el individualismo—quizá la causa principal de que aqui fracasen cuantas sociedades se constituan generalmente bien ideadas y mejor iniciadas.*)

NOTES

1. The following local written sources were used:
   Estudio Sobre La Explotación, 1969.
   Cuestionario, 1969.
   Donaciones Reales, 1962.
   Sumario de Sociodades en Hogar, 1969.

9
Reputation and Social Structure in a Spanish Pyrenean Village

The pueblo *(village) of Saburneda is the capital of the Valle de Solán, a valley of the central Pyrenees. Although politically Spanish and situated in one of the three provinces of Cataluña, geographically it lies on the French side of the range and in the past its possession has several times been disputed. Until 1925 the high pass leading into Spain was blocked by snow during the winter and the only communication was with France. It was not until 1945 that a tunnel was finally completed which gave access to Spain the whole year round.*

Unlike many mountain villages the population of Saburneda is not declining. In 1940 it numbered only 654 people but by 1966 it had reached 1,260. This increase is due to the creation of a Hydro-Electric system in the valley and to the building of the Saburneda Tunnel, both of which attracted workers from other parts of Spain, many of whom eventually settled in the village. Thus, despite the general movement off the land, agricultural decline has not led to a decrease in population as it has in many other mountain communities.

IMMIGRATION AND CHANGE

Saburneda has undergone a period of rapid change; not only the gradual development that is occurring in many other villages in the province, but sudden change largely beyond the control of the inhabitants. This can be attributed, firstly, to changes in the composition of the population due to the large numbers of immigrants and secondly to an increase in the volume of tourism.

The first workers arrived to start building the Saburneda

tunnel in 1925 and they were followed by the immigration of a semi-resident population who came to work for the Hydro-Electric Company after the Civil War. I would not suggest, however, that we can see this as a period of integration as compared with a prior period of isolation, for it is difficult to estimate how isolated the valley actually was before 1945. Isolation is always emphasized by the inhabitants and by people in other parts of the Province when talking about the valley (they say that it was *como una caja cerrada con llave*—like a locked box), but labour migration to France, cattle trading and a general lack of economic self-sufficiency all brought the valley into relationships with France and open to influences from outside. In fact when people describe the valley's past isolation, they are really talking about isolation from Spain, a fact which indicates how much more important ties with Spain now are.

Up to 1925, however, the composition of the population remained stable. Almost all the inhabitants could regards themselves as '*solanés*', i.e. belonging to the Solan valley, except for a small group composed of Civil Guard, militiamen and a few state officials. The economic base of the community was small scale peasant agriculture but many men from families whose incomes were inadequate were forced to migrate to work during the winter as agricultural labourers in France. Some members of the family stayed behind to look after the cattle and the seasonal migrants returned in summer for the harvest. During this period the returning migrants brought influences from France into the community but few people who married while working in France returned to the community to live. Very few outsiders became resident in the village through marriage or occupation while there are several examples of people who married and settled in France. Change during this period was a gradual process related to labour migration and initiated by insiders whose period of residence in France had brought them into contact with outside influences. It had no very far reaching social or economic effects.

The sudden arrival of a large group of resident outsiders who had to be assimilated into the community accelerated the process of development. By 1930 the population of Saburneda included 169 single workers and 16 family units (a total of 65 individuals) from other parts of Spain who lived in special housing just outside the village and who fall into a clearly definable category of 'outsiders'. In the village itself were 130 people whose place of birth was outside the valley and 36 people of Spanish nationality who were born in France. Of these only nine men and twelve women had, in 1930, been resident for more than five years, indicating how sudden the movement into the town was. The building of the tunnel marks the opening of a period in which the importance of the relationship with France declined. Goods that could not be obtained in the valley began to be bought in Spain and the provision of industrial jobs with the Hydro-Electric Company led to a decrease in migrant agricultural work. The economic changes brought about by new work opportunities and the new market that immigrants provided for different sorts of services within the valley, favoured conditions for the development of the tourist trade which had been encouraged by easier communication.

How has Saburneda adapted to change and what has its effect been on social relationships? I shall examine this question by discussing the nature and function of personal evaluation within the community.

The inhabitants of Saburneda characterize the qualities and actions of others in terms of a series of dimensions. During the course of frequent assessment people come to be known by others both directly and indirectly. A 'reputation' is created for them out of a multitude of events and actions past and present. The smaller and more homogeneous a community the more likely it is that people's judgements about others will be similar, that most people will be in agreement when they evaluate their neighbours. Continuous testing against the opinions of others means that extreme judgements can be modified and in the course of time a level of consensus is reached. However, in a community the size of Saburneda, in which, moreover, there is a high degree of occupational differentiation and great variation in standards of living, such a uniformity of public opinion is only reached under exceptional circumstances. During the course of daily life the inhabitants mix with a restricted group of people: for women, chiefly neighbours and kin, for men work-mates and bar companions. Clearly they share with them some common elements in the assessment of what constitutes 'desirable' action, but there is no value orientation to which *all* the inhabitants would subscribe. Some elements are shared by many people, others by few and there are different scales by which actions are assessed.[1] Sometimes an event occurs which is of interest to the whole village and is discussed more widely so that personal opinions are tested against others. But the occasions on which village interests unite are rare.

In Saburneda, the number of outsiders, many of short residence, has meant that more people are known about than known. Thus knowledge of the reputation of others is a means of assimilating them into a coherent, ordered world without necessarily knowing them well. However, personal evaluation also serves another function: an assessment of the behaviour of others can be understood as a claim on the part of the speaker to a particular moral position and status. It is designed to tell the hearer not only about the other person concerned (alter) but, more importantly, about the relationship between the speaker and that person (ego and alter). The nature of personal evaluation, of the way people characterize others and the criteria they use to do this, is an indication of the way the divisions within society are perceived. In a community which lacks formal organizations or affiliation to units larger than the family it reveals the main principles by which choices are made and actions governed.

As Redfield says in his discussion of peasant values, the value orientation, the 'view of the good life' that peasants have cannot be solely understood from a consideration of the way they view themselves.

> The townsman and the gentry form an aspect of the local moral life—form it by reflection, by the presence of example, by the model these outsiders offer, whether that model be one the peasant seeks to imitate or to avoid, or whether he merely recognizes both its likeness to and its difference from its own ideals.
> *Redfield* (2), p. 75

Similarly in Saburneda the influx of people from outside, coming not only from rural areas but also from the poorer parts of towns, brought into the community many different 'models of reality' and ideas as to what constituted the good or the bad life. Redfield presents a largely static picture of the relationship between the values of peasants and the values of others with whom they come into contact. The peasants he describes either imitate or avoid. For the inhabitants of Saburneda such a simple choice is not possible; nor are the 'outsiders' so separable by distance or by

N

class as those he uses as examples. Rather they are neighbours[2] in the village, whose style of life, obligations, working hours and financial rewards are different from those of the peasants.

There are now only forty families of *payéses* (peasants) in the village; their way of life, and standard of living is markedly different from those of shopkeepers or wage earners. It has been suggested that many peasant societies share 'an integrated pattern of dominant attitudes' (*Redfield* (2), p. 61, quoting *Francis*, p. 278), which emphasize the virtues of productive work over profit, maximize the use of labour rather than minimize the cost,[3] and feel an intimate and reverent attitude towards the land. If this is so and if we are to understand change in peasant societies we must look at the way in which such values are related to technical factors. Although this has commonly been assumed, some writers have tended to concentrate on changes in techniques as a product solely of changes in patterns of choice.[4] This is to oversimplify the pattern. Rather, we should examine the processes through which evaluations change, thus resulting in new choices. There are two reasons why this is important. Firstly, changed choice is the end process of a long and complicated process of re-evaluation. Often it is constrained by factors existing at a different level which while permitting a new assessment of conditions, make a new choice of action impossible. The farmers of Saburneda, for example, cannot choose to install milking machines, for in most cases they lack the economic resources to do so. They have, however, been made aware by agricultural experts and the local vet that such changes are desirable because less labour is needed to milk the same number of cows enabling herds to be increased or labour freed for other tasks. This has meant that they now feel that they are putting more labour into their farms than is justifiable but remain constrained by lack of capital from using machinery. Choice in farm mechanization is limited by such considerations and remains largely unchanged, but the relation of labour to economic returns is now conceived of in a different way. There are many occasions on which a new evaluation of the situation cannot result in a direct response. It is therefore necessary to consider evaluation as it is to consider choice, for there is a wider range of situations in which assessments change than there are in which new choices are actually made. Changes in assessments of various kinds may eventually influence choice in other spheres—such as the decision to stay on the farm or leave for an industrial job. Secondly, as studies of innovation and of status and debt in peasant communities have indicated, new courses of action are often influenced by the individual's perception of his relationship with others or by his awareness of their evaluation of him.

THE IDEA OF A MORAL COMMUNITY

The village consists of tightly packed houses grouped round the church and the two squares and extending for a little way along the banks of the river. The houses and barns are intermingled and most of them are joined to each other in a twisting pattern of streets. In recent years the original unit has been extended, and new houses have been built on fields round the edge of the main nucleus, but it is still possible to walk from one side of the village to another in the space of a few minutes. Within this compact area a bank, a small hospital, a town hall and administrative offices for the valley, a barracks, a post and telegraph office, and a water-powered factory for carding and spinning wool (which is owned and run by one family) are all to be found. There are also twenty-two bars, seven hotels, and several shops. Finally, in addition to the state-run school, there is a *collegio* (fee-paying secondary school) run by nuns and monks.

That there is a diversity of occupations and interests is evident. Although the village as a residential unit is clearly defined as distinct from other villages, there are many different levels on which people are 'members' of this community. The figures I quoted previously on place of birth in 1930 have now greatly changed. In 1968/9 of a total population of 1196, 415 people were born in Saburneda, 181 people were born in other villages in the valley, 180 were born outside the valley but within the same province and 420 were born in other provinces of Spain. Thus, a total of 596 people were born in the valley and 600 were born outside the valley. It would be possible to define membership of the community in terms of this statistical information and to create a continuum using place of birth of parents and length of residence in the village. However, this alone could not accurately describe the way the inhabitants themselves perceive the village and each other. In many peasant communities where farming is the dominant occupation, it is possible to make a distinction between residence and 'full membership' of the community. This distinction can be conceived of in terms of land or house ownership, or ties of kinship with other residents. Usually the concept that is used to understand the community is one that includes not only the idea of shared rights and duties but also that of the community as an ethical system, a shared pattern of norms and expectations against which actual behaviour is measured and by which it is constrained. The distinction between the community and the outside world is seen as a difference in the *qualities* of relationships at the different levels: relationship between people within the community being characterized by equality, a shared moral code and a personal ethic, those between the community and the outside being unequal, impersonal and free from moral constraints. It has been suggested by *Redfield* ((1), p. 109) following Per Grasslund's account of the Scandinavian village Kråkmarö that 'a village dies when it ceases to be whole'. However, although many of the traditional relationships in Saburneda are dying or being transformed and, as I shall show, many upheavals and changes in relationships between individuals, much suspicion and mistrust, can be seen as the result of conflicting moral codes, it seems likely that the community will continue to flourish, if in a new form.

One of the defining characteristics of a community has been that it is a moral community. Such a concept, while it may deal successfully with the traditional peasant village, is misleading when applied to the largely post peasant society of Saburneda. What is more important is that social relations no longer constitute a moral community.

The idea that it is unrealistic to see the village as a whole, within which relationships and activities are qualitatively different from those outside, was usefully expressed by Hanssen in his concept of an 'activity field' which he used to analyse various differentiated village communities in Scandinavia. He stressed the point that certain groups in the community had more intimate connections with the population of the surrounding countryside than with each other (*Hanssen, quoted in Redfield, (1),* Chapter VIII) and distinguished a separate activity field for each grouping within the village, thus enabling the differentiation of activities and relationships to be recognized. In that there are distinct economic and class groups within Saburneda, such a procedure would also be applicable. Furthermore, many of the families of immigrants in the village lack ties of kinship with other inhabitants and remain more intimately connected with kin in other parts of Spain, in spite of the fact that they visit them only occasionally. Hanssen uses the concept in connection with overt social behaviour such as co-operation and transaction but it can usefully be applied to the consideration of prestige and moral evaluation. For in Saburneda, not only the activities, but the worth of a man, depend on the group he belongs to in the community. In this sense there is not one moral community, but many.

In the past a greater homogeneity of values existed despite the fact that there were wide differences in wealth and class. The wealth of the old rich families in the village was based on ownership of land. The system of primogeniture which prevails in most of Cataluña meant that many of the non-inheriting sons of those rich families were given careers as doctors or lawyers. Education, wealth, and class were congruent, and the structure of power and leadership followed the same lines. Now, none of these families are left. In some cases all the children preferred a career in the city and the lands were sold or rented, in others the families were left without heirs. The largest house in the village stood where the main square now is. It was surrounded by high walls and had its own chapel and fields stretching away on the best flat land. Finally only one daughter was left; she never married and remained alone in the house until just before her death when she sold the house, chapel and lands to the company who were at that time engaged in building the tunnel. The land was needed for the road that joined the main road from France running through the village centre. Very little of the land that was sold passed into the hands of farmers but was used for building since it was near the village. The old rich families were not replaced by peasant families because only a small amount of land entered the agricultural market. Instead the wealthy of the village became the new generation of shopkeepers and entrepreneurs, many of whom had come as immigrants and begun by working for a wage. Thus, the old pattern: land→wealth→education→power→prestige became transformed into: money→power. This brought about a consequent change in the criteria on which the system of moral evaluation was founded.

The lack of a single moral community, then, is not only due to the fact that there are differences in wealth and class within the village, for these seem always to have existed. Nor is it only related to the presence of outsiders or the greater differentiation of occupation that are now to be found. Rather it is to do with the changing assumptions about power which lead to a moral dilemma about the worth of men.[5]

In conclusion, I would like to suggest that insofar as people within the village live in close proximity and have to contend with the actions and personalities of other residents, whether or not they know them well, the village represents an arena within which moral evaluation must be made. People judge the actions of a fellow villager and the actions of someone outside in a different way. Or rather, in the case of someone who lives in Saburneda they feel bound to act on the judgement differently for such a person's behaviour relates to their own, and the assessment of it relates to their assessment of themselves. In other words the farther a person is removed from the individual's own social milieu, the less his actions can be discussed as part of the language of claims in which he tries to present himself vis-à-vis other members of the community. This is particularly true where sexual morality is concerned. For example, during 1969 a cattle dealer who came from the provincial capital but who was well known in the valley was stabbed and badly wounded. This incident took place in the large, state-run hotel, the Parador Nacional, that was built a few years ago on the mountainside overlooking the village. The cattle dealer was said to be *un juerguista* (a playboy) and because of his wealth he had the nickname '*Pesetas*'. He had reputedly been attacked by one of his many mistresses because he refused to give her as much money as she wanted (it was said '*quiso más de los verdes*'—she wanted more green ones, i.e. 1000 peseta notes); the previous year he had been attacked for the same reason by a different woman. There was very little criticism of this event, in marked contrast with the reaction to other events which I shall describe later in the paper. Apart from a general feeling that it represented the violence of the contemporary world, people were inclined to find it amusing rather than shocking. It was thought that '*Pesetas*' was lucky to be rich enough to attract so many *novias* (girl friends), but that he ought in the course of such long experience to have learnt how to get rid of them when they became a nuisance. As he had so many it was obvious that sooner or later one of them would become jealous. The social distance between the actors in this drama and the residents of the village was such that their behaviour did not represent a threat to expectations of how people would behave within the village.

Thus there is a sense in which people find the behaviour of other residents in the village particularly relevant to themselves, and more relevant than that of people outside. What I want to stress, however, is that because of the diversity of the population, social consensus about what behaviour is permissive varies from individual to individual. For some people this consensus might include only those who were resident in the village, for others it would also include those who were members of other communities in various parts of Spain. As we shall see in the next section the community means different things to different people, and it is difficult to isolate a set of criteria which objectively define what *los del pueblo* (those of the village) consists of. Furthermore, it is more useful here to see 'moral community' as a sphere of action in which moral claims are made, rather than as it has traditionally been used to express a set of shared attitudes and expectations. Shared values operate at some levels and not at others. As *Myrdal* points out (pp. 16–17) even behind the behaviour of the individual,

> there is not one homogeneous set of valuations, but a mesh of struggling inclinations, interests and ideals. Some of these are held consciously and some are suppressed for long intervals, but all of them work to move behaviour in their particular direction. There are no solid 'attitudes' and behaviour normally becomes a moral compromise. Valuations are, so to speak, located on different levels of the moral personality, in the main corresponding to various degrees of generality of moral judgements. . . . In the course of actual day-to-day living . . . a person will be found to focus attention on the valuations on one plane of his moral personality while leaving in the shadows for the time being, the often conflicting valuations on other planes. The basis of this selective focusing is plainly opportunistic.

While I would agree with Myrdal that we cannot talk in terms of a homogeneous system of values for the individual, even less for a community as a whole, I would suggest that in so far as a group of people pursue a similar way of life, associated with the exploitation of the same resources, it is likely that some at least of their 'inclinations, interests and ideals' will be held in common and that in their assessment of other members of the community they will refer to the same general criteria of evaluation.[6]

The distinction between the levels of generality of moral judgements is an important one, for it may be useful to see that in the homogeneous peasant community concepts of a high level of abstraction and generality such as an ethic of equality or co-operation may be shared while particular values existing at a more 'pragmatic' level may more usually regulate behaviour. As a community becomes diversified and many alternative ways of exploiting resources become available so that the basis for authority and decision making changes, values held in common will decline and be called upon less and less to regulate community behaviour, so that the idea of a common construct or moral community becomes increasingly inapplicable.[7] As I have pointed out those aspects of the moral order that relate to the legitimacy of power have, in Saburneda, undergone considerable change, resulting in various, sometimes conflicting systems of ranking by which the status of individuals is measured.

ETHNIC BOUNDARIES: 'SOLANÉS' AND 'OUTSIDERS'

We have seen that changes in the composition of the community are at least forty years old and the material results of change at least twenty years old. Many of those who were in-marrying immigrants in the nineteen thirties have been resident now for more than half their lifetime and have children and grand-children who were born in the valley. The distinction between '*solanés*' and 'others' is now clearly harder to define. The experience of immigration and the transfer of power to a new section of the population is central to an understanding of change in the village. I shall now consider to what extent a distinction between insiders and outsiders is still relevant to a discussion of social relationships, and how it is a significant categorization for the inhabitants themselves. The broad dimensions will be familiar to anyone brought up in modern western society. In Saburneda as much as in an English community an idea of binary qualities, good/bad or mean/charitable provides a framework for relating oneself to other people.

The basic unit is the nuclear family. There are only family, not group loyalties and no corporate group larger than the family. Although co-operation with people who are not relatives is often necessary, the self-sufficient family is regarded as a fortunate one, both financially and socially. The 'S' family, for example, who have two grandmothers living in the house and two adult sons, are able to run a garage and repair workshop, a small grocery store and two flats which they let. They also let rooms in their house in summer, the wife mends stockings for people in the village and the sons are part-time driving instructors. They admit they are lucky in having sons rather than daughters and compare themselves with other less fortunate families who either have to hire men for a wage to run a business or sacrifice their independence by being dependent on help from other people.

Although people avoid co-operation with others, try to maintain their independence, and do not participate in formal organizations or corporate groups, they recognize that two distinct groups or categories do exist within the village. Membership of either group is as hard to specify as membership of the community and varies according to context, but the qualities that define each group are clear. The two groups are broadly conceptualized as '*solanés*' and 'not-*solanés*'. They exist as a kind of ideal type from which the speaker wishes to distinguish himself.

There are three main dimensions by which people define the qualities of '*solanés*-ness'; these are moral, social and pragmatic. In moral terms people say that the *solanés* are *hipócritos* (hypocrites), and *avaros* (mean), and they are *atrasados* (backward). They stress that the *solanés* are inward looking and ungenerous with others and that they suffer from '*amor del suyo*' (self-centredness). Maria P. whose parents came to the village when she was one year old is married into a family of rich peasants who also keep a bar that is patronized almost exclusively by farmers. She and her husband and their small daughter live with her husband's parents and grandparents who are still the owners and controllers of the house, the land and the bar. She says that, although she knows it is wrong, such a situation means that she and her husband are merely waiting for the death of the parents in order to gain some financial independence, for at the moment they have nothing of their own and are dependent on the charity of the older generation. The parents are still waiting for the death of the grandparents for similar reasons. At times, she says, she has considered leaving and going to get a job in the city, but her husband finds it impossible to make a choice between her and his parents. Although he is 'not quite like *solanés*', having been brought up in France, he suffers from that *falta de iniciativa* (lack of initiative) that she claims is typical of the *solanés* mentality. Furthermore, he is afraid of losing his inheritance if he deserts the house and because they both realize that life would be hard for them in the city, they have never gone. Her comment on this is to ask 'why are the *solanés* so attached to a piece of land that they think they will die if they are separated from it? Plenty of people have started with nothing and survived. The trouble with the *solanés* is that they can't make any effort, they are dependent on their land to go on providing for them in the same old way.' Their way of life, too, is different from her own. While *orgullo* (pride) is condemned, as we shall see when we come to consider social groups, a certain pride in oneself is thought by Maria P. to be an important quality. When she married, she says, her husband's family should have provided her with a properly furnished room; it is the husband's job to buy the furniture for the home while the wife is supposed to bring the linen as part of her *ajuar* (trousseau). But she herself was forced to save and buy the small wardrobe they have and to decorate the room which was unfit to live in when she first entered the house. All the small improvements that have been made she has done with her own hands without help from her husband's family. The *solanés*, she says, are *los más malos de todo* (the worst people in the world). The reason for working hard, she believes, is so that the future shall be better for one's children and she is unable to understand the 'grasping' mentality of the *solanés*, among whom each generation tries to keep everything for itself. Her criticisms not only extend to the failure of the *solanés* family to meet their obligations but to their general habits and style of life. 'At meal times they eat straight from the pot, without any manners, and never bother to set the table properly or put a table cloth or table napkins.' Because she thinks it important to eat *'como debe'* ('as one should') she fetches a table napkin for herself and they ridicule her. 'Where I come from, women serve the food, but they sit at table with everyone else in the proper way, but the *solanés* woman never sits at table to eat with the men but remains standing and eats out of the saucepan.'

There are thus several ways in which Maria P. feels that the *solanés* are different from herself and in which they do not fulfill her expectations of how people *ought* to behave. Although she has lived in Saburneda practically all her life, she maintains the idea that she is 'from Andalucia' and contrasts herself with those who are 'from Saburneda'. She recognizes a general concept of '*solanés*-ness' from which she wishes to distinguish herself.

Comments like these are common from those who have married into *solanés*' households and are partly related to the fact that until now separate residence for married couples has been rare so that the in-marrying partner is dependent on the family financially. In many cases even an in-marrying man who came to the valley originally to work for the Hydro-Electric Company will eventually work on the family land or in the family shop, especially now that many company workers have been made redundant. This is not universally true, but in many cases even those in some other employment remain resident at home. In farming families in-marrying men were often not only dependent on the families of their wives but they were also treated as apprentices, who had to learn a new occupation. Quite often, as the case of Maria P. showed, the house and the land are in the hands of the grandparents and the husband must fight for status and independence.

Evaluations which refer not to the moral life and the performance of obligations within the household but to the wider social behaviour of the *solanés* are also made. The secretary of the village, for example, described them as anti-social (*no hay sociedad*) and *desconfiados* (lacking in *confianza*, or trust, with other people). When he arrived in the village, he had found *una gente muy rara* (very strange people) and his only friend for a long time had been the lawyer who was also an outsider. In this context it is interesting to note that the mother of the secretary was in fact a *solanésa*, but that he had spent all his youth outside the valley and only returned when he was made secretary. Although, therefore, by descent half *solanés*, his evaluations stress his desire to dissociate himself from them. I shall return to this point later when I come to discuss the ascriptive nature of ethnic boundaries. The idea that the *solanés* lack *confianza* in their relations with others occurs in many contexts. The converse of this, that it is dangerous to trust them, is also expressed. It is said that a '*solanés* will slap you on the back in friendship one day and knife you in the back the next'. This idea of the double face is expressed in a refrain which runs:

Solanés

Falso y cortés

('*Solanés*, treacherous but polite.') This notion was interestingly explained by one man who said that the *solanés* distrusted and hated even each other, but because at certain times of the year they needed the help and co-operation of others they would pretend to be on good terms with them.

As I have already mentioned all sections of the population avoid co-operation and try to minimize it as much as possible; however, of all the groups in the village the farmers are the most likely to need extra help at times of pig-killing and harvest and now because of diminishing family size and emigration they may have to look outside the nuclear family to find it. As an explanation of their hypocrisy the idea has only speculative value but it interestingly underlines the distinction people draw between social relations that result from working the land and those that result from other types of occupation.

Related to this are those evaluations which I have called pragmatic. These relate to the performance of various skills and also to the ability to perform in the contemporary world. They are often connected with specific issues in which the peasants meet attempts to change their methods by the various authorities. For instance, it was proposed that in accordance with the government scheme for *ordenación rural* Saburneda and various surrounding villages should be grouped together to form a collective, which would own machinery and handle marketing in common. This scheme raised a great deal of protest from the *payéses*. The mayor, who had been one of the chief authorities in favour of the scheme, was conciliatory in public, but privately accused the peasants of being *routinarios* (routine-minded, or resistant to change) and *conservadores* (conservative) and lacking in moral fibre (*falta de espíritu moral*). A similar criticism was expressed in relation to the business activities of the *solanés*. One informant said, 'There won't be any progress in this place until the *solanéses* learn what business really means. Look at that hotel over there. The people who own it were farmers, but they had a bit of money, so they opened the hotel, but the old man still comes in from milking and walks through the dining room where all the guests are sitting with his boots all covered with muck from the stable. There's stupidity for you.' Another said that if anyone tried to do something new and better in a *pueblo* he was sure to be held back by the *solanéses* because they were so lacking in initiative and could never agree about anything. It is commonly said by those who wish to be thought of as not *solanés* that the *solanés* find great difficulty in co-operating even though it is necessary to them. The failure of the *lechería* (co-operative dairy) in Saburneda is a case in point. Critics said that the *solanés* wanted more than their fair share of everything and yet were not willing to play their part or take the risks involved. The only reason that things are working better now that the valley has joined a bigger co-operative in another part of the province is that the peasants are completely dominated by the people who are in charge there and all they have to do is obey orders, so there isn't so much scope for disagreement among themselves.

In various ways then '*solanés*' is an ascriptive category distinguishable in moral, social and pragmatic terms. However, although such ascription is based on the set of descriptive criteria that I have outlined we should not treat such criteria as if they provided an 'objective' definition of a group. The cultural features that are used in definition may change over time, just as the group may change. What is important is that the criteria used form a set of signals, chosen in the particular situation as being socially relevant. As we have seen, a definition through descent of membership of the group is given little relevance: while making a generalized evaluation of the characteristics, informants often make an exception for their own *solanés* husbands or wives, for example, saying that they are 'not really *solanés*', having spent a long time outside the valley. In this sense people may vary the cultural content of their ascription according to context.[8] Before considering the significance of the cultural forms that are chosen by people to discriminate between what is *solanés* and what is not *solanés* and putting forward some hypotheses about why such ethnic boundaries persist in Saburneda despite the length of contact and intermarriage, let us look at the extent to which people define a general category of 'outsider', or 'not-*solanés*'.

When I asked at the beginning of my stay who were the people who owned the gardens (*huertos*) that are to be found in and around the village I was told, '*todo los del pueblo*' (all those of the village); as this was clearly not the case, I asked 'Where do the people of family X have theirs?' and the answer was 'Oh *they* haven't got one', '*son de fuera*' (they are from outside). In this case the speaker defined an 'outsider' or 'not-*solanés*' by the criteria of land-ownership. While the family in question were defined in this respect as outsiders, on other occasions they were regarded as part of 'those of the village', as in fact they regarded themselves.

The assessment of the 'outsider' is less homogeneous than that of the '*solanés*'. Broadly speaking it revolves round ideas about acquiring and using money and about moral responsibility. Stories are often told about the 'disgraceful' poverty of many of the workers who arrived in the thirties and forties. They came with *ni una peseta* (without even a *peseta*), without clothes and shoes and were given charity by the local population. They were *desgraciados*, a word which means literally 'unfortunates', but which is often used of a person who is continually on the receiving end of charity. It is frequently pointed out by those who wish to be regarded as 'insiders' in this respect, that these *desgraciados* have made money and become rich, often at the expense of the local population. It is said that they were able to profit more from the new work opportunities because of their lack of commitments: they forgot about the wives and families they had left behind and just worked for themselves. It must be emphasized here that the 'outsider' group as a whole is composed of people from many different regions of Spain. Sometimes this diversity is recognized and sometimes it is ignored. The notion that the outsiders deserted their wives and families in order to make money which they then spent on gambling and drinking is particularly applied to the *gallegos* (those from Galicia, a region of western Spain, which is noted for high emigration. So much so that Spanish immigrants to South America are said to be known as '*gallegos*'). When discussing the connection between making money and lack of commitments, the speaker who claims local affiliation implies that he may not be well off, he may not have done so well but at least he has kept up the obligation of providing for his family and its old people in a way that the *forestero* (who left his family behind) has not done. The factual basis of this argument is almost impossible to check; although the figures given earlier suggest that in 1930 of a total of 234 men only 16 had brought their families with them, it is impossible to know how many of the others were married and what provision they made for their families. Many married workers at present resident send regular money back to their homes. But the idea remains that the *foresteros* could do as they liked; not only were they free from financial responsibilities, but they were also far from the eyes of their native *pueblos* and could, therefore, behave as they liked in other ways. In contrast to this the local population were tied to the land. Not everyone who would like to be a *jornalero* (wage-earner) could be one, especially if he was a *proprietario* (a land owner). This is still the case today. In 1969 a man died who had lived in Saburneda for 35 years, but came originally from another part of the region of Cataluña. He had been an employee of the Hydro-Electric Company. However, his *solanés* wife had had three inheritances from different parts of her family and owned a great deal of land. After the funeral people speculated on what would happen to the family. Most of them thought that the eldest son would not be able to take up the option that he had been offered on his father's job in the Company but would have to work the land. They said 'you earn more with the Company, and more easily, too, but the lands cannot be lost'.

Although the terms chosen to define the two categories of ascription that I have outlined here cannot be seen as objectively delimiting the two groups they nevertheless significantly reflect features of the social structure of Saburneda. One of the basic distinctions is that made between 'occupiers' and 'settlers'. Those who came into the community were the landless. They were, therefore, put in an inferior position by the local population, even though they had frequently better working conditions, pensions, medical assistance, subsidized food and often higher wages. Such benefits tended to be seen by the *solanés* as a piece of good fortune which did no necessarily carry very high esteem.

Many of the evaluations refer to ownership of land or lack of it. They underline the fact that the speaker, even if not well off, has the solid worth of property behind him and that the many examples of wealthy outsiders are the result of unfair advantage. I shall return to this later in a wider discussion of the moral evaluation of wealth.[9] Those outsiders who now own land in the village do so either because they married into a local family, or because they bought their way into the community. The dependence that this is felt to create is sometimes used as a weapon. An outsider may be referred to, for example, as *el gallego de Casa Fransussetta* ('the *Galician* from the house of Fransussetta) stressing the fact that he is only a resident, not the owner of the house.

The cluster of words and expressions used to refer to each category do not represent opposites, but they can be seen to be complementary and as a reflection of the different experience of cultural contact. The terms used to refer to the *solanés* stress unwillingness to participate in social relations, they are ungenerous and lacking in *confianza*, they are unable to enter into the modern competitive economy. Such evaluations are related to the inability of the *solanés* to manipulate the new resources that became available, leading to an attempt to withdraw from the corresponding social relationships. Those that refer to the outsiders express the feeling that they are usurpers who have taken advantage of a diminished moral responsibility. Each set of assessments evaluates the opposing category by the qualities in which the speaker feels strongest, and the categories persist because the economic differences on which they were based are still applicable.

REPUTATION AND SOCIAL GROUPS

Marked differences of wealth between the inhabitants are of long standing. The community is occupationally and economically heterogeneous and there is no 'ethic of equality' that is applicable to the community as a whole. Because of this diversity of interests the need to co-operate in *reciprocal* social relations is limited to a small group of kin, neighbours and equals. Transactions which take place outside this group are either purely economic, or controlled by an often ambiguous relationship of subordination/superordination in which rights and obligations are not always clear. Furthermore, for each individual there are many people in the community with whom no transactions take place and whom they know only slightly. The distinctions recognized between *solanés* and non-*solanés* are cross-cut by others between *payéses* (peasants) and *comerciantes* (shopkeepers, hotelkeepers, and all those engaged in 'business' generally); betwen rich and poor; and between *personas de carrera* (professional people) or *personas de categoría* ('important' people) and those who are not. Such categories make up the language of claims through which reputation is assessed.

Within the small co-operating group great care is taken to try to repay obligations. Favours done and help given by one member to another are carefully accounted for. This often means that any ties that an individual member has outside the group can be an embarrassment. Favours done for such an outside person are usually concealed in case one of the members to whom debts are owed should *sabe mal* (lit. 'know badly', this expression can be translated as 'to be offended', and thus to think badly of the person who has done the favour for the outsider). The annual pig-killing, for example, is done by a small group of kin or neighbours. The owners of the pig give a present of meat to the men who have helped with the killing and the women who have helped to make the sausages. Sometimes the owner may want to give a piece of meat to someone who has not helped. This is normally done with great secrecy because such a gift offends against the common interests of family and group and could provide an opportunity for the other members to *sabe mal*. It is felt that the resources available to the family and group are limited and should not be made available to other people. The idea of *sabe mal* expresses this fear that people may think badly of the person who neglects his main obligations. People in the village often say that there is *mas malicia* (more malice or ill-will) today than there was in the past, and that this is true even within the family as well as within the community in general. There are more occasions on which people can *sabe mal* and accuse other members of prejudicing group interests to favour outside interests. *Malicia* refers not only to the active expression of ill feeling but also to the need to watch other people more closely.

The diversity of interests is most clearly shown in the relationship between the *payéses* and the *comerciantes*. While there is no

o

direct conflict between them, members of each group make claims against the other to allies or third parties. Each group says that the other is profiting at its own expense. The peasants say that the shopkeepers no longer serve the needs of the village but have put prices up to meet the level that tourists from France are willing to pay. 'The more they gain, the more we suffer'. Families are smaller now because of the emigration of some members, the large number of bachelors among the farming sector of the population and the generally lower birthrate, so that the peasants rely more on bought goods and produce less in the home. Thus they are increasingly dependent on the shopkeepers and have to comply with the rise in prices. They say too that commerce has altered the form of public events in a way that is detrimental to the farmers. Sebastiana P. said that her brother Cisco would never find a wife because he could no longer meet girls at village dances. Since the mayor had opened a night club in the village there were no public dances except for the annual fiesta in September. 'Peasants like us can't afford to pay the ridiculous prices that they charge in the club', she said, 'and how else can you get to know girls? *Aquí pesetas mandan— here money rules.*'

In return, the *comerciantes* accuse the peasants of charging an unreasonable price for milk. Most non-farming families have a long-standing arrangement with a farming family to buy milk, but they complain that the peasants are increasingly reluctant to keep to these arrangements because they can now sell their milk to the large co-operative outside the valley for a secure monthly income. During the summer there is a great demand for milk from the hotels in the village, but it is in the summer that milk is scarcest. Most families send the majority of their herd up to the high pastures, as labour during the harvest season is too scarce to allow time for looking after the cows. This is related to the shortage of labour in the peasant households. Only the larger families have enough manpower available to be able to keep their cows down in the village during the summer months. The *comerciantes*, however, say that the peasants are too lazy to bother with the cows. That they could keep them in the village if they were prepared to work harder. The mayor complained that they were getting more *gandulo* (lazy) every year. They no longer harvested enough fodder in the summer to last them through the winter, so that they were forced to buy prepared feed from the co-operative, a thing they could not really afford to do. They should be spending the money on fertilisers if they spent it at all, certainly not on trying to remedy the laziness of the previous summer, he said. All they wanted to do, he continued, was to sit in the bars, becoming more alcoholic than they already were. The *comerciantes*, too, accuse the peasants of no longer serving the needs of the village in preferring to sell what milk they have to an outside organization. Many of them claim that the peasants are very rich but are so mean that no one would know. Pilar E., a small shopkeeper, pointed to a couple passing in the street during the harvest, with a cart piled with hay, and said to the group gathered in her shop, 'You'd never believe they had all that money. She still works the land and goes around looking like a gypsy. If I was as rich as that, I'd have my hair done properly and dress in good clothes.' Joaquina V. said that she had given up her cows to go and live with her married daughter, just as the people who owned cows were all becoming millionaires—*es así la vida*—that's life.

The claim that other people *hacen trampas* (practise deceptions) is common. Sebastiana P. said that Antonia M. who works the wool factory with her father-in-law and husband was *una bruja* (a witch) because she always returned less wool to clients than they had sent for processing. '*She* says that the weight of the wool always goes down a little when it is washed, but don't you believe it. If it never went down in the past, why should it go down now?' Antonia M. says, however, that the wool is of such poor quality now that it is surprising it doesn't disintegrate completely after it has been washed and spun.

Another *trampa* is adding water to the milk. Non-farmers often accuse farmers of this. Maria M. who buys her milk from Sebastiana P. said you could tell she had been putting water in it because when it was heated it didn't boil over. Sebastiana said that she knew 'some people' accused the peasants of doing this, but the peasants wouldn't be so stupid. Anyone could tell when there was water in the milk so who would try to do it?

The milk that the peasants send to the co-operative is priced according to its fat content which is recorded at each delivery. Milk sold locally, on the other hand, is sold at the same price regardless of quality. Thus, against the advantages of the security of the monthly cheque that is paid into farmers' accounts by the co-operative, must be weighed the fact that a local selling price of 9 or 10 *pesetas* per litre is often comparable with 7 or 8 *pesetas* that the co-operative will pay if the fat content is not very high. It seems therefore that the reason many peasants prefer to sell to the co-operative is not a purely financial one. They prefer the impersonal transaction to the personal one with the claims and counter-claims it involves. Sometimes clients in the village do not come to fetch the milk when they say they will, or they may build up a debt. Sometimes they expect the peasant to take the milk to their house. In many ways the peasants feel that the co-operative provides a way out of this and allows them to retain their independence.

It can be seen that money is a theme which runs through many of the kinds of evaluation that I have discussed so far. Material attributes are a frequent topic of conversation, and are often the prelude to a moral comment. The reasons for this will by now be becoming clear. Saburneda is not a face-to-face community in the traditional sense. It has become a highly competitive one and there is often little knowledge of the family background or history of those who have become most successful in the community.

Thus the poorer section of the community often attribute wealth to miraculous good fortune or coincidence, gambling or a love affair. The wealth of Marcelo S. who is one of the richest hoteliers in the village, is described in the following way:

Marcelo's parents came originally from Aragon. From there they emigrated to France and opened a restaurant. By chance, one of the clients of this restaurant was a mule dealer from Saburneda.[10] Over the course of time they gave him credit and he got heavily into debt to them. He and the wife had a love affair and it was suspected that the restaurant had also been a brothel. The dealer's debts got greater and greater and eventually he died in dubious circumstances and left everything he had, including his house in Saburneda, to the couple. It was thought that he might even have been murdered by them in the hope of this. Soon afterwards they left the restaurant in France and moved to Saburneda where they opened a hotel on the site of the mule dealer's house. They were both *lista* (clever), and from the capital they had been left they made a fortune. People remember that round her waist the wife used to wear a chain holding many keys. When she died it was found that the keys were for several chests and cupboards in the house that were packed full of millions of notes. No one could say quite how much there had been but they knew that Marcelo, the son, had spent three days counting it. As a final touch of drama, the story says that at the funeral a mysterious stranger appeared who was the image of the dead woman and who was clearly the illegitimate son who had come to claim his share of the fortune.

Such semi-mythical stories are used by people to question the legitimacy of the power that '*las vacas gordas*' (the fat cows, i.e. the rich people) wield in the community. Another story said that the three richest men in the village had become rich when they robbed a group of Polish refugees who were in hiding in a hermitage in the mountains during the Second World War. One night the men from Saburneda had gone to the hermitage and told the refugees that the Civil Guard were on their way to capture them and that they should leave as fast as they could. The Poles fled, leaving all their jewels and money behind which the men, having told a false story, divided among themselves. People like this, the teller of the story said, might be rich but they were *sin verguenzas* (people without shame).

The third major distinction that is recognized in the village is that between *personas de carrera* (professional people) and others. Most of the professional people, such as the judge and the notary, are not locally born but are posted to the valley for a period of time. Together with the doctors and various visiting professionals such as architects and engineers they form the local élite. A *persona de carrera* is a person with education and thus almost always a person from a wealthy family who is himself wealthy. A distinction is drawn between this and the idea of a *persona de categoría*, which could be translated as 'a person of importance or consequence'. Such a person is recognized as having power without necessarily having a professional position. Thus while a *persona de carrera* is almost always also a *persona de categoría* the reverse is not automatically true. The first term can be seen to represent various qualities possessed by a person, the second refers more specifically to a person's activities in his relations with others. For example, the most powerful person in the village, the mayor, is regarded as a *persona de categoría* but not as a *persona de carrera*. His father was a lawyer and therefore regarded as a professional person but the mayor himself before becoming a hotelier and businessman was an army captain.

The distinction between these two terms was traditionally expressed by the title 'Don' followed by the Christian name of the person concerned. The mayor would never be called 'Don José'; when people wish to be deferential to him he is referred to as 'Señor Pepito' (Pepito being the diminutive form of José). Thus the form of address reflects the fact that the power that is bought by wealth is seen to be different from that given by birth or education. But the use of the term 'Don' and the attitude towards the village élite is no longer the same as it was in the past. 'There are no *real* Dons in the village now,' said one old woman. 'In the past there were several people who you had to address like that, but now everything has changed. Some people say Don to the vet and the doctors, but they're not *really* Dons, not like in the old days, and anyway *son todos peseteros* (they're all after money).'

Familiarity and distance cause tensions in the relations between the élite and other inhabitants of the village. In this respect it is easier to be an outsider. The two doctors, who are locally born, are sometimes accused of being *orgulloso* (proud) and they are allowed to show less superiority in their dealings with people than others. Joaquina V. described how her mother and the mother of one of the doctors had been neighbours in one of the nearby villages. 'They were in and out of each other's houses all the time,' she said, 'and when the doctor was a child I often looked after him and held him on my knee. We knew the family very well, we had *confianza* (trust). A year or two ago he came here to see me when I was ill and we were chatting in the usual way when suddenly he said to me "*no digame más tu*" (stop calling me "*tu*"). I was angry; after all, as I said to him, I'd known him since he was a baby. I was twice as old as he was, and our families had always been on good terms. In Barcelona the doctors are different, here in the country they're too proud.'

Older people often compare the respect they say they felt for the village élite in the past with the way they feel now. People who are *instruido* (educated) are admired because education opens the way to wealth and success. It is said '*los instruidos siempre corren*' (people with education always get about—i.e. education gives you a chance to shape your own life, it gives you freedom of movement) but it does not call for the same respect as it did in the past. An event that became a village talking point for some time illustrates this.

One night at about twelve o'clock a young man who worked as a ski instructor at the ski station at the head of the valley was leaving the mayor's club with a French girl. As he crossed the road he was run over and knocked unconscious. He was taken to the hospital. The next day as the news became known people were shocked to learn that the car had been driven by a French priest who had been having supper with some friends at a hotel in the village. On leaving, the hotel owner had advised him not to drive as he had been drinking heavily, but he took no notice, got into the car and drove off at great speed. A few moments later his car went out of control and knocked down the instructor. For two days it was said that the man, though still unconscious, only had a broken leg and should recover quickly, then on the third day the news became known that he was dead. He had died in an ambulance that was taking him to France for an emergency operation for a brain injury. Word went round that neither of the two doctors had been able to attend him at the beginning because they had been barred from the hospital after a quarrel in which one of them had hit the other over the head with a chair. The instructor had been examined by a very old and only partly qualified doctor who had been brought over from another town. He had only diagnosed the broken leg and had not discovered the injury to the brain. Finally, on the third morning, the parents of the instructor had become so worried that he had still not regained consciousness that they had gone to the *Juzgado* (the legal offices) and asked the judge to make a special order that one of the doctors who had been banned from the hospital should be allowed to enter to examine their son. This was done, and after seeing him, the doctor immediately ordered that he should be taken to France for a brain operation.

As well as the general feeling of grief and tragedy that was felt throughout the village, people's attention focused on the behaviour of the two doctors. Many people commented that it was an indication of how little you could rely on people in authority to behave as they ought to. The doctor who had been finally called in was, it was felt, undoubtedly a good doctor, in the medical sense, but what was so bad was that he should have behaved in such a completely irresponsible way. The quarrel was felt to be directly responsible for the ski instructor's death. Several speculations were made about the exact nature of the quarrel between the doctors. Most agreed that it had to do with money in some form or other. The most popular account was that one of the doctors had felt resentful that the other had treated all the patients who had been injured in ski-ing accidents, and therefore had made much more money in the ski-ing season than he had, and that furthermore, *he* was the doctor officially responsible for the hospital while the doctor who had, in fact, treated the skiers was not. 'It was all a question of *envidia* (jealousy),' said one man, 'and those in authority should be above that.'

Decisions that effect the general development of the village are not in the hands of these *personas de carrera*, that I have described, but are controlled by the wealthy businessmen of Saburneda. They sit on the village council, which has only one representative of the farming sector of the community, and they are the group with the most power to affect the lives of other residents. They, more than the professional group, are regarded as *las vacas gordas*, and they are often accused of putting their own commercial interests before those of the village in general. But, despite the claims made against them, their power is undisputed; public opinion is not an effective sanction on behaviour. As one man put it while talking about Marcelo S. '*Lo que dice Marcelo, lo hacen*' (What Marcelo says, goes). Most claims, in fact recognize the power and question its legitimacy but are unable to change it. Josefina S. lets rooms in the summer to visitors to the mayor's hotel when the hotel itself is too full to take them. She complained that the mayor never settled his bill with her so that eventually she has to ask him for the money. When she asks him he tells her to come to his hotel at such and such a time and when she goes he is either not there or he keeps her waiting a long time. She says that she has done him a favour in putting the people up even if it is to her financial advantage, and that he should come and pay her, rather than expect her to go to him. 'The trouble is,' she says, 'he's in debt, because of all his grand schemes, and he doesn't want to pay up. He thinks he can do what he likes with people. I'd rather have nothing and know that I didn't owe anyone anything than have all the hotels in the world and the debts *he's* got.'

Many people in positions of authority are said to *chupar* (lit. 'to suck'). This means that if they are administering money they secretly suck it away for themselves. Many people in the valley invested small amounts of money in the ski station and complained that after three years they still had had no dividends. All the profit had been sucked away by the administrators. When the *lechería* in Saburneda failed, many farmers found that they had lost the money they had contributed towards it. It had been sucked away by the people in charge, such as the vet and the engineers. No doubt the people in charge of the new co-operative would *chupar* as well.

During the *Fiesta Mayor* of 1968 (the Festival in honour of the village patron saint) the shopkeepers came into open conflict with the village. Organization of the *Fiesta* was, for the first time, taken over by the village council instead of being left to the young men of the village. A large tent was hired and put up in one of the squares for dancing. But the price of entry was so high that many people went to the mayor's club or the bars instead. Clearly the shopkeepers on the council stood to lose by the lack of success of the public dance almost as much as they could hope to profit by their increased trade. But many other people in the village said that it was a way to *chupar* council funds from which money for the *Fiesta* was drawn while increasing their own personal gain. The outcry against the council was so strong and the failure of the *Fiesta* so evident that the following year the young men again took charge.

CONCLUSION

The three main distinctions between *payéses* and *comerciantes*, between rich and poor, and between *personas de carrera, personas de categoría* and the general village population are the most important categories used by the residents of Saburneda to define themselves and other people. In conclusion I want to emphasize that such evaluations are not static but continually measured against events. When the mayor first opened his club, his reputation worsened, mothers refused to let their daughters go there, he was accused of bringing immorality into the village. The club survived because it was not dependent on the local population and enough French people and skiers went there to make it pay.

Gradually people in the village saw that the club was popular, that people who were enviable in other ways, who had a certain status, went to the club and they began to follow suit. Soon girls from outlying villages were allowed to come down to the dances at weekends. People became proud of the club and praised the mayor for his initiative in bringing more people into the valley. Then various incidents, a few fights, drunkenness, a car accident in which a girl who worked as a receptionist at the club was involved while in the car of a married man she had met there, and the death of the ski instructor as he came out of the club, all began to change people's assessments once more. Stories about the mayor's debts began to circulate, there were rumours about his own behaviour. *'De esta casa no sale nada de bueno'*— nothing good comes out of that house, said one woman.

Each set of events and evaluations changes people's expectations and their reaction to subsequent events. I have suggested that the three distinctions outlined above and the distinction between *solanés* and outsiders, are not to be seen as rigid categories but rather that they form a framework which people use to define and justify their own behaviour. The change in population and the changing economy have led to a new basis for power and authority. Whereas before it was based on land and family, now it is based on the profit to be made from various kinds of business activities. This does not carry the same moral legitimacy and in their evaluations people try to claim a different kind of status for themselves.

NOTES

1. cf. *Firth* (1), p. 120. 'Values do not exist as isolated entities—they link as systems with some degree of integration for every individual. At the same time the value systems of different individuals must present some common elements in order that comunity life can go on.'
2. The Spanish term for neighbour is *vecino*. This is also the term that designates full legal rights in the community, dependent on residence for at least five years.
3. The same definition is used by *Franklin*, Chapter 1.
4. cf. Firth's account of 'conductive' and 'convective' change (*Firth* (1), p. 86). 'Two effects can occur. One is a process of what may be called social convection. When some members of a society change their behaviour from what has been recognized as an established pattern,

the reactions are likely to involve other members too. By imitation, by resentment, by the need to repair the breach in their accustomed ways, they tend to modify their own conduct likewise. The other effect may be called a process of social conduction. A change in established patterns tends to bring unforeseen results in its train. The functional interrelation of activities is very delicate. So people who have adopted an innovation may find themselves facing a situation to which they must conform, though very much against what they would have chosen in the beginning could they have known. These new situations, in which unwanted changes are enforced on some members of the society and unforeseen effects encountered by others, pose fresh organizational problems, so the stage is set for further efforts at change. The essence of the dynamic process lies in the continuous operation of the individual psyche, with its potential of unsatisfied desires—for more security, more knowledge, more status, more power, more approval—within the universe of its social system.'

5. cf. *Burridge* (2), Chaper 11. In his account of millenarian movements, Burridge discusses the way that changes in the system by which money is controlled and ordered lead to changes in the moral basis of power.
6. For a further examination of this cf. *Kelly* in which he discusses the relationship between 'personal constructs' and 'cultural constructs'.
7. cf. *Burridge* (2), p. 163. 'Moral dilemma implies dissonances in basic assumptions about power. These in turn can be seen in stresses and strains in social relations, and are particularly expressed in the prestige system in terms of which the worth of man is measured, integrity earned and redemption gained.'
8. cf. *Barth* (2), p. 14. 'Ethnic categories provide an organizational vessel that may be given varying amounts and forms of content in different socio-cultural systems. They may be of great relevance to social life, or they may be relevant only in limited sectors of activity.'
9. Compare also the concept of the 'limited good' (*Foster* (4)). The original inhabitants exploited a fixed amount of natural resources. The fact that new resources from industrial work and from tourism suddenly became available, was thought by them to be 'unjust' in that they were part of a completely different system.
10. Mule dealing was very important to the valley in the past.

10
Social Mobility and Social Control in a Southern Italian Village

According to Rossi-Doria, one of Italy's leading agricultural economists, the agricultural system of the central uplands is economically absurd.[1] Land in this zone is best suited for pastoral farming, but most of it is used as arable. The main crops are wheat and vegetables, and yields are very low. Very little is produced for the market. Property ownership is widely diffused and land is highly fragmented.

Until the beginning of the nineteenth century Pertosa,[2] a hilltop village in the central Apennine uplands of southern Italy, had a predominantly pastoral economy. In the late eighteenth and nineteenth centuries, however, there was a population explosion throughout southern Italy. In Pertosa the population rose from 2,663 in 1807 to 5,021 in 1911. This rise in population had two immediate and important consequences. First, large tracts of land which would have been better left as forest and natural pasture were brought under the plough. Secondly, as pressure on land increased, large landowners, who until the middle of the nineteenth century had mainly run sheep and cattle farms, gradually became rentiers. Rent-racking proved far more profitable than cattle farming; large estates were converted to arable, split into tiny plots and rented to land-hungry peasants. But despite the emergence of a more labour-intensive arable economy, for the last eighty years at least, Pertosa has housed a population which could not conceivably be supported by its agricultural resources. This had resulted in widespread unemployment and underemployment. In the peak years of unemployment of 1946 and 1947 almost one-half of the registered labour force was out of work. Consequently, many Pertosini were obliged to emigrate. From

*1880 to 1914 between a hundred and two hundred emigrants left
the village each year, for the most part going to the United States
and South America. Since 1958, similar numbers have taken jobs
as seasonal migrants in Germany, Switzerland and France.
Pertosa, like most other communes of the interior, has become a*
paese di passaggio, *a village of passage, a village in which most
peasants are born, grow up, marry and die, but from which they
are absent for the greater part of their adult working lives.*

*A score of landowners own about two-thirds of the cultivable
land; the rest, highly fragmented, is mostly held by peasants.
It is rare to find a family that owns no land, but few have more
than twenty acres. Since land is of poor quality, until very recently
most peasant families were obliged to rent or to share-crop extra
plots of land belonging to the village upper class. Only in the last
five or six years, in which seasonal migration has come to assume
large proportions, has this system begun to break down.*

SOCIAL CLASS

Until the early nineteen-fifties it was possible to discern a fairly
straightforward three-class system of stratification in Pertosa.
The social classes, the gentry, artisans and peasants, corresponded
quite neatly to the main occupational categories. They could
be distinguished in terms of income, patterns of consumption,
housing, dress, speech and recreational associations, and with very
few exceptions class endogamy was practised.

At the top of the social hierarchy were some twenty families of
rural gentry, the *signori* or *galantuomini* as they were normally
called. Their power and position were based in part on their
control of land, in part on their monopoly of scarce educational
skills which enabled them to act as brokers between village and
state. They were the only class which received secondary
education, and the local professionals, lawyers, doctors, schoolteachers and the more important local government officials were
recruited from their ranks. In politics they normally provided the
mayor and *assessori* (aldermen) and filled the secretaryships of
the main political parties. About three-quarters of the gentry
could trace the origins of their family fortunes to the beginning
of the nineteenth century; the rest had achieved their position
just before the First World War.

Next in the socio-economic hierarchy came the artisans (*mastri*) and a few shopkeepers, together about a hundred and twenty families. In terms of income and style of life they were far nearer to the peasantry than the gentry, and like the more prosperous peasants they usually owned enough land to meet most of their subsistence requirements. Almost invariably they had some educational qualifications, and even their wives were literate. Some artisans and shopkeepers were also patrons in their own right, but usually on a small scale. Peasants depended on them for credit and small political favours and, because of their ties of illegitimate kinship with gentry families,[3] they sometimes acted as intermediaries between peasants and the village upper class. Many artisans were also active in local politics, and they were fairly frequent members of the council. The origins of this class were somewhat mixed. A few came from families which had practised the same trade for over a century, but most were either the descendants of the illegitimate offspring of nineteenth-century gentry families or the children of early emigrants who had been apprenticed to a trade. In this period, the distinction between artisans and shopkeepers was relatively unimportant; both came from very much the same sort of families and had similar incomes and styles of life.

Last of all came the peasants (*contadini* or sometimes *cafoni*[4]) who constituted about 90 per cent of the population. Within this class, however, there were important social gradations, based in part on the ownership of land and houses, in part on social honour. Since there was relatively little economic specialization in Pertosa, it was difficult to make any firm distinctions between peasants in terms of occupation. In fact, besides being small-holders, most peasants filled most of the occupational roles available in the local economy at some stage of the life cycle. The peasant hierarchy of prestige could be thought of as a continuum; at the bottom were the dishonoured and the landless, at the top families whose honour was unimpinged and who had sufficient land to meet their needs. The position of individual families on the scale was fluctuating and precarious; the misconduct of a daughter, the death of a household head, a bad harvest and a score of other factors of this sort could lead to a rapid descent.

In recent years it has become increasingly fashionable amongst Mediterranean sociologists to analyse social differentiation in terms of prestige ranking models. Some of them have also argued that in Mediterranean peasant societies it is inappropriate to talk of class or stratification.[5] In Pertosa, however, a class model is not only analytically helpful, but it also corresponds fairly closely to the way in which villagers perceive the social order.

The Pertosini model of the system of stratification is partly explicit, as, for example, when peasants talk about the differences between *signori* and *cafoni*, or discuss the way in which they are exploited by artisans. More commonly, however, it is expressed in the idiom of cultural symbols. Thus, for example, until very recently women from different social classes were expected to dress in different styles. Peasants wore a plain tunic dress, which they covered in winter with a cotton shawl; artisans a dress, canvas apron and a woollen shawl; the wives of the gentry, normal European-style frocks, winter coats and hats. These differences were not only highly visible, but were also enforced by the sanctions of public ridicule and gossip. Thus, in 1964, I saw a peasant woman who was returning to the village from Germany replace a smart winter coat with a flimsy shawl as soon as she arrived at the local railway station. She explained her behaviour by saying that she didn't want it to be thought that she was putting on airs, or to risk the derision of the *signore* (upper-class women). Similarly there are important differences in speech, dialect and intonation between the various social classes.

Social class is also one of the main determinants of mate selection. Generally speaking, marriages in Pertosa are still arranged by parents, although nowadays children's preferences are more readily taken into consideration. The main principle in choosing a marriage partner is summed up in the saying '*Paro para piglia*' (equal marries equal). Spouses must not only come from the same social class, but should also be of roughly equal economic and social standing within it. There are, of course, exceptions to this rule, but they are of little structural importance. Thus, pretty or particularly well-endowed girls sometimes marry men of a higher social class. But since women take little part in public affairs and on marriage assume the status of their husbands, such marriages, whilst giving rise to comment and gossip, can be easily fitted into the village social system. On the other hand, I came across no cases of upper-class women marrying down.

An example of the strength of the rule of homogamy can be

found by examining extra-village marriages, which usually occur in situations of acute status inconsistency or when it is difficult to find a spouse of equivalent standing. Thus, dishonoured but rich peasant families seek to marry their daughters to people in nearby villages. Similarly, in recent years schoolmasters of peasant origin have, without exception, been obliged to take brides from outside Pertosa.

In Pertosa honour plays no part in the class system. All Pertosini with whom I discussed the matter agreed that upper-class families, however dishonoured, remain members of the gentry. Correspondingly, peasant households, however morally respectable, do not improve their class position. This point is well summarized in the local proverb '*Le corna dei signori sono di paglia*' (Gentlemen's horns are made of straw). In respect to artisans and peasants, the economic and social standing of a member of the gentry is unaffected by the conduct of his wife, daughters or sisters.

On the other hand, each of the social classes is internally ranked on a number of scales, and amongst artisans and peasants honour is one of the most important of them. Thus, when I asked a number of peasant informants to put in rank order a pack of cards, each bearing the name of a peasant family, all assigned bottom place to the household of a fairly wealthy peasant who was known to have committed incest with two of his daughters. Nevertheless, although in exceptional cases high standing on one scale can be cancelled out by poor performance on another, there is a strong tendency towards status consistency. In Pertosa, as in many other Mediterranean societies, wealth and honour are normally closely linked.[6] Unless there is clear evidence to the contrary, it is assumed that prosperous peasants are also honourable; and poor families are generally held to be of low moral repute.

During the last decade, the threefold system of stratification which I have been describing has been modified in two important respects. On the one hand the gap between the classes has narrowed; on the other, two incipient classes have emerged. Nowadays one frequently hears upper-class Pertosini complaining that their ex-*cafoni* earn as much as they do, or that they can afford to buy bigger and better cars. These complaints are exaggerated, but it is nevertheless true that the disparity of income between gentry and peasants is declining. Emigrants have neither security of tenure, fringe benefits, nor pleasant working conditions, but they often earn as much as local civil servants. Conversely, the income which the gentry derive from land has conspicuously declined in the last few years. Moreover, the barriers dividing peasants from artisans and shopkeepers have in part broken down, largely as a result of emigration. Most peasant families now have a fairly regular source of cash income, and no longer depend so much on credit provided by shop-keepers. As the demand for their skills has declined, many artisans have been compelled to seek work outside the village, and nowadays their work situation is often identical to that of the peasants. Indeed, today marriages between peasant and artisan families are becoming increasingly common.

The two incipient classes to which I have referred both developed in response to recent changes, in particular as a result of growing state intervention in village affairs. The first consists of schoolteachers and civil servants, the sons and more occasionally the daughters of artisans and peasants who chose to invest in the education of their children. Although they work side by side with professionals from gentry families, and to a great extent share their recreational associations, so far, the latter have consistently refused to provide them with marriage partners. Indeed, one of the most important recent developments in local politics has been the growth of overt hostility and in-creasing competition between the gentry and the new profes-sionals.

The second incipient class is made up of a few artisans (especially builders and building contractors), the wealthier shop-keepers and merchants and the minor salaried employees of various local authorities. Like the new professionals, members of this class have peasant and artisan backgrounds. Similarly, they are beginning to associate more with each other than with people below or above them, and to set themselves apart from the classes from which they came. Thus, in 1963, they founded their own 'traders' association (*circolo dei commercianti*), and increasingly they are marrying amongst themselves.

In Pertosa there is little class conflict at least in any regular or organized form. In part this can be explained by the importance of vertical patron-client ties which cut across class loyalties, in

P

part by the nature of the social classes themselves. All the social classes are characterized by intense internal competition for economic and political resources. Since most people are obliged to combine many different occupational roles in order to make a living, few families have identical interests or common life chances in the market. Moreover, in the eyes of most Pertosini success and social mobility are achieved not through co-operation but by manipulating in one's own favour social relationships with peers, and by attracting the support of powerful upper class patrons.

SOCIAL MOBILITY

The bulk of social mobility in Pertosa has come about in response to the expansion of economic and political opportunities over the last eighty years, as the village has become more tightly integrated into the national economy and the national political framework. The first phase of overseas emigration in the years immediately before the First World War brought mobility of two types; first, upward mobility on the peasant scale, secondly a movement of peasants into the ranks of artisans. Most of the early emigrants invested their savings in houses and land. Some of them, however, went on to try to marry their daughters to artisans and to have at least one son apprenticed to a trade. In fact, almost one-third of the present generation of artisans and slightly more than half of their wives had peasant fathers who had emigrated. This process was costly, and in most cases it proved economically disadvantageous, since there were already too many artisans. It was costly not only because peasants had to forgo the services of their children on the land, but also because they had to provide their daughters with substantial dowries, and make series of gifts to the artisans to whom their sons were apprenticed, in order to ensure that they would be properly trained.

The social mobility prompted by the expansion of the political frontiers of the village can be most easily illustrated by examining the careers of members of the two incipient classes. Since the war state intervention in village affairs has greatly increased, particularly in the fields of education and the social services. In Pertosa the number of schoolteachers has risen from a dozen to fifty, and in the same period communal and provincial employees have tripled their numbers.

Most of the minor salaried posts available in Pertosa are in the gift of the commune and the provincial authorities, and are distributed on a political spoils system. These jobs are highly prized by peasants and artisans alike, partly because by village standards they are well paid, partly because they carry regular salaries, pensions and sickness benefits, and fair security of tenure. With very few exceptions their present holders received them as a reward for political services. Normally, they are staunch party activists who are able to guarantee the votes of extensive networks of kin and friends to their political patrons. Similarly, most prosperous contractors and tradesmen have been successful because of their skills in political manipulation, for their businesses, in part at least, have been founded on lucrative government licences and contracts.

In 1965 there were about seventy schoolteachers and *impiegati* (civil servants with secondary education) living in Pertosa, of whom nearly two-thirds came from artisan and, more occasionally, peasant families. In more than half the cases in which the children of artisans became schoolteachers the mother was of a higher class than the father, usually the illegitimate or only partially recognized daughter or grand-daughter of a member of the gentry. In these cases the mother not only sought to recapture her own lost social status by encouraging her children to study, but could also count on the advice and help of upper-class kinsmen. The latter were usually prepared to lend books or give extra lessons, and often used their influence to find a place for the aspiring student in a seminary.[7] Of the other schoolteachers of artisan and peasant origin, four or possibly five have been financed by kinsmen living abroad, two were the only children of prosperous peasant families, and two belonged to households which were fortunate enough to have a steady income in the form of a war pension. Most of the rest were the younger brothers and sisters of employed schoolteachers, for once a newly qualified teacher has found work, he is expected to help his younger siblings.

As the result of the expansion of educational facilities in Pertosa and nearby towns in the last decade,[8] education is now seen as one of the main means of achieving social mobility. An increasing number of peasant and artisan families, especially those who receive remittances from abroad, are investing in the higher secondary education of their children. So far, they have generally preferred to provide schooling only for sons, although a small numbers of girls are enrolled in the teacher training college in the next town. In the next few years, however, it is probable that more and more girls will receive secondary education, for a teaching or professional diploma costs less than a dowry, and is equally, if not more, acceptable to potential husbands.

Although the political and economic changes of the last eighty years have provided the most ready avenues of mobility, the social classes in Pertosa have never been completely closed. Throughout the nineteenth century it appears to have been possible for the children of well-to-do peasants to become artisans, and a handful of peasants and artisans rose to the ranks of the gentry. The latter process took at least two generations: in the first, a family acquired land and property, in the second, education. Intermarriage with established gentry families occurred only after the second generation. Indeed, in terms of overall numbers and in the amount of land under its control, the village upper class has remained remarkably constant over the last hundred years, rising peasant and artisan families having replaced and bought up the estates and mansions of bankrupt gentry.

PERCEPTIONS OF MOBILITY

During the course of my fieldwork in Pertosa, I was intrigued by the sort of explanations which were used to account for the rapid social mobility, both upwards and downwards, of certain families. Upward mobility was attributed to one of three factors: conspicuous good fortune, cheating (*imbroglio*) and the power of *raccomandazioni* (patronage). Downward mobility was occasionally explained in terms of ill-fortune, but usually it was summed up in the phrase that the person or family in question was *troppo buono* (too good). Let me give some examples.

The good fortune theory normally explains how an ancestor of an upper-class family found a treasure hidden by bandits. Similar theories appear to be widely diffused throughout southern Italy and indeed in most peasant societies.[9] Moreover, they appear to have a long history. In 1878, in the course of the first major parliamentary inquiry into the conditions of agricultural labourers in southern Italy, the commissioner for the province of Potenza remarked on the strange, and in his view mistaken, popular legends which were used to explain the origins of the wealth of the local gentry. Thus, he wrote, 'When one consults popular tradition one always finds at the origin of every large fortune a legend, treasure hidden by bandits, found by chance in the corner of an old castle or in a newly acquired piece of land, or sometimes even a saddlebag full of gold buried by a long-dead military commander.'[10] The commissioner was sceptical of this explanation and hastened to add that although small hoards of treasure had been found from time to time the prosperous provincial gentry had acquired their fortunes in other ways. Their ancestors had bought ex-monastic or ex-feudal lands cheaply at the turn of the century and had let them at high rents, or else had held lucrative government posts and had invested the profits of office in land.

Even today, similar stories are told in Pertosa and in most of the nearby communes. For example, one of them tells how Nicola Rossi, the great-grandfather of one of the richest landowners in the village, made his fortune in this way. The latter, a poor peasant, found a rich hoard of treasure whilst pruning an olive tree. He used it to buy land which has ever since brought prosperity to his descendants.

Although it is obviously difficult to assess the accuracy of these stories, on closer examination most of them appear to be false. Thus, when I checked with the land registry records (*vecchio catasto*), I found that the father of Nicola Rossi was already a substantial yeoman farmer in 1807. In the course of the next fifty years, he and his sons frequently bought up small plots of land from their neighbours and encroached on the communal demesne. This method of acquisition was far more consistent with the re-investment of savings accumulated by good management and hard work than with the spectacular purchases that might be expected to follow a sudden fortune, especially in a period in which large quantities of church and feudal land came onto the market at relatively low prices. Ultimately, however, it is of little importance whether these treasure tales are true or not. The point is that they are widely believed to be true by most Pertosini, whatever their social class.

One of the most conspicuous examples of social mobility is that of the brothers Bianchi, the sons of a prosperous blacksmith, who bought up the estates of the village's largest landowner just after the end of the First World War. Popularly their success is attributed to their skills as *imbroglioni* (cheats). There is a saga of stories which tell how they organized blackmarket commerce in wheat during both World Wars, how they cheated their peasants over the measurement of grain and in payment of wages, and how they avoided the expropriation of land during the period of land reform.[11] Whilst many of these stories are in part true, it is doubtful whether the commercial ethics of the Bianchis were any different from those of other landowners. The difference lay in their success, for the most part due to the careful administration of their estates. They were one of the few landowning families that worked their lands directly and personally supervised the day-to-day running of their estates.

The assumption that good fortune and skill in cheating are the prime elements in upward social mobility has a close parallel in the explanations which are given for the rapid decline of certain families. The Amodios were undoubtedly the richest family in Pertosa in the nineteenth century. When Pasquale Amodio died in 1908 he left an estate which, converted into present-day values, was reputed to have been worth about £500,000. In 1919 the family was declared bankrupt. According to one of its surviving members, the main reasons for bankruptcy were economic fluctuations of the share market, and the devaluations of the *lira* during the First World War. Within Pertosa, however, a rather different interpretation prevails. The decline of the house is seen as the result of the reckless gambling and gullibility of the head of the family. He is reputed to have played cards with farms as the stake, and his bad luck has remained proverbial. To this explanation is added the fact that he was *troppo buono*, that he let himself be cheated too easily.

A more recent example of economic decline is that of the Rossi family, which in the last three years has been obliged to resort to a series of expedients in order to stave off bankruptcy. The reasons for its difficulties are threefold. In the first place, Don Vincenzo Rossi, the head of the family, has had to find considerable sums to pay the dowries of his sisters. Secondly, he has been lax in the administration of his estates. Lastly, as a result of the scarcity of labour in the last few years, large landowners in general have found it difficult to make a profit. The explanation given in Pertosa, however, is almost entirely focused on the second of these causes. Don Vincenzo is *troppo buono*. He has allowed himself to be cheated by his peasants and farm managers.

The third local explanation of mobility which I want to examine is the *raccomandazione*. Most civil servants, schoolteachers and minor communal and provincial employees are exposed to the charge that they owe their jobs and their success in public examinations (*concorsi*) to the *raccomandazione* of a political patron. To this charge is sometimes added that of *imbroglio*, as, for example when schoolteachers are accused of having bought their teaching certificates. Although it is true that appointments to minor posts in the gift of the commune and the provincial authorities, particularly jobs such as road-members and ushers for which no real skills are needed, are made on the recommendation of influential political leaders, these charges are more difficult to sustain when applied to schoolteachers or civil servants. I am not trying to argue that *raccomandazioni* do not exist in this sphere, but that accusations of corruption are often greatly exaggerated. Since most competitors in public examinations are furnished with recommendations, they often cancel each other out, and the most able candidates are appointed. It is, however, very difficult for a successful candidate to prove that the *raccomandazione* carried no weight, or to deny that his success was due to the influence of his patron.

The explanations of mobility which I have been considering are all highly selective. They are interesting as much for what they fail to explain as for what they explain. All portray the process of mobility in ambiguous and unflattering terms. Implicitly, they deny the value of personal merit and endeavour. The importance of hard work and able administration is also ignored.

That hard work and personal endeavour should be discounted as factors in mobility is not particularly surprising. In Pertosa manual work has always been associated with low status. Indeed, one of the basic social divisions is between those who work with their hands and those who do not. The word which in dialect is used to designate work is '*fatica*' which may be used either as a noun, for example, in the phrase, '*Tienn fatica?*' (Do you have any work?), or as a verb. The nearest equivalent in English is the army term fatigue, which is used to describe a routine and unpleasant manual task, offering little hope of reward and an expectation of punishment in the case of failure to perform it properly. But in Pertosa *fatica* as used by peasants and artisans has a fairly neutral tone. For really unpleasant work there are two special words, *cunsarr* and *sacrificio*. The former literally means to work as a day labourer under a tyrannical master, and by extension has come to mean any especially hard work. The latter is most frequently used to denote the work situation of emigrants cut off from their families. Work, then, is seen as part of the human condition, a monotonous and repetitive set of tasks associated with the annual cycle of agriculture. Whilst it is a necessary and valuable quality in a man that he should be a good worker, work in itself promises no reward.

Perhaps the quality which villagers most often associate with the socially mobile is *furbizia*. *Furbo* can be translated as crafty or cunning. In Pertosa, however, it means rather more. A man is *furbo* if he succeeds in manipulating the mutual rights and obligations of a particular social relationship in his own favour. The institution of friendship is often used for this purpose. A man makes a series of short-lived friendships with the intention of exploiting the rights and privileges of the relationship without giving anything in return. If he succeeds he gains the reputation for being *furbo*. His partner who allows himself to be taken advantage of is called *fesso*, soft-witted. The polite form for *fesso* is *troppo buono* or *tre volte buono* (three times good).

Let me give an example of these concepts in action. In 1964 a shopkeeper became mayor of Pertosa. This in itself was exceptional, since all previous mayors had been either gentry or professionals. On this occasion, however, they had quarrelled amongst themselves, and Tizio was elected as a compromise candidate. Since he knew that he was unlikely to be elected again, he felt free to exploit the advantages of his office exclusively in the interests of his own family. Tizio's wife's sister was engaged to Caio, a *geometro* (a sort of land surveyor), who was out of work. The mayor decided to provide his future 'brother-in-law' with a job as *tecnico comunale* (clerk of works). Although there were a score of qualified applicants for this post, most villagers had very little doubt who would be successful, especially when it became known that the mayor was to be president of the examination commission which was to make the appointment. The actions of the mayor were generally described as *furbo*; he was a man who obviously knew how to turn a favourable situation to his own advantage. In the event, however, the examination turned out badly. Caio's rivals protested to the provincial authorities. In order to avoid a scandal the outside examiners decided to make no appointment. Shortly afterwards, the father of Caio's fiancée commented to me, 'You know what this village is like—full of *invidia* (envy). It's bad enough his not having got the job, but we are being ridiculed as *fessi* as well.'

One of the main points which comes out of this incident is the intense competition for jobs in Pertosa. Unemployment and underemployment are not confined to the peasant and artisan sectors of the economy, but are equally found at higher social levels. Quarrels between professionals over clients and jobs are just as common as disputes between peasants over rights in land. Success in either sphere can be achieved only at the expense of others.

Upward social mobility is, therefore, seen as the successful manipulation of social relationships. This theme is implicit in almost all local explanations of mobility which I have considered. People prosper not through selling their skills in the market, nor by exploiting the economy, but by taking advantage of their fellows. Thus, the Bianchis succeeded by cheating their peasants; schoolteachers and civil servants find work not because they have the necessary ability and educational qualifications, but by manipulating political connections. Conversely, the Amodio and Rossi families declined because they allowed themselves to be exploited. Seen from this standpoint, the process of mobility is clearly socially disruptive. The socially mobile are a constant source of danger to those around them, for their success is achieved at the expense of others. It is not surprising, therefore, that the terms in which their success is depicted are partial, ambiguous and often downright hostile, nor that they should be subject to a wide range of sanctions.

SOCIAL CONTROL

The sanctions which are invoked against the socially mobile can be subsumed under the general heading of *invidia* (envy). *Invidia* is expressed in many different ways, which tend to vary according to social class. Amongst peasants and artisans it is closely associated with a form of witchcraft known as the evil eye (*malocchio*). It is believed that an envious glance can lead to illness or even death. Animals and small children are especially exposed to the dangers of *malocchio*. Obviously the socially mobile are most likely to attract envy. Thus, for example, in the peasant neighbourhood in which I lived my richest neighbour was an ex-muleteer who had become a building contractor. Although he lived in a large, well-furnished house, his only surviving child was invariably dressed in rags. As his wife explained to me, she had already lost a baby daughter as the result of the envious glances of her neighbours and had no intention of exposing her son to the same danger.

Another context in which the villagers speak of *invidia*, is to describe a form of economic behaviour which at first sight seems absurd. New economic enterprises, especially if they seem to be successful, quickly attract imitators to the point at which they cease to be profitable. Thus, a fairly prosperous one-man taxi firm which was set up in 1954 now has a dozen competitors. Similarly, in the last few years there has been proliferation of shops selling consumer goods: radio and television sets, refrigerators, gas cookers and so forth. Indeed, all villager entrepreneurs complain bitterly of the extreme competitiveness of the market, which they attribute to the envy and lack of enterprise of their rivals, who prefer to compete in established markets rather than find new outlets for their activities.

Amongst the new professional class and the gentry, who are sceptical of witchcraft and who rarely engage in commerce, *invidia* takes other forms. Normally it is directed at the families of rivals and colleagues who appear to be on the verge of success. Common examples are anonymous, defamatory letters written to a fiancé's parents when a girl is about to make a good marriage, and unsigned letters sent to the superiors of colleagues accusing them of corruption or other forms of misbehaviour.

If one examines the social context in which accusations of *invidia* are made, it is clear that they are directed at near status equals. Peasants may well be envious of the gentry, but they do not practise sorcery against them. Similarly, I heard of no cases in which the gentry accused peasants of political corruption, or set out to destroy a suitable marriage contract. *Invidia* is confined to rivals for very much the same sort of economic and political resources. Indeed, intra-class competition, competition between near equals, is far more intense and sustained than conflict between the social classes. Furthermore, in Pertosa, as in other societies in which resources are scarce and social visibility is high, this competition not only takes the form of trying to secure for one's own family a major share of these resources, but also of denying and attempting to limit others' access to them. Thus, one of the main strategies for maintaining and even enhancing one's own prestige is to denigrate and deny that of others. To this end, malicious gossip, *invidia* and perhaps even theories about mobility are all grist in the same mill.

CONCLUSION

In this paper, I have attempted to analyse the way in which Pertosini perceive and describe the process of social mobility, and to show that their model of society depicts a closed and relatively static social order, in which economic and political resources are limited and fixed, and in which success can be achieved only at the expense of others. In the village ideology mobility is seen as a form of deviancy, and the socially mobile are subject to a wide range of sanctions. But I have also suggested that this model corresponds only in part to reality. With the expansion of economic and political opportunities in the wider Italian society, the resources available to members of the village are virtually unbounded. Even in the nineteenth century the social classes were never entirely closed. And, although I have insufficient data to measure rates of mobility, my guess is that in the post-war period the rate of mobility in Pertosa is not greatly different from that of most Western industrial societies. Indeed, as I tried to show in my analysis of village explanations of mobility, the plausibility of the Pertosini model depends on a partial interpretation and careful selection of the facts.

Furthermore, the mechanisms of social control, which I described in the previous section, have never been fully effective; in part because they could be directed only against persons who were permanently resident in the village and in constant interaction with other villagers, in part because each social class tended to have different sanctions. By leaving the village, peasants and artisans were not only able to tap the resources of the wider society, but also escaped the various social pressures which would have tended to direct their savings and newly acquired capital into socially approved channels. On returning to Pertosa, provided they had sufficient capital to set themselves up as gentry, they were largely immune from the sanctions traditionally invoked against peasants and artisans.

This process can be well illustrated by re-examining briefly the three local explanations of mobility which I described earlier. The good fortune, *imbroglio* and *raccomandazione* 'theories' each refer to different historical phases of mobility,[12] and all three describe conspicuous inter-class mobility, that is, the process whereby peasants and artisans rose to gentry or professional status. But although each of them depicts a different path to success, their protagonists have an important element in common: all of them seem to have been absent from the village in the critical period of their careers in which they were building up capital and resources. Thus, in the period 1810–1840 the Rossis appear to have lived permanently in the countryside.[13] Again, the brothers Bianchi are reputed to have acquired the capital with which they eventually bought their estates by running a station bar (which they are said to have used as a centre for blackmarket commerce in grain) in another part of the province. Similarly, many of the new *professionisti* were financed by kinsmen living abroad and acquired their qualifications and first jobs outside Pertosa.

In both structure and content there are remarkable similarities between these three theories of mobility and the various types of *invidia*, which I have already analysed. In so far as I can tell, the stories of treasure, *imbroglio* and *raccomandazioni* seem to have originated and are certainly re-told and re-affirmed by near status equals. At least, amongst the professionals and gentry the same terms (*imbroglio* and *raccomandazioni*) which are used to explain conspicuous social mobility are also used as mechanisms of control. But there are also important differences between them. In the context of an on-going competition between peers for status, resources and prestige, accusations of commercial sharp practice and political corruption are potent weapons of control, warning off potential economic partners and political allies. As *ex post facto* explanations of mobility, however, they are far less effective. At most, they provide a negative comment, a denial of the legitimacy of the newly-won status of the successful, and serve to re-inforce and perpetuate the Pertosini belief that mobility is harmful and socially destructive and can be achieved only by those who are prepared to take advantage of fellow villagers.[14]

NOTES

1. *Rossi-Doria*, pp. 2–34.
2. The name of the village and all proper names used in this article are pseudonyms.
3. In the nineteenth century, it was a fairly standard practice amongst upper-class families for only the eldest son to marry. During their lifetime, younger sons enjoyed the usufruct of the share of the estate, which, on death, returned to the main line. This practice was designed to maintain family patrimonies intact, and to avoid the consequences of the abolition of the laws of primogeniture. Not surprisingly, however, it was not entirely successful. Younger sons often took peasant or artisan mistresses. Occasionally, the offspring of such unions were legally recognized. More often, however, male children were apprenticed to a trade, and females were provided with a dowry and married to artisans.
4. In this period the term *cafoni* (yokels) was still used in a neutral non-derogatory way. Even in 1964 I occasionally heard peasants using it to describe themselves.
5. See, for example, *Pitt-Rivers* (3), pp. 81–2. Also, *Stirling*, p. 222.
6. See, for example, *Campbell*, p. 317.
7. Many village schoolteachers were educated in seminaries, not because they had any intention of becoming priests, but because this was the cheapest form of secondary education.
8. A *scuola media*, providing three years' secondary schooling, was set up in Pertosa in 1964. A teacher training college was opened in the next town in 1965.
9. See, for example, *Pitt-Rivers* (3), p. 52. Also *Djilas*, pp. 143–4. Throughout this section of this paper I am also clearly indebted to *Foster*, 1965b (2) and (4).
10. *Atti della Giunta per l'inchiesta agraria e sulle condizioni della classe agricola (The Jacini Enquiry)*, Vol IX, p. xxv (Potenza, 1883).
11. Another variant on what might be termed the *imbroglio* theory of mobility purports to explain the conspicuous social mobility of a very small number of ex-emigrants. They are reputed to have made their fortunes as members of criminal associations in the United States.
12. Treasure tales appear to be confined to the period 1800–1880; the *imbroglio* theories for the most part to the inter-war years; the *raccomandazioni* theories to the post-war epoch.
13. My source of information for this statement is a letter of 1836, preserved in the communal archives, in which the head of the Rossi household, asked to be excluded from the *lista degli eliggibili* (i.e. the list of persons suitable for election to communal offices) on the grounds that he lived permanently in the countryside. I should perhaps add that

today, as in the past, the countryside is very sparsely settled. Very few Pertosini are prepared to live outside the densely populated and highly nucleated central settlement area known as the *paese*, and it is only in the *paese* that the range of sanctions, which I have described in this paper, are operative.

14. The author would like to express his gratitude to the following institutions which financed the research on which this paper is based: The Central Research Funds Committee of the University of London, the University of Michigan, Ann Arbor, and the Mediterranean Research Committee (University of Kent; School of Oriental and African Studies; London School of Economics and Political Science).

11
What are Signori?

Losa lies at the northern edge of the Maritime Alps in Italy. It is situated half-way along a valley which runs westwards to the French border and lies 800 metres above sea level. The provincial capital, Cuneo, is 15 miles away to the east. Cuneo has a number of light industries. At the foot of the valley there is a large cement works. In the mountains around the valley the state electricity operation has numerous enterprises.

Losa has a population of around 800 people divided between approximately 260 households. Less than one-fifth of these keep themselves by agriculture, and even in these households the men are likely to seek subsidiary employment at certain seasons of the year. The heads of only two households in this category are under 40 years of age. The rest of the working population earn wages in the factories of Cuneo, at the cement works, in the employment of the electricity corporation or elsewhere. Many of these have kept a foothold in agriculture. About a dozen people own retail shops; six households are supported by artisans, carpenters, blacksmiths, and masons; finally as many as fifteen households can be considered middle-class in that they run their own prosperous firms or are professionally qualified men in salaried employment.

Losa is a Piedmontese word which means 'slate'. Up until the last war the ancestors of virtually everyone in the village now, rich and poor alike, were peasant farmers filling the slack of the agricultural year by quarrying and humping down the steep mountain-side two-inch thick slabs of stone, some a yard square, to roof their houses and cattle byres and to sell to builders from outside the valley.

This essay analyses the concept 'signore' as I heard it used in Losa in the autumn of 1968 and shows how its meaning changes both as time passes and according to the status of the speaker and his auditor. The meaning of the concept is given by defining the contexts in which it would be appropriate to use the word 'signore' *either as a term of address or reference.*

RANK

'*Signore*' is a term which suggests rank. In some contexts it means 'Our Lord'. In others it is like the English word 'gentleman' and it invites a contrast with those who are not gentlemen, and implies a judgement not only of difference, but also of superiority and inferiority. It is therefore necessary to make some preliminary remarks about ranking systems.

To rank a set of objects means to place them in order of magnitude according to some criterion; that is, according to some attribute which they all share. There are approximately 260 households, the members of which have their residence registered in Losa. All of them have some kind of income so that they could be ranked according to the size of this income; they could be ranked according to the amount of money they spend each month on groceries; or according to the quantity of water they use each week; or the family members could be laid end-to-end and the aggregate length of this extended family could be used to set families in a rank order.

The people of Losa do not indulge themselves in this kind of exercise. They frequently speculate about each other's income, but always with reference to a small number of people. Once they get beyond two or three subjects they stop talking in a factorial fashion, in terms of a scale of more and less of some given quality. For larger universes the ranking is done by placing subjects into categories, making binary judgements in order to do so. *Signori* are distinguished from *non-signori*. There is not a scale of *signorilità* (gentlemanliness) on which notionally everyone could have a place. This does not, of course, mean that there can never be any dispute about who is and who is not a gentleman. It does mean that the concept itself appears not to be under dispute, in the sense that people behave as if there is a broad consensus about its meaning. In fact there is an important half-hidden disagreement.

Factorial reckoning to set the households of Losa in, for example, a rank order by monthly income, would take into account a single attribute—the *lire* coming into the house each month. Binary judgements could also be made by a single attribute. But the judgements which decide whether or not a man is to be considered as a *signore* refer to several attributes and ways of behaving. A gentleman is well-off, uses his wealth generously, is magnanimous, refined in behaviour, well-educated, doesn't keep cows in a stall under his house and so forth.

One of the problems in analysing a ranking system of this kind is to discover the rules which relate these different characteristics to one another. At first sight the whole business is as mysterious as that which, in English university examination boards, reduces a string of marks—$A-$, $A-$, $B+$, BC, C, D and so on—to upper second class honours rather than lower second class honours. The people of Losa act like the examination boards insofar as the end product is not a profile (good on quality A, poor on quality B, superb on quality C and so on) but a single unified judgement which in some mysterious way averages out the relevant qualities. How do they do it? In particular, how do they do it without the explicit and strenuous efforts through which examination boards attempt to assess the total performance of a candidate?

The answer is that the people of Losa do not make elaborate calculations to score up the points, or to make plus and minus judgements on a variety of different scales. For them 'Handsome is as handsome does'. For them the indicator is not the collection of attributes which the *signore* possesses, but the transactions which they have with him. The qualities and attributes which the *signore* is said to possess are no more than statements of the way they expect him to behave towards them: the qualities of a gentleman are epiphenomenal upon the transactions which he undertakes.[1]

In the next section I shall be giving my evidence for the assertions that the people of Losa make ranking judgements in a binary fashion and not in a factional fashion and also that no single attribute is used when talking about *signori*. To conclude this section, let me summarize by explaining Diagram One. At the top level the concept of *signore* is represented by a number of qualities (A, B, C etc.) which Losa people say constitute *signorilità*. These qualities are realized (i.e. transformed into expectations

Q

about social interactions) in different contexts—with whom the *signore* is interacting, for what purpose, and so on. In different contexts the qualities are differentially realized (or—to preserve the notion of 'meaning'—have different degrees of relevance) and this is crudely indicated by the use of capital letters as against smallcase letters.

Diagram I

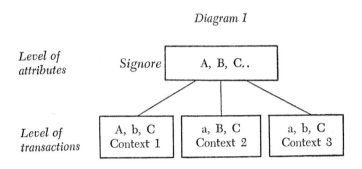

I do not claim that this is new. If you wish, you may read 'status' as the top box and 'roles' as the bottom boxes: or you may think of it all in terms of Goffman[2] and his metaphor of the players selecting their parts. But whether old or new, the framework is useful because it enables us to start from what the people of Losa say and do (not tempting us to foist our own categories upon them) and then to get behind apparent inconsistencies to the structures in which the concept '*signore*' has meaning. Furthermore, the framework is of use because it can handle change, up to a point. One has only to make the series of contexts diachronic: for example, they could be three elections at five-year intervals for the municipal council.

COMPONENTS OF 'SIGNORE': NOT WEALTH ALONE

The first task is to show that *signori* cannot be identified by the possession of a single attribute (other than, of course, *signorilità*, which would answer none of our questions). At first it seemed as if there might be one such attribute, namely wealth.

I first encountered the term when the ladies in whose house I stayed were showing me photographs of relatives who had migrated overseas. There were some in California who were ranchers and the pictures showed, in the background, large houses, sumptuous cars and other signs of material wealth. My hostess told me how her father had been to America, had come back and had always regretted it. 'Look at my cousins and their children,' she said. 'They are real *signori*.'

On another occasion I asked someone to tell me what the *signori* were. 'Generally', he said, 'when people use that term, they mean the rich. Those who aren't *signori* are the *poor*.' Then he added quickly, 'Of course there aren't any real poor these days, except perhaps one or two old people.'

Another informant, using the local idiom, said: 'There are three kinds of people here: *famio d'sgnuri* (the family of *signori*); *famio che sta beng* (the family which is doing nicely); and *pauridiau* (the poor devil).' Then he gave me examples to go into each category.

The final example is a description of how life changes, from a woman in her thirties, the wife of a schoolmaster, sitting in her marbled drawing-room, all chrome and glass and modern furniture. 'You've met my father and mother? They used to sleep in the cowshed in the winter, because it's warm. They look at me and my sister and the kind of house I live in and tell me that we are *signori* now. And my daughters—they are going to be even more *signori*.'

Although at first I thought that wealth was going to be the main criterion and that I could equate *i signori* with 'the rich', even these examples (except the *pauridiau* one) leave open the possibility that it might be the style of life made possible by wealth, rather than wealth alone, which marked the *signori*. This was quickly confirmed by the case of the man who inherited a fortune.

The lucky man and his wife were already well on in years when they had their windfall. An uncle who had migrated to America died childless and left them, so it was said, seven or eight million *lire*. At the time they lived four miles up a side valley in a near-deserted hamlet. They moved down to Losa, having bought an apartment in a modern block of flats. They stayed there two nights and eventually acquired an ordinary house in the village where they keep a couple of cows, and, so it is rumoured, sleep in the cowshed in the winter time, because, unlike the centrally-heated flat, the cowshed is warm without being suffocating.

These people must be among the richest in the village. But they are by no means *signori*. Wealth alone, therefore, is not the criterion for *signorilità*.

The other components in the concept were gradually clarified for me in interviews, in particular one with an elementary schoolmaster (who in certain contexts is reckoned a *signore*) and several with a man in his fifties who in no circumstances could be reckoned to be of that rank. Between them I got the impression that there were three main elements as follows:

Benessere. The *signore* is well off. But a man born into a family of *signori* would have that rank until he died, even if he became poor (and providing he met some of the other requirements). But the rank would not survive indefinitely without wealth. This is because it is not the riches that count but the transactions that are mounted with the riches. The *signore* is *generoso* (open-handed). He helps individuals with his charity and makes donations to the church and its institutions and gives generous contributions to the various communal causes. Examples will be given later.

Livello culturale. The *signore* has to have certain attainments and refinements and live up to an appropriate standard. What counts is the possession of non-manual skills, or at least the means to live without getting one's hands dirty. Education beyond the elementary level has to be paid for in Italy, so that by and large those who get education in a place like Losa are also those whose families were well-off. In fact *grado sociale* (social rank), my informant insisted, was an exact reflection of educational attainment. By this criterion, therefore, the schoolteachers, the doctor, the priest, the accountant, the few graduates and so on are all *signori*.

Autorità. The *signore* possesses some degree of authority. Old people, one informant said, look with respect (*guardono con rispetto*) on the priest and the schoolmasters and the doctor and other professional people. When he was a child he used to be told to greet the *signori*, and that was because the *signori* then had authority.[3]

There are three components which informants placed, so to speak, in the upper box on our Diagram 1: wealth, cultural attainments and authority. The transactional equivalent of wealth is its use for what the moment can be called charitable ends. This will be discussed in more detail in a later section, when we also take up the more complex problem of the transactional equivalents of cultural attainments and authority. I have not, of course, adequately described the components of the concept *signore*. My purpose so far has been to demonstrate that no single criterion will suffice as an indicator for the category *signore*.

BINARY JUDGEMENTS

My next task is to show that ranking judgements are made in binary fashion into discrete categories and not through a scale in factorial fashion, composed of units which are infinitely divisible for purposes of measurement.

At first sight some of the statements which I quoted in the previous section look as if they might be factorial. Is there not a continuum implied in the woman who scaled her parents (not *signori*), herself and her family (*signori*), and her children's chances of being even more *signori*? Is not also a continuum implied in the range of *signori* families, those who are doing well, and the poor devils? Certainly there is the notion of going up and down, a ladderlike quality about these statements. But I do not think there is a continuum. The ladder, so to speak is divided into compartments, so that the climber is located not by asking how many yards, feet, inches etc., he is from the top, but by two 'yes/no' questions:

Is he on the top half of the ladder? Yes/No?
If not, is he on the top half of the remainder? Yes/No?

For the second statement given by informants and quoted above, this fits exactly:

Is he *famio d'sgnuri*? Yes/No?
If not, is he *famio che sta beng*? Yes/ No?

The other statement—the woman comparing herself with her parents and her children's prospects—gives rise to some difficulties, for it seems to imply that there are degrees of *signorilità* ('more *signori*' or the 'real *signori*' of a statement quoted earlier). It also implies relativity: compared to my parents I am a *signore* but compared to my children I may not be a *signore*; this again supposes degrees of *signorilità*. Perhaps this is resolved if we bring in the idea of contexts. There are two possible solutions.

The speaker was thinking in one dimension only and using the word *signori* to refer to material possessions and style of life, within the given category of *signori*. Both she and her daughters by this criterion were *signori* (but they would be better off than she was—a factorial statement) while her parents were not *signori*, an interpretation which brings us back to the binary mode of expression.

It is not worth following this particular topic further, although it is very tempting to speculate whether or not all categories which have to be used to order social interaction—those that a man carries round in his head—must be limited in number and therefore identifiable in a short series of binary questions. The question that precedes taking part in a transaction is not just 'Where is he to be placed on a scale from 0 to 100?' but rather 'If we scale him at 51, is that above or below the line of reliability or gullibility (or whatever is the relevant expectation)?' In any case I think we can continue the investigation, simply by asserting that the concept *signorilità* is in the same class as 'big' and not in the same class as 'height'. It is nonsense to ask 'Does he or does he not have height?' since no-one is without that attribute. But it is not nonsense in Losa to ask if the members of a family are or are not *signori*.

INDICATORS FOR RANK

To contrast two concepts, as *signori* and *non-signori*, is certainly to separate them, but not necessarily to rank them. There have probably been sufficient clues so far for the reader to accept the statement that *signori*: non-*signori*: :high:low. In this and the next section I produce the evidence for this by describing some of the transactions through which the qualities of *benessere* (wealth) and refinement and education (the *livello culturale*) and *autorià* are realized. These transactions take the form of asymmetrical exchanges, usually deference and respect in return for something more tangible.

Indicators of prestige and deference are to be found in forms of address and reference. The alternative vocabularies are titles (*Signor, Cavaliere, Signora, Madama, Suor* etc.), surname, given name or diminutive, or nickname or certain combinations of these. Other indicators are given in the grammatical alternatives of *lei* as against *tu* or *voi*—the respectful as against the familiar forms. The same signals are conveyed in forms of greeting, familiar *ciaou*, the neutral *salute* or *salve* and the formal *buon giorno*. Apart from this there is a wide range of deferential behaviour in, for example, not speaking until one is spoken to, holding open a door, responding in whatever code the other person initiates a conversation (Italian/Piedmontese/the Losa dialect), running messages and a hundred others. Notice that none of this behaviour (except perhaps some of the items envisaged in the final category) is in itself a sign of superiority or inferiority. One may respond to 'Signor Bianco!' with 'Signor Lovera!', to 'lei' with 'lei', to 'tu' with 'tu', 'ciaou' with 'ciaou' and so on. These are all signals of equality, of the absence of rank, and in that case the choice between e.g. a reciprocal *tu* and a reciprocal *lei* indicates distance and formality as against, in the former case, familiarity. It is only the transaction which can indicate rank and it does so when, for example, a greeting of *buon giorno* receives in return a *ciaou*, or a *lei* is met with a *tu*.[4]

Apart from these verbal indicators of rank, there are also exchanges through which the person who has offered deference and respect and prestige receives a more tangible prestation. The recipient of the *signore's* generosity may be an individual (or his family) or it may be the community at large; the gift may be material (a loan or a gift of cash, of wine, of clothing, the repair of a bridge railing, a sum of money for a new organ in the church and so on) or else it may be in the form of services, especially the service of putting someone in touch with a resource otherwise denied to him.

The *signori*, then, are *benefattori*. The man who is poor or sick or down on his luck may regard them as a source of help and ask them for money to pay off a debt, to pay hospital fees or school fees, and so on. One very rich man in Losa has many people in the village who, over the years, have become his *debitori* in this fashion. The same man makes an annual cash gift to the home for aged people which the nuns run in the village. He also supplies wine for the nuns and their patients throughout the year. The home itself was the bequest of a famous son of the village, a successful engineer. The new war memorial and the new school were built by a local contractor whose bid, for charity reasons, was much below that of any other builder. Everyone (except a few determined anticlerics) gives to the church, and the *signori* are, ideally, especially generous. The true *signore* asks for nothing material in return. Neither for the public nor the private donations: what he receives is high rank.

Apart from the direct use of their wealth, *signori* may become benefactors either through their skills or through their connections. The ability to write a letter in correct Italian or to fill in a complicated form is not possessed by most peasants even today. Even fewer had this skill at the time when it was most required—when the war ended and widows and the disabled learned that they might get a pension if they went about it in the proper way. The former parish priest, some of the schoolteachers, and the lady, now dead, who was postmistress at that time, accumulated a great deal of credit from providing this service.

Finally there are services which the *signori* provide through their connections with other *signori* in the world outside the village.

A carpenter in the village has two grown sons. The elder son, who is married, is employed in his father's workshop. The bachelor son wanted a job elsewhere. He heard of a vacancy in a state hospital about fifty miles away. It was discovered later that there were over eighty qualified applicants for this job and it is firmly believed in the village that the young man got the job because his father was able to enlist the help of one of the local *signori*, who has what are called *le braccia lunghe* (long arms). This man's younger brother is a priest and the secretary of the bishop who wrote a letter to the appropriate authorities testifying to the suitability of the Losa carpenter.

There are other similar stories.

Very often there is the notion that somehow the *signore* was able to twist the regulations to help the man who thereby became his *debitore*. When I asked an informant what *le braccia lunghe* (long arms) meant, I was given the following hypothetical story:

Suppose I fall sick and cannot work properly any more. I cannot get a pension because I am ten years too young, and that's what they tell me when I make the application. So I go to X and tell him my difficulty and say that having so many friends he can surely do something for me. So he writes me a letter and tells me where to go with it. Through that letter I get my pension. That is what 'long arms' means.

Twisting regulations is a cause for congratulation, not misgiving, and such an affair would undoubtedly add to the credit of a *signore*.

In short, a *signore* is someone who has more resources, more skills and more connections than I have and is willing to use them on my behalf. I could not return the favour by doing him a similar service; nor could I pay him in cash; instead I pay him in deference and various small quasi-menial services. This transaction between us is what marks him out as a *signore*.

DISTANCE AND HOSTILITY

To call a man 'Signor Lovera' or 'Signor Giordana' is to indicate formality and distance. It indicates respect, either from a posture of inferiority or from the posture of distance that is accorded the stranger. But the term may also be used in the way that once in our society 'My dear sir ...' was used to indicate a slightly respectful impatience, to indicate that one is addressing someone whom one dislikes, even despises, but to whom one will not accord the familiarity that round abuse connotes.

I heard the term used in this way during the fiercely fought election which took place in Losa during November 1968. There were two contestants, *Lista no. uno* and *Lista no. due*, of which I will have more to say later. List Two had held an election meeting, inviting the leaders of List One to come out and debate their record as the immediate incumbents of the office of mayor (*sindaco*) and the majority on the municipal council. The meeting flopped to some extent because the leaders of List One stayed in their houses and avoided public debate. But a few of the more aggressive stalwarts of List One did turn up. They did not heckle, but they stayed behind when most of the crowd had dispersed and I listened in while two of them conducted a heated argument with two members of List Two. The List Two representatives were *signori*, one an elementary schoolmaster and the other the manager of a branch bank: the List One people were peasants. They used the Losa dialect and virtually all of what they said went over my shoulder. But some parts I could follow. They were civilized. Each had their say with eloquence and dignity, pitched, it seemed to me, rather high for the audience of five or six people who stood around. They seldom interrupted one another

242 What are 'Signori'?

and they did not try to shout each other down. When they felt moved to protest at what the other was saying, while he was saying it, they laid their right hands over their heart (in one case the man took off his hat and laid that across his heart) and said '*Ma, signore . . .*'('But, my dear sir . . .')

So there is an instance of '*signore*' being used in a fashion which if not actually abusive, is respectful only in a mocking fashion.

On another occasion I heard the term used in contempt and hatred. It came from a peasant looking at the printed *Lista no. due*. 'Vote for them? Not me! They're all the richest in Losa. Not one of them knows how to handle a hoe. They're *signori*.'

This is not, at first sight anyway, a statement about difference and asymmetrical transactions. It is a statement about conflicting interests, about enmity. What it breathes is class warfare, the rich against the poor, the privileged against the under-privileged. But in fact the situation is not so simple, for the enmity grows not out of direct antagonism, but out of the idea that the *signori* abuse and profit illicitly from their position as mediators with the outside world, and that it is the community and the individuals within it who pay the price and so are exploited.

The idea that relationships with outsiders are governed by the law of the jungle starts with merchants and middlemen who buy the peasant's potato crops and sell him seed potatoes and various other agricultural requirements. There were several such men in Losa, one at least with the status of *signore*. The stories of how they were said to have cheated were many. They buy potatoes at one rate and sell them at 50 per cent profit a month later. They sell you seed potatoes supposed to have come from the Venice region, but they are really seed from the next valley with false labels fixed on the bag. They get wind, through their friends outside, that a company wants to buy up the fields below the village to quarry the mountain above them. So they buy these fields at twice their present market value and sell them again a year later at six times the price they paid for them. Because they know how to manipulate the world outside, they, the *signori*, are indispensable, for the peasant cannot get what he needs without their help. But they are not content with deference and prestige and a reasonable profit from the transaction. They take the profit that should come to the peasant and while he stays relatively poor, they get richer and richer.

We are not concerned objectively with the truth or falsity of these accusations of sharp practice, but with the no less objective fact that people *say* this is the kind of thing that *signori* do. *Le braccia lunghe* (long arms) became a term of abuse in the November election, used by the supporters of List One against the members of List Two, which was rich in *signori*. It was said that they had used undue influence in the prefecture to bring about an early election before the mayor's term of office was finished. The assertion that such connections could only be to the good of the community because they would be used to bring work and subsidies to the valley and to the village was countered by the argument that anyone who appeared to be helping the community in this way had his own axe to grind and, if there was a deal he got his *mancia* out of it (his tips, his baksheesh, his bribe, his rake-off) and that the cost of this was borne by the community.

In this way we have added another context and so another meaning to the concept *signore*. The *signori* are those who have resources or skills or connections with the world beyond the village. You can enter into transactions with them—indeed, if you need something from the world outside, you must do so, for there is no other access. But the price you pay for such a transaction is not just the deference and the prestige which is, so to speak, normal. They are middlemen, rewarding themselves with big profits for small efforts, pretending that their private gain is public service.

SPEAKER AS CONTEXT

A concept, we have been saying, gets its meaning from the context in which it is used. So far we have been identifying these contexts as different kinds of transactions between different sets of people:

The *signore* might use his
wealth for private charity or for public benefaction
      or his
connections to assist an individual or the community.

These are, so to speak, the 'agreed' range of meanings which can be attached to the concept *signore*. Everyone agrees that a *signore* is well-to-do and has reached a certain level of cultural attainment, testified to by his educational qualifications and/or his style of life. But beyond these meanings are the components which add distance and hostility to the concept, and to understand these we have to take into account that part of the context which includes the question: Who is the speaker and to whom is he speaking? In other words 'meaning' is relative: it is always construed with a (sometimes unspoken) 'for someone'. There is my meaning and your meaning and his meaning of a particular concept. To the extent that these meanings overlap, we have an agreed meaning and this is usually what should be meant by the unqualified phrase 'the meaning of *signore* is . . .' But beyond that central area are meanings determined by who is the speaker. Diagram 1 could be used to illustrate this, substituting the word 'speaker' for 'context': each speaker modifies the set of components made available to him in the upper box. There have already been several examples of this. For instance, the woman ranking her parents, herself and her children's prospects was emphasizing almost wholly the wealth and style of living aspect of *signorilità* and leaving on one side the obligations to use that wealth in a certain way. The ingredients, so to speak, are standard, but there is a variety of possible mixes.

The possibilities for further analysis and further research arising from this are considerable; so are the problems. One could take a variety of statuses (men/women; old/young; *signori*/non-*signori*;) and ascertain their picture of a *signore*. Then one would have to find out that there was a relationship between their definitions and the central meaning, and work out the rules for getting from one to the other. Finally, one would want to explain why particular meanings were related to particular statuses.

In the rest of this essay I propose to carry out this exercise in a limited way, concentrating on the three marked status categories out of the following range:

I have not taken a sample of those who might be considered *signori* and systematically worked out the range of interpretations of the concept among them. Instead, I will consider some of the things said during the heat of the November election about the leaders of the two rival lists. Like candidates anywhere they stressed their good record in the past and made promises about what they would do, if returned. There was a great deal of talk about the numbers of personal *debitori* which the leading figures on each list had, arising both from acts of charity and from the use of 'long arms'. (After the election there was a great deal of bitter gossip and speculation about beneficiaries who must have voted for the other side.) As for public benefactions, a crucial issue arose from the evident superiority of the members of List Two in the ability to make connections with the provincial and other external authorities. The propagandists of List One stressed the *mancia* (the rake-off), dug up all the scandal they could about a prominent member of List Two who had been a merchant and was himself a former mayor, and succeeded in rallying behind them a number of ordinary people on the vaguely stated theme of not being pushed around by outsiders. In this context the *signore* (List One could boast only of its leader in this status) looks like the protector of the village against the world outside, and the whole stance is based on the premise that village-outsider relationships are governed by the rules of the jungle and it is generally the villager who gets eaten. The propagandists of List Two took the opposite point of view. The world outside was a world of resources which could be used for the benefit of everyone in the village. It is possible to enter into a moral relationship with officials of the province and the state enterprises and church dignitaries and this relationship need not be a predatory one. The role of the *signore* is not only to dispense charity and benefactions but also to make sure that the infinitely greater resources of the province and the state are made available to the village. A particular bone of contention was tourism, and the development of trout fishing. In short, the propagandists of List Two had a 'modernized' version of the *signore*'s public duty: not charity alone, but also brokerage.

In a sentence, List One's *signore* closes the gate to keep the dangers out; List Two's opens it wide to let the benefits in.

Of course no-one knows exactly how individuals voted. But

there was a general opinion that a larger part of the older section of the population, who are also the *contadini* (the peasants), voted for List One (the gate closers). Correspondingly, those who were salaried workers or wage-labourers working outside the village and being either part-time peasants or having no land at all, were said to have voted for the gate-openers. How would each of these categories define a *signore*? My text to be explained is a statement by an informant, which ran as follows:

> Perhaps the old people still look at *signori* in the old way. They look up with respect at the mayor or the teacher or the priest. But the young people and the people of middle-age don't look at them any more as authorities.

When we consider the *contadini,* this statement is not without its difficulties. Firstly, they voted against the list which had on it a preponderance of *signori*, taking just the 'basic qualities' meaning of wealth, education and cultural attainment. Secondly, the statement quoted earlier—that the speaker was not going to vote for a list of *signori*—was also made by an old person and a peasant. Yet at the same time, it was said that the leader of their own list (the gate-closer) had a degree and was employed in Turin and they needed someone like him to give them leadership. For them such a man still has authority. They regard him with respect. Obviously this had to do with his gate-closing activities. I will return to this question in the final section of this paper.

There is a corresponding puzzle with the young, the non-*contadini*. They no longer look with respect at *signori* nor grant them authority, but they are said to have voted for **Lista no. due,** with its high proportion of *signori*.

We are, of course, dealing with two different realizations of *signore*. The informant's statement leaned heavily towards what might be called the 'internal' aspect of *signorilità*: wealth and refinement, benefactions and charity, protection from outside dangers, and the authority that flows from or is a return for all these transactions. The workers and clerks had their eye, one guesses, almost wholly on the 'long arms' and regarded the *signori* as potential middlemen.

WHAT THE 'SIGNORI' THINK OF 'CONTADINI'

Before concluding, I want to examine the meaning which *signori* (that is, certain members of List Two with whom I discussed this question) give to one of the sub-categories of non-*signori*, namely the *contadini* (the peasants). I begin with an anecdote told me by a Losa *signore*.

> I was walking last summer through one of the Tetti [hamlets—this one about three miles up in the mountains from Losa], when I noticed the lintel of a cowshed. There was a date carved on it and I suddenly realized that it must have come from the old *municipio* (Town Hall) in Losa. I found the owner and asked if I could buy it. He said that his four brothers [all abroad] would have to agree, since he only had a fifth share in it and all he could do was cut off a fifth and sell it. That"s what they're like. I'd have given him a good price. It's worth nothing to him. If they did cut it up, it would obviously be worth nothing at all. I should have sent Menico up for it. If he'd said he needed it to prop up a piece of guttering, they'd have given it him as a present.

Menico is a friend and dependant of that *signore*, no longer a peasant but a bluff, forceful, horny-handed quarry-supervisor and on good terms with most people. This anecdote carries a lot of messages. The storyteller, as I remember, was intent on conveying to me the lack of enterprise to be found among peasants. But it is not simple stupidity. It is compounded with a bloody-minded skill at using traditional values (in this case the rules of inheritance) to cut off their own noses to spite the faces of people like himself who were trying to improve life for peasants. That was the point of his speculation about how easily his friend Menico could have obtained the stone, if he had wished.

This resolute lack of the entrepreneurial spirit among the *contadini* is a frequent topic of conversation among the *signori*. Their agricultural techniques are said to be antediluvian; they like using a hoe when there are mechanical potato-lifters available to them. Dairying is running down, but if they ran a co-operative they could all benefit. They will not experiment with new crops— just potatoes and rye and some vegetables in the garden. They cannot see that better tourist facilities, as in the neighbouring *comune*, would raise the demand for locally grown vegetables, would send up the price of building land, would make jobs for people in the village and everyone would benefit. (When we suggested a communal cowshed and dairying enterprise, they said that all we were interested in was getting the smell of the cowsheds away from the village streets. They want a closed community; they do not want change; they cannot see what is good for them; they represent people who try to help them.)

In short, for the *signori* the definition of that term now includes a component equivalent to what we have been calling 'gate-opening'. Conversely, the word *contadino* has come to mean for them an obtuse and obstructive person, who, nevertheless, has the right to be aided to better his lot. Specifically, the peasant has to be taught that he is living not at the turn of the century, but in the second half of the twentieth century. This, indeed, is the point, as we will see in the concluding section of this essay.

THE DECLINE OF PEASANT LIFE

In the mountain areas of northern Italy in particular—and in many other areas in Europe as the recent book by *Franklin* convincingly argues—the tide of industry, including industrial agriculture, has swept away the foundations of peasant life. For governments the 'peasant problem' no longer is the economic problem of how to grow enough food, but a social problem of how to keep occupied and content the peasant classes, particularly those over the age of forty and therefore the more difficult to re-train for other work, and how to shield peasant agriculture from the vastly superior competitive power of industrial heavily capitalized agriculture.

This process began in Losa after World War II and probably did not make itself seriously felt until the late nineteen fifties. I have discovered no dramatic benchmarking event about this time and I am relying on what informants say about how the place has changed. I do not mean that before this time the village stood on its own, isolated from the nation around it. Since before the turn of the century it has been exporting people to North America and South America and the South of France. But this does not seem to have altered radically the peasant way of life followed by those who remained in the village.

I have a description of life in the 1920s, covering approximately the decade following World War I. They lived on potatoes and rye bread. They drank milk. Wine was for feast days only. They kept larger herds of cattle than they do now, and more sheep: they manufactured and exported cheese. The things they bought —some clothes and their boots and utensils—were bought at the annual fair. Compared with families at the present day, families at that time were self-contained: so too was the village and its hamlets. The productivity of the farm was not the main concern: the farm was there to feed the family and provide enough surplus to meet its other needs and to give everyone an occupation.

Keeping cattle and sheep and working the land without the aid of machinery involves long hours of heavy and often dangerous work, alike for the women as the men. By now this kind of life has almost entirely vanished. Even those who still derive their main income from agriculture, find life less exacting. This is communicated in a hundred different ways, to even a casual enquirer. Then a shower of rain when you were out with the sheep or the cattle left you soaked to the skin: now you can carry one of those cheap lightweight nylon coats and come home dry. You can get a tractor to plough the land. The high dangerous pastures no longer need to be mown and the hay brought down. So the tale goes on: life is easier now, even if you are still farming.

But there is a strange ambivalence about the change. Men travel in buses and cars and on scooters: but they value intensely their ability to walk in mountains and they admire the hard endurance which this requires. Women do not romanticize the kind of life that has to be lived when there are cows in the stalls and they are intensely proud when they managed to get their house what they call *aggiustata* (equipped with a modern toilet and a bathroom and central heating, the glass-fronted drinks cabinet and modern furniture and sometimes a washing machine and usually a television set). But all I met still retain in the kitchen a wood-burning stove and on this they cook, using the gas stoves only if coffee has to be prepared in a hurry. The heat from the wood, they say, is better for cooking: it doesn't destroy the flavour. They all keep small kitchen gardens: the majority of them keep rabbits and chickens and there is an immense (and, it seemed to me, not always rational) pride in their ability to put on the table food grown or prepared at home. Even those who are now wholly out of the peasant way of making a living yet seem to be

R

proud of their peasant heritage, to value the powers of physical endurance that a peasant needs to survive, to value even the very particularity of their own Losa dialect. Several men pointed out, mingling amusement with a kind of pride, how the vocabularies changed once you moved even a couple of miles up or down their valley, let alone cross the ridge into another valley. All these seemed to me to be messages about the value of their lost or vanishing way of life, and of the particularity of their own community within that culture. But at the same time they do not want to put the clock back: to get rid of the motor-cars and the scooters and the television sets and the power-saws and the pensions and the security and the prosperity. They look both ways. But there is a difference between the old and the young. For those under forty or those older but already wholly committed to employment in industry, the dilemma is no more than those symbolic gestures about home-grown food and cooking over wood. Their natural posture is looking forward. But the old look back and are hurt and resentful because every day more and more things forcibly turn their heads in the new direction: even to farm, let alone to live, you need more and more equipment and supplies from the outside world.

In the past—even up to this last war—the *signori* sat at the gateway to a closed little community and a closed culture. Migrants went out—and a few came back—but enough were left to keep peasant life intact, held, no doubt, by the vastly greater security whch peasant agriculture offered in comparison to pre-war industry. The *signori* were not trying to change anything. Their transactions were the traditional ones: charity and benefactions exchanged for prestige and authority. They were part of the peasant's moral community insofar as their rank was not grudged them.

But now things are different. The gateway is wide open. The *signori* keep it open. If the old people who are still peasants hate the *signori* that is because the latter stand for the opening of the community and the ending of peasant culture. If they are accused of sharp practice—of robbing the community through the rake-off—that too is partly a symbolic statement about their role in integrating the village into the larger world. It is also a statement that *signore* no longer represents a status within the peasant's moral community. He is a person with whom one makes contacts in order to manipulate the world outside: less perhaps a *grado sociale* (social status) than, metaphorically speaking, a *grado di lavoro* (occupation).

The attempt to exclude the *signori* of List Two from the moral community of the peasants showed itself in comments which followed the election. Some supporters of List One expressed vociferous disgust at the behaviour of the leaders of the other list.

> They are supposed to be the educated ones. It's true that no-one on our list except the mayor has got beyond elementary school. But our people behaved like *signori*. The List Two people are the educated ones yet they were out on the streets shouting abuse in public and stirring up all kinds of unnecessary dissensions. These were administrative elections, not political elections. It was a disgrace to see them divide a small community like ours.

These comments reveal very clearly the theme of what makes a good community (one in which there is no dissension) and how the new style of *signori* destroy the community by importing the style of the so-called political elections[5] (i.e. provincial and national elections) into the community, where harmony should prevail.

NOTES

1. See *Marriott*, pp. 133–8.
2. See *Goffman* (1), *passim*.
3. *Autorità* was given by informants as a quality of the *signori*. It does, however, differ from the other two attributes—wealth and refinement —in that it can be perceived *only* in exchanges.
4. In fact this seems to happen only between people of different generation (e.g. the pupil's '*Bon giorno*' receives in exchange a '*Ciaou*' from the schoolmaster); and not always then (e.g. parent and child use '*tu*' symmetrically). These forms of address seem more often to signify distance/familiarity, rather than high/low. Rank is more usually signalled through the third code—the many kinds of deferential behaviour. See also the discussion of long-term changes in *Brown and Gilman*.
5. The bureaucracy provides the distinction. Elections at the level of the *comune* are called 'administrative': provincial and national elections are classified as 'political'.

12

Political Behaviour and World View in a Central Italian Village[1]

This chapter concerns a village called Colombaio[2] in the western hills of central Italy. About 700 people live there. It is the largest village and the administrative centre of an agricultural commune. Before the early 1950s, almost three-quarters of the land of the commune was owned by a small number of landowners, who let out their land to sharefarmers in the institutional framework of mezzadria *contract common in Central Italy. The farmers lived on the land they worked. The village served as the administrative, marketing, and social centre of the surrounding countryside. Most of the families who lived in the village depended on agriculture for a living, both as agricultural labourers and as cultivators. Most of them owned a small amount of land, but few had enough to provide more than a part of their subsistence requirements. Consequently most families depended on seasonal paid labour in agriculture and in the wood industry and on access to small amounts of land rented on short-term leases from landowners.[3] Thus, in both the countryside and in the village, there was a high degree of economic dependency on a small number of people. The large landowners in general lived in the cities of the region rather than on or near their land. A few middle-sized owners lived in Colombaio and one of the large landowners had his administration there. There were a small number of professionals, office-workers, and schoolteachers. The people in these categories were the high-status people of the village. There were a small number of traders and artisans, considered to be of middle-status. Finally, there was the majority of village families dependent on agriculture as cultivators and as wage labourers.[4]*

In the Italian land reform of 1950, a large amount of the land in the commune was expropriated and redistributed in small farms, mainly to people of local origin. Accompanying the re-distribution of land was a large investment in roads, bridges, houses and farm-buildings. Land was deep-ploughed, vines and olive trees were planted. New settlers even had the kitchen cutlery provided. To administer this programme, a Local Centre of the regional land reform agency was set up in the village, and in the first eight years or so of the reform forty to fifty officials of the agency, most of them outsiders to the area, lived in the village. Between one and two hundred local men were given employment by the agency during this period. In the mid-1960's the stage of active intervention came to an end, and the Centre at Colombaio remained open mainly to administer the outstanding accounts of the assignees with the agency.[5]

During the active period of the reform the agency managed the allocation of vast resources, and through the manipulation of these resources was able to keep the assignees heavily dependent on it. In this way it was able to influence the farming practices of the assignees, many of whom had little experience in managing a farm unit; and it could also carry out the anti-communist politi-cal objectives of the reform. Thus, the high degree of economic dependency in the pre-reform economic organization was trans-ferred to a state agency in the post-reform organization, a state agency which appeared to have unlimited quantities of resources at its disposal and which was prepared to use these resources to achieve political as well as economic ends.

Since the reform, farm incomes have risen considerably. Olives and wine-grapes have been added to the pre-reform pro-ducts of livestock and wheat as the principal products of the zone. Nevertheless, net migration from the countryside has occurred at the rate of just under two per cent per year since the mid-1950s. While this does not mean that agriculture is being abandoned wholesale as it is in the mountain communities de-scribed in other chapters of this book, it does indicate that the future of agriculture in the area is uncertain: the reform created farms, many of which are probably too small to continue to provide a level of income high enough to compete effectively with levels of income in industry. In the village, the effect of the reform and of the more general economic changes taking place in Italy during the same period was to reduce dependency *on agriculture. Pre-reform sources of income in agriculture were cut off and new sources of income in non-agricultural activity opened up. Today, less than a fifth of the active male population of the village depend mainly on agriculture, either as farmers or as labourers. Over a third are employed as workers in construction, manufacturing, and similar kinds of activity. A quarter are self-employed artisans and traders. Just under a fifth are professionals, teachers, and office-workers. In addition, about ten office-workers and fifteen teachers work in the village but live in nearby towns.*[6]

This completes a brief review of the main economic changes which have occurred in the area of Colombaio within the last twenty years. There have been large increases in the quantities of some kinds of resources available to the Colombesi (people of Colombaio) and large changes in the distribution of these resources. These changes provide the background to the processes of interpersonal behaviour described below.

This essay is about political behaviour; about the way people compete with each other for esteem and allocate the resources they control. Patterns of political behaviour in the village emerge from a set of shared beliefs about how other people allocate resources, and a set of derived rules about how in these circumstance's one's own resources may be best allocated and the resources of others best controlled. These beliefs and rules define suitable strategies in the small politics of reputation-management. They condition action in the larger politics of voluntary organizations and competition between political parties. And, through their relevance to action in these contexts, they have important consequences on economic development and innovation. The object of the essay, then, is to show how the beliefs and rules of resource allocation are relevant to these processes.

WORLD VIEW AND SOCIAL ACTION

Two propositions about resource allocation explain much of the social life in Colombaio:

(1) The behaviour of those *outside the family* is believed to be motivated by the desire to achieve their own advantage.

(2) The world of people is seen as stratified, with responsibilities divided.[7]

The first proposition expresses the pervasive feeling that those outside the family will not hesitate to sacrifice the interests of others in order to follow their own, however friendly or impartial they may appear. The belief is conscious: the Colombesi themselves voice it and use it to explain particular cases. The second proposition states the basic principle by which the world of people is divided up and ordered. Unlike the first, it is not stated as a generalization by the Colombesi, but it is implicit in comments on particular people and in actions. These two propositions appear to be basic premises of social interaction: they are basic in the sense that taken together they are sufficient to explain a wide range of social regularities.

Social behaviour may be seen as decisions to allocate time and other resources between alternatives.[8] Patterns of action at the community level are then the deposit of the decisions of many individuals in the community. The problem of explaining the patterns is the problem of explaining the bases on which the individuals make their decisions. What people do, how they make allocations, depends on several kinds of factors: on environmental constraints, which limit the range of alternatives available; on the standards used to evaluate alternative outcomes; and on the way in which the presence of other people influences an individual's allocation decisions. My subject is this last factor, the way in which people in Colombaio adapt to the presence of others. In Colombaio the way the world of people is divided is expressed in the second premise; and the principle by which others are believed to behave is expressed in the first.

Those who see people outside the family as concerned to achieve their own advantage will tend to be wary and distrustful in extra-familial relationships. They will not necessarily conclude that to protect themselves from others they must behave according to the same principles as they believe others use. For one reason, there are, as we shall see, cultural mechanisms by which a person who has few opportunities to take advantage of others is able to give himself high self-esteem and to claim esteem in the opinion of others. The effect of the belief will be to make people wary of entering into confidences, of revealing information which could be used against them. The second premise defines certain kinds of action as the business of certain categories of people. In particular, it defines 'public action' as the business of high-status people. The rule of effective action in these circumstances, as expressed by the Colombesi, is: 'It is better to wish well of others, depend on no one, and stay in your own house,' Colombesi, in fact, do not work together very much outside the family. Extra-familial relationships are informal, shifting, seldom involve more than two persons and involve little exchange of economic goods or assistance. People do not often visit one another. Women meet casually in the course of the daily round and stop to exchange gossip. Men have informal contact in the bars. In appropriate contexts—the bar and the home—there is great emphasis on politeness and generosity in extra-familial relations, expressed particularly in the offering of drinks.

These patterns result from the cognitive premises about the world, and the conditions of the economic organization of the village. One who believes that others are out for their own interests will adapt to this situation by not getting too closely involved with them and will give the impression of wishing them well by being polite and generous. Further, there is no large economic advantage to be had from frequent extra-familial contacts. The economic organization of the village permits most households to be self-sufficient consumption units. When a family requires labour in excess of its own, as may happen in those families which still get part of their income from agriculture, labour is hired or exchanged, usually hired. Thus, within the range of choice perceived by the Colombesi, there is little economic advantage to be had from more exchanges between households.

This is the setting for the business of small politics. There is little stable contact between families, but people are very concerned about their good name. Much of what they say about each other can be seen as part of the competition for esteem: for self-esteem and for esteem in the eyes of others. The rules and the processes of this competition derive from the two basic premises. I approach the problem of competition by considering who is criticized by whom, and how. This should not be taken to mean that what people say about each other consists only of criticisms. But since the balance is heavily weighted towards the negative, I begin from this side.

WORLD VIEW AND THE COMPETITION FOR ESTEEM

In criticizing others, the Colombesi implicitly order people according to a number of criteria. The most important is the status of the person criticized in relation to that of the person making the criticism. Most of the cases of criticism I heard were from low-status or middle-status people. Let us begin, then, with what low-status people say about high-status people.[9]

High-status people tend to be critcized by low-status people 'on the flat', on their attributes and behaviour as holders of certain jobs. The theme of the criticisms is that they are two-faced; they are *gentile* (decent) to one's face, but in reality are insincere, dishonest, selfish and unfair. They are people of whom one has need, and whom one fears because of the resources they can control. In allocating these resources, they are believed to follow the pragmatic rule: seek one's own advantage. And they are thereby believed to break the normative rules[10] of impartiality, honesty, and public service without special reward. They are not believed to have a sense of duty to the organizations for which they work or to the people who are their clients: what they do depends on how much they can get out of it for themselves.

Low-status people criticize other low-status people 'in the round', on their behaviour as family-members and as potential or actual friends. They are the focus for criticisms of untrustworthiness, meanness, sexual looseness and irresponsibility in family obligations.

The difference in the content of criticisms is associated with other differences. For example, criticisms of high-status people tend to be more standardized through particular stories (told to demonstrate the grounds of criticism), while the criticisms of low-status people by other low-status people are more varied. High-status people also are more openly and readily criticized than are other low-status people.

Middle-status people criticize those of high-status more in the round than do low-status people: on their behaviour both as holders of particular positions and as family-members and potential or actual friends. They say that high-status people consider themselves superior to everyone else and are miserly despite their wealth. Thus, a middle-status person may criticize a particular high-status person for wanting to receive the formal *lei* form of address, and for considering himself *grande* (important) because he has a degree. But a low-status person would not question whether the high-status person should be given the *lei* or doubt that a degree merits respect.

Sometimes low-status people criticize those of high-status over their performance outside their jobs. A high-status man whose wife works as a teacher is criticized for being so much interested in money that he sends his wife out to teach, thereby making her sacrifice her responsibilities as a mother and home-maker. High-status men who are known to have changed their party allegiances are criticized like anyone else who changes political allegiance: they changed, it is said, because they profited, never because of a 'genuine' change of convictions.

Status is not the only criterion affecting the criticisms made. It makes a difference whether a high-status person is an insider or an outsider.[11] Much is known about the family background and the relatives of high-status insiders. Much of the criticism, particularly that made by middle-status people, is of the dishonesty involved in getting their jobs, their wealth, or their houses. The bad behaviour of relatives may also be used against them. On the other hand, less is known about the family history and relatives of high-status outsiders. While they are assumed to be out for their own interests as much as the high-status insiders, the criticism is less rounded and less detailed. However, there are a few cases where a high-status outsider is exempted by some low-status persons from the general condemnation. In these cases, the high-status outsider has done something good to the low-status person. In one case, a high official of the commune administration carried letters to a woman of the village from her sister, a nun in a village some distance from Colombaio, when he passed through this village on his way to Colombaio. In another case, a high official of the land reform agency showed unexpected sympathy when a low-status man was called to discuss his large debt with the agency. In both cases, the low-status people concerned evaluated the high-status people as 'not malicious' (*non è cattivo*). In both cases, the only direct interaction they had with high-status persons was on these occasions.

Outsiderness also influences the evaluation of low-status people. Women may be identified as outsiders, or as children of outsiders, in order to explain their shortcomings. 'What else can you expect of someone from there?' The country-dwelling farmers are recognized in most contexts as a separate and generally inferior category of people by village dwellers: they are said to be lazy but well-off, overfavoured by the state at the expense of the village people, and ignorant and behind the times in agriculture and in their general outlook on life.[12]

Kinship also affects patterns of criticism. Close kin are not criticized, but presented as good people who follow the normative rules of family and marriage, friendship and work. This range is generally confined to siblings and parents. Beyond this there may be criticism, but it is muted. This commonly extends to the children of parents' siblings, and their children, but may go further. The typical preliminary remark to a criticism of their behaviour is: 'Even though we are relatives. . . .' Kinsmen thus tend to be protected and reasons are found why the behaviour for which they are criticized is not in their control but is caused by a petulant and spendthrift wife or by an impulsive temperament. In talking about kin, people distinguish more carefully between what is known to be true and what is rumoured: kin tend to be given the benefit of the doubt.

Finally, the sex of the person criticizing others is relevant: women tend to gossip more readily than men, and men tend to confine their criticisms to other men.

These regularities depend partly upon the purposes of the criticisms. The Colombesi compete with each other for status and moral worth. The post-war economic changes, in particular the land reform, presented new opportunities for social mobility. Most high-status people living in the village today have come from lower-status origins. Those who feel that they have missed these opportunities, who have seen others getting ahead while they remained where they were, are concerned to defend themselves and to explain the situation in ways which preserve their self esteem. The basic strategy is to claim that the successful person follows his own advantage and sacrifices the interests of others, and, by morally condemning this, to imply that one would not do the same oneself. In this way the first of the two basic premises is relevant to the processes of small politics. Given this basic strategy, the regularities in criticisms follow from differences in opportunities open to people for the manipulation of resources, and from differences in the kinds of knowledge available about people.

A person's status is defined in part by the resources he can control or influence. High-status people can influence important resources: they are people whom others have need of or whom others may have reason to fear.[13] At the same time, most people of high status signal their eminence by keeping out of the informal social life of the village. For these two reasons high-status people tend to be the object of job-based criticisms by low-status people: it is in the course of their jobs that they allocate resources sought by others and have contact with low-status persons. Within the category of high-status people, the distinction between insiders and outsiders corresponds to differences in the knowledge available about particular persons' past and present lives. The high-status insiders are mostly people who have been seen to be mobile. Accordingly, the criticisms made of them deny the legitimacy of their high status. The ways by which they came to possess the bases of their status—in particular their jobs and their wealth—are claimed to have been illegitimate, due to the relentless and dishonest pursuit of self-interest, to the manipulation of others through political ties and *raccomondazioni* (a patronage system). It is their badness and good fortune (fortune in having highly-placed relatives, for example) rather than their abilities, which are used to explain their upward mobility.[14] The argument implicit in the criticism is: 'He was low [or middle] and now is high. Therefore, he must have done things which are bad, things which I would not have done. That is why he is high and I am not.' These criticisms are made especially by middle-status people, who see their relations with high-status people more in terms of rivalry for the same position than do low-status people. Thus, the criticisms of high-status people that they consider themselves superior to everyone else tends to come from the middle-status people. High-status outsiders are in general criticized in much the same way as high-status insiders, but in less detail. And, because of the lack of knowledge of their family past and their relatives, small acts which are seen to run contrary to the general assumptions of how high-status persons behave may be sufficient in the case of high-status outsiders to gain them an overall evaluation as 'good' people. The same acts would not produce the same effect on the overall evaluation if they were done by high-status insiders.

In short, the implication of the criticisms made of high-status people by those of low-status and middle-status is that the former do not behave according to the normative rules for those of high status. Rather, they behave, and in the case of insiders, have behaved, so as to get what they can for themselves. The next step in the argument relates this to a judgement of the moral worth of a person.[15] The behaviour of a high-status person is said to confer on him a low moral worth. It is implied, on the other hand, that the criticizer, because he would not have done what the high-status person is alleged to have done, is of high moral worth. It is then implied that it is better to have a high moral worth and low status than to have a high status and low moral worth.

Criticisms of low-status people by other low-status people are somewhat different. They make use of the same normative rules by which the criticizer ranks himself as high: rules of the family and marriage, of friendship and work. The same standards define the criticizer as high and the criticized as low. Low-status persons do not, by the definiton of status, have opportunities to manipulate many other people: nor have they been mobile. Consequently, the first premise is used differently from the way it is used against high-status people.

The case of a 'good man', the only person who was presented to me by many Colombesi as good, confirms this argument. The man died soon after the end of the Second World War. In the first four decades of the century he was one of the most conspicuous men in the village. He started the Consumer Co-operative and administered it for forty years until his death. He administered the religious confraternity during the same period. He organized and directed the long drawn-out campaign to reclaim rights to certain land (*usi civici* land) which had been held jointly by the people of the village some centuries ago but which had lapsed and been taken over by the big landowners. For many years he took evening classes for the young people of the village. He gave assistance to people in their dealings with the state. At first he was presented to me as a thoroughly good man (*un uomo per bene*), an initiator, an administrator, a co-operator; as one who educated himself, acquired a large experience of the world, and was happy to use this experience to help others; as one interested in helping 'the people'; as one who, when he saw something unjust, got angry about it and did something to right it; and above all, as one who was born poor and died poor, as one who 'did not make love with money'. No other person was described in such terms. In particular, no other person was described as 'an initiator', as having personal merit as the basis of his leadership, and as more interested to help 'the people' than to help himself.

However, in later discussions I learnt that the man had in fact been strongly criticized. Towards the end of his life he bought a small piece of land and at the same time he apparently began to appear less willing to help others than he had previously been. What happened is stated by an old man who knew him:

> When people saw that he, from the nothing that he was, began to go up a little, immediately they went against him. They said that he worked for his own interests, that he had frauded. When people saw him changed in physical condition, in his clothes, they said: 'You have stolen.' Rather, he had earned.

Thus, towards the end of his life, when he began to demonstrate a modest comfort, he was criticized for following his own interests at the expense of others. Economic improvements lowered moral worth. The same criticisms are made today of those known to have been socially mobile. Today, however, this man is presented by those who knew him as the epitome of goodness. It is not surprising that in a small community where people compete to evaluate each other in terms of moral goodness and badness, excellence is represented by someone dead and safely out of the competition.[16]

We have seen how two basic premises about the world of people influence the processes of small politics in Colombaio. The basic strategy for lowering another person's moral worth and increasing one's own is to claim that the other person is following the pragmatic rule of doing what is in his own advantage, whatever his claims to be following the appropriate normative rules. The way this belief is used depends on the relative status of critic and victim. Status defines people mainly according to the kind of resources they control and so according to the degree to which other people depend on them. It defines the kind of knowledge wanted about them, and influences the knowledge which is available. The outsider attribute controls the knowledge available about background and family connections. The kinship attribute defines the range of people who cannot be criticized without giving information which could be used to attack one's own good name. In addition, the extent of direct contact between people, which may vary independently of variations in these attributes, modifies the kinds of criticisms by modifying the kinds of knowledge wanted and available.

WORLD VIEW AND THE COMPETITION
BETWEEN FESTIVAL ASSOCIATIONS

If this argument is sound, these same premises should be used in much the same way in other types of interpersonal competitions within the village. The competition of a recently-initiated village festival provides evidence for this. The first was held in 1966. Since 1967, the principal event has been a competition between three festival associations (*contrade*). Each association builds a float, the floats are paraded before a panel of judges, and a prize —a silver cup—is awarded to the winning association. The three associations are based on territorial divisions of the village which existed before the festival but had never been organized into formal associations. The prize was won by Cassero Association in the first year and by Molino in the second. Before the festival in 1969 there was considerable interest in the outcome of the third competition. In the event, Cassero won again. The people of Molino and the people of Pescina, the third association, immediately set about denying the legitimacy of the victory.

It was said, first, that Cassero Association had bought the judges. The judges were all outsiders, most of them in public positions. Three of them went to lunch in houses of Cassero people, and it was there in the secrecy of the houses that the deal was made. A figure of L.10,000 a head circulated.[17] To demonstrate the truth of the accusation, it was pointed out that some people of Cassero were going around claiming that they had won the prize two hours before the parade of floats began. Secondly, it was said that the victory went to Cassero for political reasons. The head of the panel of judges was the Communist President of the provincial administration. He was one of the three judges who ate in houses of Cassero people. He was assumed to have preferred the Cassero float, because most people in Cassero (it was said) are Communists, because the two outsiders who painted the Cassero float are well-known Communists, and because the theme of the float, 'Peace in the World', is a theme which appeals to Communists. He was able to influence the other six men of the jury because they all have positions in which they are likely to have need of him at some time or other. Hence the jury voted for Cassero. As a result of this process of reasoning, a group of Pescina men gathered in a Pescina bar after the result of the competition was announced and began chanting *'Viva Mao!'* waving imaginary Red Books in the air. The buying of the jury and the influence of politics were the main explanations used to account for the success of Cassero by those who lost. These were not explanations generated in the heat of the moment and later discarded as unrealistic. People seriously believed that Cassero had got the victory by these means. The implication of the explanations is that the victory was not merited, just as high-status people are not high through merit. Cassero people did not use a moral defence. They argued that it would have been so difficult to buy the jury that it was a preposterous suggestion; and that, if anyone could have bought the jury Pescina could have, since the rich people live in Pescina, not in Cassero. They denied that there are more Communists in Cassero than in other associations, and so maintained that there were no grounds for favouritism from the head of the jury. Cassero's defence did not deny that if there are the opportunities, people will behave as the explanations of their victory said they had. Their defence was that they did not have the opportunities and the jury members had no incentives.[18]

During the weeks preceding the festival, the Colombesi talked of their own and other associations. What they said and the way they said it is much the same as the way they evaluate themselves and others. For Cassero people the main rival was Pescina Association, because many of the high-status people live there, because it borders on Cassero, and because it was thought likely that Pescina would win, since it was the only association so far without a victory. Cassero people reckoned up the good (+) and bad (−) attributes. They emphasized that most of the people in Cassero were born in Cassero (+) whereas most Pescina people are outsiders (−); that Cassero is like a big family (+), whereas Pescina is less compact (−); that there is friendship and familiarity, mutual assistance and generosity between the people of Cassero (+), whereas there is indifference to others, distance and formality in Pescina (−); that Cassero people are all poor (+), whereas Pescina is in the area of the *signori* (−). Pescina people tended to agree that Cassero was more compact and enthusiastic. High-status Pescina people attributed the difference in the associations to the fact that Cassero people were born in Cassero and grew up there, whereas Pescina people in general did not grow up in Pescina. Low-status Pescina people attributed the difference both to this and to the presence in Pescina of too many high-status people, who held themselves *in grande* (behaved like important people) and caused great distance (*distanza*) and indifference (*menefregismo*) between people in the area. In the competition, however, Pescina came last by a long way, and Molino came a close second. Molino was now the rival to be fended off. Cassero people now talked of Molino as the area of outsiders, as the area of those who cannot see reason and justice. Pescina was talked of as the area where many of the residents were born in Cassero, but later made money and moved out into Pescina. And Cassero was described in contrast, as the area where everyone was born and grew up in the area where they live today, where everyone has remained on the same level, where everyone forms a big family.

Thus, much the same ways of ordering and evaluating people, and of explaining their success are found in the context of the festival competition between rival associations as in the interpersonal competition for esteem. In both cases, the status, outsider, and kin attributes are used to order and evaluate people, and in both cases the manipulation of people, rather than personal merit, is used as the basic explanation of success.

WORLD VIEW, VOLUNTARY ASSOCIATIONS,
AND POLITICAL PARTY COMPETITION

We have been following through the way in which the Colombesi adapt to the presence of others. Adaptation at two levels has been considered: at the level of action, in the extent and kind of extrafamilial relationships; and at the level of verbal communication, in what people say about each other. I come back now to adaptation at the level of action, and consider the patterns of allocation of time and other resources in voluntary organizations and the reasons for these patterns.

S

There are and have been several voluntary organizations in Colombaio. Some of these are of local origin, or are at least sustained mainly by local resources: a band, a religious confraternity, a consumer co-operative, a sports association, and a festival organization. There are other organizations which are branches of national or provincial organizations: a cultural circle sponsored by the provincial education authority, a branch of each of the main political parties, a branch of each of the main labour unions, and a service co-operative for farmers, initiated and maintained by the land reform agency. However, a simple listing of existing organizations is misleading. With a few exceptions, the organizations are inactive. The band, the religious confraternity, and the consumer co-operative, active and flourishing before the Second World War, have declined greatly. The Communist Party is the only political party organization which is active outside pre-election periods. The labour unions exist as voluntary associations in name only. The sports association, started in 1967, is concerned only with the administration of the Colombaio football team, which plays in the third grade provincial competition. The cultural circle, started in 1966, is run by a schoolmaster and meets once a week during the winter months, attended by five to twenty young people of the village. The most active organization is the festival association (*Pro-loco*). It was started in 1966, and now administers all the village dances, the Festival of the Village (which previously was organized by a committee selected by ballot from the members of the confraternity), and the Festival of the Grape, which it initiated in 1967. In addition to these presently existing organizations, there are others which existed for a period and then closed down. Before Fascism there was an active sports association, and after the end of the Second World War another sports association existed for a few years. Two small work co-operatives have existed in the village during the last fifty years. During the 1950s and early 1960s, two national workers' organizations (E N A L and A C L I) had branches in the village.

Several generalizations can be made about the organizations currently existing in the village. There is little interest in participation in them. In particular, there is little interest in becoming involved to the point of taking a position of authority. Their activities depend very much on one or two men who supply what leadership is necessary. These activities are very limited in scope and in the demands on the time of those formally involved. They make little impact on the allocations of time or money of the great majority of Colombesi.

This pattern is the outcome of choices based partly on two beliefs, which are the expression in the context of voluntary organizations of the two basic premises:

(1) Authority-holders in voluntary organizations are believed to be motivated to take the positions in order to follow their own advantage, whether in money terms or in prestige.

(2) The running of voluntary organizations is the responsibility of those elected to do so. It is not the business of those without a position of authority in the organization to take responsibility for its activities, to suggest changes or to check on the activities of the authority-holders.

These two beliefs reduce the incentive to become involved in an organization, as an authority-holder or as an ordinary participant. From the point of view of potential holders of positions of authority, the material rewards are small. In addition, the criticisms to which they are likely to be subjected (based on (1)) mean that they risk their reputation and are not likely to gain esteem. In Colombaio, the suspicion that a person might be serving his own interests by doing some public action is sufficient to deny the worth of his actions: public interest cannot be served by one who is seen to be profiting. Further, the losses of organizations are attributed to the authority-holders; but not the gains.

How people who have had experience of authority positions in organizations feel in this situation is expressed in the following comments:

If you, as President, send to people a notice saying that they can come and collect L.3,000, they come, but say, 'What is L.3,000? It is nothing.' But if you send them a letter asking them to pay L.300, *porca miseria*! the world explodes . . . If you try a plan which cost 3 million instead of the normal 1 million, and if all goes well, nobody says anything. But if all does not go well, they eat you! It is necessary to be always fearful: mistake if you go here, mistake if you go there. So things do not progress much, because of this criticism . . . There are many people who, if you try to do something for the collectivity, do like the dog who guards the garlic: he does not eat it and does not let others eat it. In the end the organization is closed down and the collective benefit is finished.

It is better for everyone to stay in their own house. Because if you do good to others, they won't tell you.

The most active organizations, the festival association and the festival committees, the sports association, and the cultural circle, depend largely on one or two persons for leadership. The festival association was started at the initiative of the head of the land reform agency and the doctor, both outsiders of high-status, and continues to be maintained largely by these men together with the bank manager. The sports association was started and is maintained largely by the mayor, who takes personal responsibility for it. The cultural circle was started and is administered entirely by a local schoolmaster, who is paid and assisted in the work by the provincial education authority.

From the point of view of potential participants, also, incentives are low. Public benefit is an incentive only in so far as an individual smells private gain. Hence, the often expressed complaint: 'We pay and pay, but never see anything of our money again. What happens to it?' The authority-holders are to be distrusted: they may try to evade responsibility and one may find oneself blamed for a mistake. Many men of low-status say that they feel a sense of 'subjection' (*soggezione*) when they go to meetings and find themselves face-to-face with authority-holders who are educated and who know how to run organizations. They feel unable to express what they want to say and unable to understand the workings of the organization. They are afraid that if they say something, they will make fools of themselves (*fare una brutta figura*). The conclusion is that it is better not to get involved. An active interest in organizations is the business of those with education and a regular salary and regular working hours. Thus, the two basic cultural premises influence the workings of voluntary organizations by reducing the incentives to take part, either as authority-holders or as ordinary participants. They reduce the expected personal benefit from participation and increase the possible personal cost.

The organization for the Festival of the Grape is a partial exception to these generalizations. The festival was initiated in

1966 by the committee of the newly-formed festival association (*Pro-loco*). As we have seen, the chief event of the festival is a competition between three territorially-based associations to build the best float. Compared to other formal organizations, the festival organization has a relatively large impact on the pattern of resources allocation in the village, in particular on the use of leisure time. Float-building is begun about a month before the festival and in each association a core of four or five men, helped by a dozen or so others, work on the float several evenings a week. Three or four women in each association prepare costumes to be worn on the float. The activities of the associations are financed largely by voluntary contributions from members of the associations: on average, each household gives L.2–3,000.

One explanation for this relative enthusiasm is the opportunity it gives for a legitimate and open expression of competitiveness. The float competition provides an opportunity for winning over others in Colombaio. Strictly this is a competition between equals. But the fundamental notion of hierarchy makes people think in terms of status differences. Predictably, the greatest interest in the festival is found in the area of Cassero, where most people are of low status, and the least interest is found in Pescina, where most of the high-status people live.[19]

Nevertheless the future of the festival competition, and with it the future of the festival organizations, is uncertain. The men who make the floats complain about the large amount of time it takes and it is difficult to find volunteers to take responsibility for float-building. Requests for money are resented, and generate discontent with the festival in those not actively engaged in the activities of their association. The *Pro-loco* organizers are unhappy at the amount of their own time the organization of the festival uses, and complain that people will not help them with the overall organization. A crisis point in the organization of both the Festival of the Village and the Festival of the Grape is always reached when it is necessary to find men to do unpaid work (such as manning entrance gates). Finally, relations between people of different associations tend to become less than polite, and this produces a reaction against the whole festival: it is better to stop the whole festival, it is said by many, than to have people quarrelling all the time.

Thus, the Festival of the Grape may be finished by the same

cultural factors which make the operation of any kind of deliberately concerted action (*cf. Banfield*) difficult in Colombaio.

In the past it appears that the level of community life was
higher than today, and that several organizations had a considerable effect on the pattern of allocations. In particular, in the first
half of the century, the band, the confraternity, and the consumer
co-operative were large and active organizations, with a range
and scale of activities much greater than today. The band had
about forty players, and occasionally went on tour to play in
nearby towns and cities. The confraternity arranged funerals, as it
still does today, and in addition kept a large quantity of medical
equipment and supplied organizers for the Festival of the Village.
The consumer co-operative had a large clientele, and from time to
time put up candidates for the commune council. Why was the
past different? At that time travelling was difficult and leisure
time was spent in the village. Today, most families own a car and
a TV, and so can amuse themselves independently of others.
Then households depended on one another more, because most
families were cultivators and there were occasions in the agricultural year when one family's labour was not enough and
because things which families could not make or grow for themselves had to come from others in the village. But there are other
factors too. Authority, one of the main problems of voluntary
organizations today, lay with one family of unquestionably high-
status who provided patrons for several of the organizations.
Furthermore, there was a low-status man who was capable of
administering the organization (the 'good man' referred to
earlier). Since the land reform, there has been nobody of unquestionably high status—rather, as we have seen, most of those
now regarded as high are known to have begun low, and so their
status is not secure. Nor has any capable administrator, like the
'good man', emerged.

The only political group active outside election periods is the
Communist party. It holds meetings for members about once a
month, attended by five to fifteen village men, and also small
meetings in farm-houses. It organizes a festival in the village, as
part of a series of provincial-wide village festivals of the party.
A few years ago it arranged an instruction course in grape-
growing for young Communist farmers. In general, its activities
cater for its own members only. By the standards of the other

parties it is quite active, firstly, because it has a large and well-defined category of people—the farmers, and in particular, the ex-*mezzadria* farmers—who are traditionally identified with it. Secondly, the provincial party organization is large and active, and much of the organizational and administrative skills for the village branch are provided by outside officials. Further, there are a number of local men employed by the Communist-controlled provincial administration, mainly as road-menders, and they depend for their much sought-after jobs partly on their activeness in the party at the local level. This gives the Communist party a supply of willing workers at the local level, something which the other parties conspicuously lack.

After the Second World War until the early 1960s, there was more political competition in the village than there is today. The collapse of Fascism and the introduction of huge amounts of resources with the land reform made possible greater competition. The Communists were matched by a Christian Democrat organization staffed mainly by officials of the land reform agency. People looking back on the period say that politics in the village were fierce and entered into everything; and they contrast this with the situation today, when people are more apathetic. Nevertheless, while there is no doubt that the non-Communist party organizations were more active than they are today, there were never well-developed party machines which involved many people giving up time and energy to party politics.

In spite of increased political competition and the change in resources during this period, voting trends remained stable in the commune and in the village and have continued to be stable since; stable between national, provincial and local elections, and stable over time.[20] There are several reasons. At the local level there are generally two competing political party alliances, each of which presents a list of candidates for the commune council. Both sides discourage voters from voting for particular persons in the lists and encourage them instead to vote for one or the other list in its entirety. Both sides, in drawing up their lists, find it expedient to give first priority to the representation of every geographic area of the commune in the list, with the result that the quality of the candidates in each list is very uneven. If many voters selected individual names rather than entire lists, the side which won the election might do so with only a slender majority in the commune council, which would make administration difficult. Thus both sides encourage voters to vote for a list in its entirety rather than for individual candidates. Further, local elections have little to do with specifically local problems: the alliances between the political parties at local level are determined largely by national and provincial events; the negotiations between the parties in each alliance do not concern the policy programme of the alliance, but simply the number of councillors to be given to each party; and the public campaign of both sides does not focus on specifically local problems. In short, voters are discouraged from voting for individual candidates; neither side relies on its local policy programme to attract support; and so the only remaining basis of choice is the party: one votes for the list which includes one's own party. At the higher election levels the rival candidates are generally unknown to the voters, and again the party is the only basis of choice.

These are the immediate causes of the stability in voting patterns. But there are other underlying causes. First, the increased specialization in economic activity since the land reform has resulted in a well-defined and stable division of economic interests, which provides a stable basis for political alignments. Second, with the partial exception of the Communist Party, there have been no well developed political party machines capable of recruiting support from other parties. Thirdly, the basic premises of world view operate to produce stability in voting behaviour. Politics, for many, is the business of other people, particularly other people at the higher end of the social hierarchy. Many villagers and farmers feel that politics involves them in things they cannot understand, issues they lack the education to follow, procedures they lack the experience to handle. It is a world to be watched but not actively participated in. One votes, but one does not attempt to weigh up issues. One votes for the party for which one has always voted. With this is associated the strong criticism levelled against a person known to have changed his party allegiance. Such knowledge is always an effective way of discounting a person's sincerity and honesty. It is assumed that a change in political party allegiance is never the result of a change in convictions, but always the result of a change in where the pay-off lies. In these ways, the premises of world view have the effect of stabilizing the pattern of political alignments,

In the early 1960s, with the withdrawal of the land reform agency from the village and the calming of the general situation in Italy, the political parties declined in importance at the local level. For the following few years, there was little activity in voluntary organizations of any kind: the band almost ceased to exist, and the confraternity and the consumer co-operative just kept going. From about 1966 onwards, there was an increase in activity in voluntary organizations. As the old organizations declined in importance, new ones were created. The new organizations are recreational associations, which take the village rather than sectional party interests as their focus, and bring those who participate in their activities into contact with the outside world.

WORLD VIEW, ECONOMIC DEVELOPMENT AND INNOVATION

The argument which has been set out in this essay is relevant to economic development. The land reform agency organized the assignees of land into a co-operative at the beginning of the reform, and gave great importance to the success of this co-operative, as the farmers' way to economic improvement and the good life. However, eighteen years later, the co-operative is still seen to be the business of the agency, not of the farmers. One reason is because most of the services it provides can be bought from private suppliers at much the same prices. Another reason is that the agency kept tight control over the co-operative, and the farmers have been given only a very small part in decision-making. But there are wider reasons. There is great difficulty in getting farmers to take positions of authority in the co-operative. Those farmers who do are criticized by others on the grounds that they are there to follow their own personal interests rather than the interests of all the members, and that they have betrayed the members by going over to 'them', the agency people. There exists a pervasive fear, as in organizations participated in by village people, that if one takes an active interest one will get involved in things one cannot understand and might have to pay for. It is better to leave the co-operative to the officials (who are appointed by the agency) and to those few farmers who want authority in it.

Thus, one important set of reasons for the lack of interest in the co-operative are the premises about the world of people which we have been following through in this chapter. Even if the economic incentives were made higher than they are at present, the co-operative would probably still function with difficulty because of the cultural obstacles to concerted action. The influence of these cultural factors emerges clearly in discussions with farmers about the possibility of having more co-operative relations amongst themselves: in sharing large machinery which it would be unprofitable for one farmer to buy on his own: or in forming livestock co-operatives between groups of neighbouring farmers. The farmers recognize that the returns from such arrangements would be much higher than from present arrangements *if* they worked. But they assume that, after the first year or so, some of the farmers would start to say that others were neglecting their obligations to the co-operative, and so the whole thing would break up; and it might then be more expensive for each farmer than it would have been had he not entered into the arrangement at all. These cultural factors provide the bases on which forecasts of future gain and loss in alternative arrangements are made: they lead the farmers to forecast failure. For this reason farmers remain largely economically independent of each other. To the extent that this constitutes an inefficient allocation of economic resources (in particular, to the extent that it may result in under- or over-capitalized farms), the cultural factors obstruct economic development. Similarly, the general lack of success of the land reform agency's attempts to encourage farmers to grow less grain and keep more livestock, and to adopt more modern techniques of livestock rearing, are partly the result of the lack of trust between the farmers and the agency, which in turn is partly the expression in this particular context of the farmers' basic cultural premises about the world.[21]

Nevertheless, a considerable degree of economic development has taken place in the area since the reform. This suggests that one must be careful in assuming that cultural factors of the kind considered in this essay are always important obstacles to economic development: they have an important influence on development when choices of inputs and outputs and production techniques are conditioned by the kind of interdependencies which exist between people. In Colombaio much economic development has taken place without involving these inter-dependencies to any important degree. But in the future, when higher levels of income are desired than are likely to be possible from the small land-reform farms without an increase in co-operative relations between farmers, the retarding influence of the cultural premises on development may become very important.

CONCLUSION

I have shown how widely ranging kinds of behaviour in Colombaio may be brought together and understood as a function of two basic premises about the world of people: first, people outside the family are, despite appearances, out for their own advantage; and second, people have certain responsibilities and expectations according to their position in a stratified world. These premises condition the way individuals adapt to the presence of others. We have seen how this adaptation occurs at the level of reputation-management, at the level of defending one's own good name and attacking that of others. The first premise provides the basic weapon in this competition, and the second premise decides how the weapon can be used. We have seen, further, how these rules affect behaviour outside the family, particularly in formal associations. People are wary of entering into confidences with others and wary of becoming active in organizations. We have also noticed other factors apart from the cultural premises which influence these processes: changes in the extent of economic dependency and in the opportunities for social mobility, and changes in the links between the village and the national society. Finally, we have seen how the cultural premises influence the rate and direction of economic development, through their effect on people's willingness to act concertedly for economic ends.

NOTES

1. I should like to acknowledge the help I have had from Professor Bailey, who guided the field-work and offered suggestions on an earlier draft of the paper. Field-work was begun in December 1968, and 13 months had been carried out at the time of writing. The research was financed by a grant from the Social Science Research Council and a scholarship from the New Zealand Universities Grants Committee.

2. 'Colombaio' disguises the name of a village.
3. Harvesting of cereals and olive picking provided the main opportunities for wage labour in agriculture. The work in the wood industry was concentrated in the winter months, and involved mainly charcoal-making and the cutting of railway sleepers. Most of the work in agriculture and the woods took place in the area close to Colombaio, but there was also some short seasonal migration to the western plains to work as wage labourers during the harvesting season.
4. People talking about the pre-reform period, especially the pre-war period, frequently simplify the pre-reform society into two categories: the *signori* and the *poveri* (the poor). Some traders were in the first category, other traders and the artisans were in the second.
5. For an account of the Italian law reform up to 1956, see *Barbero*.
6. The active male population is defined to include men between 15 and 65. There are about 190 men in this category. The average age of active men who depend on agriculture is 55. About a quarter of the men classed as workers are employed outside the commune and travel daily or weekly from their home to place of work. Of the people who come to work in Colombaio but live outside, all the ten office-workers are men, and most of the fifteen teachers are women.
7. My attention was first drawn to the importance of the first premise by *Cancian*, who picks it out as a basic element in the world view of the south Italian peasant. The theoretical argument of this paper owes much to Cancian's argument, and to Banfield's study of political behaviour in a south Italian village. The first premise is close to the rule Banfield uses to summarize the behaviour of peasants in the village where he worked: 'Maximize the material short-run advantage of the nuclear family; assume that all others will do likewise' (*Banfield*, p. 83). This is a way of analytically representing patterns of observed behaviour, not of saying how the peasants think. The first premise in my argument, in contrast, is a summary of how the Colombesi see other people around them. I use this premise to explain regularities in behaviour, whereas Banfield's behaviour rule is what he tries to explain. I do not say that the Colombesi act as if they try to maximize the short-run advantage of the family, but that they believe others are likely to do so. The relationship between how people believe others to behave and their own behaviour is more complicated in Colombaio than a simple 1:1 relationship.
8. I owe the analytical approach outlined in this paragraph and used in the rest of the essay to *Barth* (1). The approach is the logical extension of the approach of micro-economics to the whole of social life.
9. I use the status categories of high, middle and low in order to simplify the analysis. The essay is not intended to present an adequate description of how the Colombesi themselves perceive status differences, although my placing of particular persons in these categories is consistent with rankings made by informants in test situations.
   The division of people into status levels corresponds roughly with the division in terms of occupations, although the correspondence is not at all exact. In particular, while all the people classed as high status come from the occupational category of professionals, office-workers and teachers, by no means all of the people in this occupational category are considered of high status.
   The criticisms were made in informal discussions in a variety of con-

texts while people were telling me about the village and while they were talking amongst themselves about others. From a small number of people I was able to build up over many months a fairly comprehensive picture of how they evaluated others, and much of the argument of the paper is based on the analysis of what these people said. The many casual and less comprehensive comments made by a wide range of Colombesi about others served to check the accuracy of the generalizations. To protect the identity of criticizers and criticized, I have given only the overall results of the analysis of criticisms in the paper.

10. 'Normative rules are very general guides to conduct: they are used to judge particular actions ethically right or wrong. . . Pragmatic rules are statements not about whether a particular line of conduct is just or unjust, but about whether or not it will be effective.' (*Bailey* (4), pp. 5–6.)

11. I use the simple 'insider/outsider' dichotomy for the same reasons of simplification as I use the three-fold status division. The analysis is not an adequate description of the way the Colombesi perceive degrees of outsiderness. Since I am concerned with how the Colombesi see others in the village, I use the term 'outsider' to refer to outsiders living or working in the vilage.

12. However, the country/village distinction is not nearly so marked in Colombaio as it is in Silverman's Colleverde (*Silverman* (1)). It is not a basic criterion of the prestige ranking.

13. In ranking tests, informants commonly explained their high ranking of a particular person on the grounds that people 'have need' of him.

14. My attention was first drawn to this point by John Martin.

15. 'Moral worth' corresponds to a native concept: in discussions about how people in Colombaio could be ranked, informants distinguished a ranking according to *atto morale* from rankings according to *posizione sociale, livello culturale,* and *positione financiale*.

16. I owe this point to Professor Bailey. It is worth noting that the 'good man' has a legendary quality only for those who knew him. Few people under 30 know anything about him.

17. L.10,000=c. £6 13s. 0d.

18. In the two previous festivals there was less doubt about the legitimacy of the victory. In 1968, however, when Molino Association came first and Pescina came a close second, Pescina people maintained that Molino had somehow managed to influence the jury to change its original verdict in favour of Pescina, and give the prize to Molino. The reason for the much greater competitiveness in the third year was that Cassero's victory meant that it had won twice before Pescina had won once, and this was thought unfair by people of the other associations.

19. Of course, this does not exhaust the explanation for the degree of interest in the festival. Another important reason is that the festival's emphasis on attracting tourists to the village and on promoting the development of the area is consistent with the new interests of the villagers.

20. The degree of stability in voting patterns between local and national elections, between village and county areas of the commune, and over time is shown in the following table:

Table 1. The vote from areas of Colombaio commune in communal and national elections.

	Section (a) Colombaio Village	A village	X country	Y country	Commune
Votes cast (b) 1956 Communal elections	477	449	528	395	3,483
% going to (c) LEFT (*Lista I*)	20	23	45	67	44
CENTRE-RIGHT (*Lista Civica*)	76	62	50	27	51
1958 National (*Deputati*) elections					
% going to (d) LEFT	20	23	48	66	45
CENTRE	72	59	44	23	48
RIGHT	6	15	6	9	7
1965 Communal elections					
% going to (e) LEFT	17	14	42	64	42
CENTRE-LEFT	69	64	47	32	48
1968 National (*Deputati*) elections Votes cast	360	319	566	445	3,009
% going to (f) LEFT	21	14	42	62	43
CENTRE-LEFT	65	77	48	32	51
RIGHT	13	4	5	6	6

Notes: (a) The commune is divided into 8 voting sections. The table gives voting results from 4 sections: 2 are village areas and 2 are the voting sections into which the area of dispersed settlement between the villages is divided. (b) The proportion of those voting to those entitled to vote averages over 95 per cent in all elections. (c) 1956 communal elections 'Left' includes Communist and Nenni Socialist parties; 'centre-right' includes all other parties. (d) 1958 national elections 'Left' includes Communist and Nenni Socialist; 'centre' includes Christian Democrat, Saragat Socialist and Republican; 'right' includes Liberal, MSI, and Monarchist. (e) 1965 communal elections: 'Left' includes Communist and Proletarian Socialist; 'centre-left' includes Christian Democrat, Nenni and Saragat Socialists, and Republican; (f) 1968 national elections: As for 1965 communal elections. 'Right' as for 1958 national elections.

Table 2 compares voting patterns from Colombaio commune with those from three south Italian towns, and shows that the degree of stability in voting patterns over time is much higher in Colombaio commune than in the south Italian towns.

Table 2. Voting patterns from Colombaio commune and from three south Italian towns (a):

	Population	LEFT		CENTRE		RIGHT	
		1953	1956 (c)	1953	1956	1953	1956
Colombaio commune (d)	6,000	48	50	45	43	5	7
Montegrano town	3,400	23	18	44	62	33	20
Addo town	1,039	46	9	28	72	26	19
Basso town	6,473	45	36	46	62	9	2

Notes: (a) The figures for the south Italian (Lucanian) towns come from Banfield 1958:28. (b) For the south Italian towns, 'Left' includes Communist and Nenni Socialist parties; 'centre' includes Christian Democrat and Saragat Socialist; 'right' Monarchist and MSI. For Colombaio commune the definitions are the same, except that 'centre' also includes Republican, and 'right' also includes Liberal. (c) The figures for the south Italian towns are for the provincial elections of 1953 and 1956. The figures for Colombaio commune are for the national (senate) elections of 1953 and the provincial elections of 1956. (d) The population figure for Colombaio commune is from the 1951 census.

21. I do not mean to imply that the lack of trust between the officials of the land reform agency and the farmers is the only, or even the single most important reason why farmers have been slow to adopt the agency's suggestions; nor that the only reason why farmers have not formed informal co-operative arrangements amongst themselves is that they do not trust one another. In order to have an accurate idea of the causal importance of the cultural factors, one needs to carry out a linear-programming type of analysis of the farming system to see whether the objective profitability lies in the direction of more informal co-operation and in the direction encouraged by the land reform agency officials. *A priori*, it is reasonable to suppose that beliefs about how other people behave influence the way people make assessments of the future of economic arrangements which involve them in changes in their relations with other people and so influence whether they will adopt the new economic arrangements or not. But the matter really

requires a careful analysis of the farming system before it can be satis-factorily answered.

Given the *a priori* argument that the cultural premises do have an important independent influence on economic development and inno-vation, the argument of the paper makes a qualification to Silverman's paper on economic, social and cultural differences between Central and South Italy (*Silverman* (2)). She argues that 'an ethos cannot be re-garded as a "cause" or satisfactory explanation of behaviour'. For the kind of problem which Silverman was considering—the broad social and cultural differences betwen the two regions, in particular, why Ban-field's 'amoral familism' is found in the south but not in the centre—this position is acceptable. But for the kind of problem I have been considering—the problem of economic and social change in one par-ticular area over time—it is important to allow cultural premises an independent causal importance on the rate and direction of change.

13

The Management of Reputations and the Process of Change

It seems strange that, among the many sayings reported in this book, no-one has come up with the equivalent of 'only the good die young'. People in these communities may or may not be wicked, but they certainly see in one another sufficient evil to make the world of social interaction seem difficult and dangerous. This is stated in the solemn prose of the native of Hogar, sermonizing about the weaknesses of his fellows. The people of Auguste say the same about themselves. A similar message is conveyed in the light-hearted picture of the defeated team in Colombaio, consoling itself in the bar and waving imaginary Red Books in the air to proclaim that advantages are never honestly gained. Finally, what could be more explicit than the sad phrase *troppo buono*, used to dismiss the person who, by returning good for evil, takes Christian teaching literally and so becomes an idiot: he, I suppose, is 'too good to live'.

The discrimination between good and evil in effect distinguishes altruism from egoism. Evil actions are self-interested actions: to be good is to serve other people. But the world and human nature are such that to extend the range of people for whom one makes sacrifices beyond a very narrow limit is to slip beyond goodness into foolishness.

Statements about self-interest and public service are part of a language of claims and there is a very noticeable lack of unambiguous criteria by which to decide whether an action or a policy (or an official) is egoistic or altruistic. People do not judge by performance and results. The results which matter are not

T

so much the benefits which are seen to accrue to the community, but rather the assumed profit and loss account of the man in office. If he has made a personal loss, then he was a fool. In the communities which we studied no-one seems to be able to recall persons who benefited the community at a loss to themselves. The assumption goes exactly the opposite way; if he took office, he must have benefited from it. Reputation and profit are, in fact, believed to be inversely connected. A man who has made money has not done so through hard work and his own merit: at best he has stumbled upon a crock of gold, and more likely, he has done it by manipulating other people and so cheating them.

At the back of this lies another fundamental discrimination: between 'people like us' and 'the others'. There is a quasi-ethnic flavour about this distinction; a readiness to assume all kinds of strange improprieties, not to say perversities, about the beliefs and the way of life of 'the others'.[1] 'People like us' are defined by equality. To be born into the community and have many kinsmen there and to live by the same standards and at the same levels as they do qualifies one to be an equal and a member of the community. This equality is recognized, as most of the essays in this book show, in a willingness to undertake certain kinds of defined exchanges: principally those of services and civilities. It is also recognized in the way in which people criticize one another. In assessing a community member one takes into account the whole man: outsiders are criticized 'on the job'.

The logic of this is that evil is rewritten as self-interest and this in turn is translated into attempts to upset the existing pattern of equality. The upstart is the embodiment of evil. He is the renegade who is hated more than the true enemy.[2] Indeed, part of the antipathy which some peasants in Losa felt towards their *signori*, may have arisen from memories of the humble origins of these *signori*, none of whom were more than one generation removed from the peasant style of life.

The logic which equates superiority with egoism and evil clearly conditions the way people react towards leaders. They are themselves that much the more reluctant to take on positions of leadership and responsibility, because such positions automatically have an adverse affect on their reputations:[3] indeed, this extends even to the point of refusing to do anything at all on

public occasions, being loath to speak at—or even to attend—
public meetings. Positions of this kind are defined as belonging to
high-status people: to 'the others'. These are not the same as the
upstarts; they are people who are beyond the reach of criticism
in-the-round, because they cannot be cut down to size by
depriving them of the help and civilities extended to equals:
the point is they no longer need the help and can afford to
demand deference in the place of civilities. This does not, of
course, put them beyond criticism: they are attacked for their performance—'on-the-flat', so to speak—and they are vulnerable, as,
for example, the story of Martin in Valloire shows, because the
implementation of policy is seldom possible without some kind
of co-operation from those who receive the orders.

There is another way of looking at the distinction made in the
contrast of 'in-the-round' with 'on-the-flat'. Behaviour 'on-the-flat'
is behaviour from behind a mask. Every man has many identities:
to wear a mask is a metaphorical way of saying that a person
insists that only one identity be recognized in the affair in hand.
If he is successful, then he absolves himself of all social responsibilities other than that symbolized in the mask. The mask directs
people's attention towards the interpretation they should make
of what he does. Furthermore, the design of the mask usually
suggests one or another form of 'altruism' or 'public service'.
Authority is always masked and the mask should provide some
protection for the person in authority.[4] This argument will be
developed later in this chapter.

The rules which people follow in regulating their interactions
with one another must contain advice about the transmission of
information. Whether your aim is to protect yourself and remain
part of the community of equals, or to cut upstarts down to size,
or to rise out of the community of equals into a position of
leadership, you need the important skill of being able to control
information about yourself and others. To be a member of the
community is to allow wide access to all sides of your life, for if
familiarity breeds contempt for leaders, it also engenders equality
among comrades. The would-be leader must cut down the flow of
news about him by wearing a mask: hence our cliché that leaders
need to be remote. The general rule, covering all objectives, is
that one's reputation should be kept as close as possible to the
altruistic end of the spectrum. In Valloire Martin failed to create

the appropriate image: in the Austrian village the schoolmaster paid the penalty of ignoring (or, perhaps, being ignorant of) the signals which his activities were emitting; but in the same village the man of affairs, Bachmann, succeeded in separating himself enough and sufficiently restricting the flow of information to make his claims to leadership acceptable.

In this chapter I shall examine some of the strategies which are used in the communities where we have lived to control the flow of information. I shall also look at the way in which these strategies are likely to effect change and development.

DEALING WITH UPSTARTS

Upstarts are separated from high-status people in that the common people know so much more about their 'private' lives. It is easy to see why this should be so. Those who belong to a community live out all aspects of their lives in one another's presence and are without the shield of ignorance, which is a feature of societies like our own. The man who works in an office or a factory may genuinely not know what kind of family life his colleague has, since family and work are separate worlds. This is not the case in any of the communities which we have described, not even those in which nowadays people have diverse ways of making a living. They know all about each others' personal attributes, and can reinforce their conclusions by appealing even to the attributes of ancestors.[5] In no time at all everyone knows how much this man was paid for mending the floor of the barn, or how much that woman paid (or says she paid) for her new coat. Information cannot be recalled and it flows around like a liquid that is spilt: in the context, I suppose, the liquid is milk.

All this knowledge comes not only from what people see but from what they hear and say to one another. An event or an action is public not only to those who see it, but also to those who hear about it.[6] Indeed it is speech which defines the nature of that event: the moral evaluation, which is what matters, is of its very nature unseeable. Comment relates event and action to the 'eternal verities' (egoism, equality and so on) and just as these abstract qualities are invisible, so also are the events which are judged in their light. The map which a man has of the community around him, of what is going on and of how he should respond to others, is a map created by the spoken word, by the information circulating around his community.

In order to see how the flow of such information may be controlled, let us assume that we are being guided by an un- usually frank and articulate informant, one who is willing to spell out in detail the factors which he usually handles without giving them a second thought, in the way that a practised car driver changes gear. Something has happened in the community and our informant is calculating how, if at all, to pass on this information in such a way as to maintain or improve his own reputation, while damaging the reputation of someone else, whom our informant deems to be an 'upstart'. It will save time if our informant is called S (for 'sender') and the upstart is called O (for 'objective').

Other people are involved besides S and O in such a communi- cation event. Firstly one or more persons have to be selected as the primary recipients of the information (R for 'receiver'): If S intends that R should pass on the message then we also have to take into account A (for 'audience'). R and A clearly may vary from one situation to another and S has to make a choice both about the particular individuals and, even before that, about the extent to which he wishes the information to be disseminated and about the responsibility which he is willing to take in being seen to be the originator of the message, that is in 'signing it'.[7]

In making this general decision, a number of more particular decisions are involved. There will be a variety of channels and networks, each adapted to different kinds of information and each varying in range and direction. An event or action which is private cannot easily be posted on the notice board outside the town-hall. News leaked to the Circle of Catholic Women may not filter through to the men who patronize the left-wing bar. Even indi- viduals have their personal networks of people with whom they exchange information, and these networks will be known at least to the more astute and active manipulators in the community.

As well as surveying the range of channels open to him, S also has to think about the code which he will use. The word 'code' can be interpreted in a large number of ways, too numerous to be considered systematically here. For example, the decision to pass on the news in Italian, thus rejecting Piedmontese and the local dialect, itself conveys information to the inhabitants of Losa about the nature of the message and about who can properly be included among the recipients. At another level, the use of family nicknames in preference to titles, or surnames, or given names, itself transmits a signal about how S sees himself standing in relation to the persons referred to, and about how he sees their connection with R and (possibly) A. At a third level, the general tone in which the story is told or the argument made can, quite apart from the content, incline the listener to see scandal and tragedy as against finding it all rather a joke.[8]

There are many other levels of coding. The particular level to which I wish to draw attention is that which indicates the degree to which S commits himself to a moral interpretation of the news which he is giving. It may also be used to make an assessment of a piece of news which he has received. This is done by attaching to the news one or more of the following labels: chat; scandal; rumour; confidence; gossip; and open criticism.[9] There are obvious signals which can be attached to the heads of messages, so to speak, for making these discriminations. Some examples from English are as follows:

'It is an absolute scandal. . . .'

'I was just having a chat with George, when he told me. . . .' (In other words, 'I did not maliciously solicit the information which I am about to give you.')

'There is a rumour going around. . . .'

'Between you and me and the gatepost. . . .'

'I tell you this in the strictest confidence. . . .'

'I feel it my duty to say. . . .' (This is a signal that open criticism is about to follow and it may be transmitted on the speaker's authority.)

Each of these signals has a different tactical significance, and the differences relate firstly to the costs and benefits which S perceives in transmitting the information, and secondly to its ambiguity. Let us consider the ambiguity first.

Any message has two parts, which correspond ultimately to the fact that a message requires both an S and an R. The first part is a factual account of what someone has done or has said or is alleged to think. This part is wholly under the control of S. The second part of the message is the meaning which R chooses to read into those events or actions. This is not directly under the control of S and he has to make a judgement about how far he can afford to guide *R* (and behind *R*, the audience—*A*) into making an interpretation of the moral significance of what has been done. In other words, *S* has to make a judgement about how *R* and *A* will fit the news into their conceptions of how the world of people is and ought to be.

The skill lies in balancing the nature of the news against the existing reputation of *O* (the person whose reputation *S* is intending to assail). Some events are absolute: for example, the charge of incest, which is said to have occurred in Pertosa, must have been quite unambiguous and had only to be stated as a fact in order to be condemned. Equally, given the context of the particular Austrian village, one does not need to add a gloss of disapproval to the news that an outsider schoolmaster is opening his house for sexual orgies by the young. But notice that lovemaking by the young, when a girl takes the cattle to the high pastures (*alm*), will not necessarily receive the same disapproval and might indeed elicit only a nostalgic comment on how nice it was to be young.[10] At the other extreme from the case of incest is the sumptuous wedding in Valloire: this is as readily interpreted favourably as it is condemned.

The case of incest in Pertosa is an example of a *scandal*. There is no possible ambiguity about its interpretation, since the act constitutes a gross breach of a widely accepted norm of conduct. *S* has no need to add an interpretative gloss to the plain story. Once uttered it circulates with great rapidity and is beyond his control. He risks nothing by transmitting it, since no blame can attach to him for passing on news which everyone has a right to know. This, I suppose, is why certain kinds of newspaper, having ferreted out stories about private lives, quickly remove the seal of 'private' by attaching the label 'scandal'.

At the opposite end of the spectrum is *chat* (what in French is called *bavarder*). This is story-telling unembroidered by moral comment. It is an exchange of news which, ostensibly at least, is not intended to manipulate attitudes and opinions. There are no moral implications in what is said, or, if there are, *S* takes no responsibility for the interpretation which *R* puts upon the story. Officially, so to speak, there is in fact no *O* since chat is about trivial things and not about moral issues. An ideal topic for chat is the weather since, at least in these cultures, no-one can be blamed for that,

288 Management of Reputations and the Process of Change

Scandal is about important things and chat is about trivialities, or at least moral trivialities. They have in common the fact that S, in transmitting them, does not risk his own reputation. *Rumour* contrasts sharply, in that if S attaches this label to his message, he explicitly refuses to take responsibility for it. Like scandal, rumour commonly deals with matters of importance, either events or the conduct of persons. In the latter case, it may be a rumour about a possible scandal, but S is evidently uncertain enough about the truth of the story (or about the way it will be interpreted) to behave as if he were a mere instrument, nothing more than a channel of information, and therefore absolved from taking moral responsibility for handing on the news. It is probably this quality of being without cost which enables rumours to be spread quickly and easily.

Gossip is about persons and their conduct, and it contains an overt moral evaluation. It differs from scandal in that the moral judgement has to be made overtly, by adding it to the facts. Like rumour, it is said to spread quickly, but it does so along specific channels. A rumour may be passed to anyone: only certain people can properly be entrusted with gossip. There are two reasons for this. Firstly, S may suspect that the story will turn out to be untrue, and he also judges it to be sufficiently ambiguous for R to need a push in the right direction to make the appropriate interpretation. The message is likely to be partially 'signed', a typical opening signal being 'I have just heard from George that . . .'. To this extent S passes the responsibility for transmitting the message onto George: but, at the same time, he can expect R to hand on the message with the signal 'S has just told me that . . .'. One concludes that S reckons that there is a chance of making his interpretation acceptable to the general public (and thus doing down O), but at the same time wishes to leave himself a way of retreat in case he has misjudged the situation.[11] He backs away from an open confrontation with O.

Open criticism is distinguished from gossip in that it does exactly this: the message is signed and the challenge is issued. S feels sure enough of his interpretation to risk his credit. He speaks to an unrestricted audience. He is not merely, as in repeating scandal, climbing onto a bandwagon: he stands to gain the credit, providing he is successful, of a reputation for being brave enough to stand up and speak the truth in the public interest. For reasons to be discussed later, this kind of message is most commonly delivered from behind a mask.

All the labels so far discussed permit free or almost free circulation of the news. So far as I can see there is just one device for limiting circulation: this is the label 'in confidence'. Such messages are signed but they contain instructions to R about limiting the range of people to whom he transmits the news, or even an instruction to keep it to himself. In the strict sense such a message is signed: but to some extent protects himself, if the news should get out, by handing on the responsibility to R. In other words, the signature is rather ambiguous, and a label 'in confidence' may, in fact, be not so very different from ordinary gossip. A confidence also is something shared between close allies or friends, and the signal 'in confidence' is a claim to a relationship of solidarity. As Paine says, such relationships have a quality of 'terminality', in the sense that information and other kinds of exchanges tend to remain closed within them.[12]

To summarize. In choosing one or another of these labels to categorize his message (and in giving whatever other signals are appropriate in the culture), S has to take into account the moral ambiguity of the news. This is by no means a simple operation. Only relatively rarely does news have the clear-cut quality of scandal. Moreover, whether clear or not, S must try to see the news through the eyes of R and A, since it is from them that he is trying to elicit a response. Nor is this judgement to be made simply of the news itself: it must be seen in relation to the existing reputations both of O and of S himself in the eyes of R and A.

In such conditions of uncertainty we would expect to find devices by which S, so to speak, hedges his bets. The label of 'rumour' frees him from responsibility. 'In confidence' restricts the circulation of the news, and both it and 'gossip' blur his signature.

Of course, any of these messages, if successful, will lower O's reputation. So also will the remaining two categories, scandal and open criticism. But the first set of labels do not directly benefit S's reputation. 'Scandal' gives it a slight boost, but not much since everyone else is having a bite from the cake. Only open criticism, providing always it is successful, will directly benefit S's reputation. Correspondingly, he stands to lose most if he fails.

Of course, the situation is in fact much more complicated than this, since the active manipulator does not choose one tactic and disregard the rest, but is likely to work through a sequence, which carries him from less to greater responsibility, and consequently from less to greater reward. At each stage he gets a feedback which tells him whether or not to go further. Begin with a rumour. If that is well received, go onto gossip or an 'in confidence' leak. One can always withdraw by claiming that the gossip was really chat or that a confidence had been breached. But if this too goes well, one can go on to confront O through open criticism, proclaiming that his behaviour has been scandalous.

WEARING A MASK

As an outsider, used to the conventions of British elections, I was surprised at the reluctance shown by the leader of List One in Losa, to play the game of democracy by entering into public debate with his opponents. The man in question is far from formidable in debate and, at the time, I put his behaviour down to a prudent unwillingness to have his lack of skill shown up in public. But comments afterwards, and a reading of what my colleagues have written about other communities, show that more than simple discretion was involved. List One's leader evidently judged accurately the values of the electorate and his opponents may well have lost support by inadvertently flouting the fundamental norm that community dissension should never be wantonly and irresponsibly dragged into the daylight. The question in fact hinges around attitudes towards impersonal relationships, in particular towards holders of positions of authority.

Impersonal relationships are those in which the actors wear a mask. The intention of the mask is to seal this relationship off from any other relationship or attribute or responsibility which each of the actors may have, either towards one another or towards other persons. The authorities of the British Army, ever present to anticipate whisperings of mutiny, used to tell the recruits that it was not the man who was being saluted, but the uniform, thus hopefully dispelling the idea, derived from living in a community, that one must know a man well and take into account all aspects of his character and behaviour before granting him respect. The ethos of community exists in armies within small groups of the same rank, but evidently it does not extend upwards and downwards between ranks. Authority, in other words, is to some extent masked and must always be so.[13]

The mask limits the range of information available for manipulating the relationship. Sometimes this is in fact based upon ignorance. The parties do not have extensive personal knowledge of each other and this ignorance of antecedents and private life works as a shield. When people do not know about the difference in the rewards which they receive for equal work, there is that much the less cause for dissension.[14] When the leader's shortcomings and failings are concealed from his followers, the latter have that much the less ground for criticism and so find it more difficult to justify scorn and disobedience. Looking at it from the other direction, equality exists where there is a free flow of information about all aspects of the persons concerned. In such a situation there can be no mystery and no awe, and to be a hero to his wife or his valet, a man must really have heroic qualities.

These clichés of army manuals on leadership are exemplified in other kinds of organization and community. Even within armies there are many devices which do not find their way into the manual. For example, one of the adjutant's functions is to take the responsibility and the blame for the inevitable failures and confusions of the day-to-day running of the regiment, thus shielding the majesty of the commanding officer from the heat of continual criticism. The colonel is left in a position of remoteness and infallibility. In some societies the holders of power are literally masked, and it is from these that I have taken the metaphor. For example, secret societies in certain areas of West Africa function as organs of control. The secrecy—and the masks themselves—engender terror.[15] The victims do not know and cannot calculate what the mask might do and so are inhibited from deviance and prevented from organizing resistance. In a more complicated way the Klu-Klux-Klan used masks to uphold its chosen values in the face of rival authorities.

The man wearing the mask of authority or the member of a secret society is absolved from all social responsibilities other than that symbolized by the mask or contained in membership of the secret society. He is kinsman to no-one and a friend to no-one. He has the single authoritarian (usually threatening) relationship towards those under him. The 'hard' behaviour required in authoritarian transactions, especially in bureaucratic situations, requires a single-interest relationship (that is, a mask). As soon as one takes into account the fact that the victim has other roles and other obligations, the 'hardness' is likely to be mitigated. To repeat, authority has to be faceless—or at least to show the single consistent face of a mask.

But masks, either in the literal or metaphorical sense, do more than this. Besides cutting away the fat of 'whole persons' and leaving a relationship with the muscularity needed for effective command, the masks themselves are also likely to symbolize common values. Masks represent those qualities which lay on the right side of our matrix: they stand for duty, the community, the society, *dharma*, continuity and stability. In lives that would otherwise be 'nasty, brutish and short' (but far from solitary) the mask is Leviathan. The collection of masks stand for public opinion, or the State, or the Community. Furthermore masks make possible communication between local leaders, such as M. Martin in Valloire, and the world of resources outside the community.

Here emerges our version of the paradox which has tantalized philosophers down the ages. The mask and the uniform (and for that matter the 'saint', the person who is *troppo buono*, the idiot who is too good to survive) stand for the community and its fundamental values: they represent morality as against self-interest and the individual: indeed, one of their tasks is to bring deviants back into line. On the other hand membership of a moral community is achieved to the extent that one is treated by other persons 'in the round': to have a single-interest relationship with a person is to be used by him and to use him as an instrument, that is, not as a moral being. On the one hand a moral relationship is achieved by dealing with whole persons and rejecting impersonal interactions: on the other hand morality is ultimately safe-guarded by doing just the opposite, by making impersonal interaction with the guardians of morality.

Like gifts and poison, this dilemma is built into human inter-actions: it can never be finally resolved. But different kinds of community and society find different compromizes between the extremes of wholly masked and wholly unmasked patterns of relationship. Let us now look at the pattern which is found in the communities described in this book. What needs to be set in the context of the noticeable lack of public spirit, the reluctance to serve the community, coupled with a profound lack of Christian

charity in one's expectations of other people's motives and behaviour, is the extreme cynicism about the masks which those in
authority wear. They have achieved their high status through the
kind of trickery to which no decent man would stoop: they
continue, in their positions of authority, to benefit themselves
at the expense of the community. Leaders are not inevitably
regarded in this way. The late Dr. Ambedkar is literally wor-
shipped, as if he were a saint, by the Jatavs of northern India and
by other Untouchables.[16] Why did M. Martin in Valloire or the
mayor of Auguste not rise to these heights? Indeed, at least some
of the people in all four countries described in this book, Italy,
Austria, France and Spain, have shown themselves capable of
blind obedience to leaders. But there are no signs that *local*
leaders ever perceive even a glimmering of the light of their own
charisma.

What matters to the leader of a community is the amount and
kind of information that circulates about him. The leader risen
from the ranks is in a particularly difficult situation, since a great
deal is known about him and his antecedents and he cannot
achieve the mystery required for leadership. Of course, covert
criticism of the kind which was discussed earlier only bites if
the leader still needs services voluntarily given by his followers.
The ultimate sanction upon a deviant is to cut off exchange
relationships with him: if a would-be leader is in a position to
do without these exchanges, then, so far from harming him, the
separation will help him in his struggle to be recognized as a
leader.

People in high-status positions—those who have moved into a
different league or who have first appeared before the community
in that guise—are relatively immune from envy and gossip and
backbiting. They are allowed to protect themselves with a mask.
In the little community of Pellaport the mayor stands on a
ladder, changing bulbs in the lamp-posts and swapping badinage
with people in the street below. It seems that this would be
inconceivable in Colombaio, where the mayor is treated with
deference and certainly I never saw the mayor of Losa with his
shirt-sleeves rolled up. The bigger the community, the larger
the stock of *outside* resources at the disposal of people in authority.
They do not depend on those whom they lead:[17] on the contrary
the people depend upon them and have to pay the tribute of

allowing privacy. The postmaster in the Austrian village is another case in point.

But this does not explain why officials in Colombaio or the unfortunate would-be leader in Valloire should be considered dishonest. Why the cynicism?

Obviously one answer is that they may in fact be dishonest. There are variations from one country to another, but it is fair to say that peasants, almost everywhere in the world, could make a case to say that they gave more than they ever got from the world outside.[18] But the definition of 'exploitation' is a subjective matter, a matter of belief, and we still have to explain why peasants should have this belief.

The ultimate explanation is the definition of a moral being. The denial of morality is the person who is *sauvage*, that is, the man who refuses to enter into exchange relationships with other people. The wholly moral person is the one who gives *and* receives. Christ-like figures give but do not receive in proportion, and consequently are less than whole beings. The same is true of any kind of leader. Authority requires a mask. A masked relationship cannot be truly one of reciprocity. Therefore, leaders, like saints, may become objects not of awe and reverence, but of fear and contempt.

This contempt is expressed by pulling away the mask. The mask of public service should be worn, so to speak, for the benefit of an audience of outsiders. Where an official is not protected by ignorance, then his fellow villagers stand like a chorus *behind* him, and his mask can only be worn to the extent that they collude. The mask itself must be left undamaged because it symbolizes the values of altruism and public service, on which community life should be based. The mask is left undamaged, and self-respect is reasserted by jeering at the contemptible qualities of the whole man who wore the mask. To refuse to do this to those who want to administer or reform the community from behind a mask (and thus to grant the man behind the mask the status which the mask demands) is, in the end, to deny the community: to be a renegade.

It follows that to win unswerving and unthinking loyalty and obedience from peasant followers, a leader must first extract them from the web of community relationships and the associated values. It is sometimes said that peasants make good soldiers, easily divesting themselves of the tight concern with self which is the negation of an *esprit de corps*. But to the extent that peasant soldiers have been tough and disciplined, these qualities have nothing to do with their definitions of morality or their fine loyalties: mostly the toughness came from the hard austerities of peasant life, and the discipline from a sense of helplessness arising from a lack of skill and experience in manipulating market relationships.[19]

This view of the world is a fact: indeed it is a rock which should feature more prominently than it does on the charts which guide the movements of politicians and planners who aim to change and develop peasant communities.

'EVERY MAN HAS HIS PRICE'

To understand why a man chooses to respond to a command or a suggestion in a particular way, we have to see this choice not as an act of selection but rather as a process of reasoning towards selection. To do this is to take a cognitive approach towards the study of social behaviour and social change. We have to find out how the actor 'words' the world around him, how he makes plans to respond to situations and to other people, how he makes sense of what has befallen him; it is not enough merely to observe what he does; we have also to know what is the meaning (to him) of what he does.

It is strange that one should feel the need to say this, for this process of reasoning towards selection is a part of everyone's immediate experience. The need arises because planners and policy makers, especially those who are themselves economists or who have been associated with economists, make a grand simplifying (and stultifying) assumption that 'every man has his price'. I quote from a preface by Arthur Lewis:[20]

> Many countries have indeed attitudes and institutions which inhibit growth, but they will rid themselves of these attitudes and institutions as soon as their people discover that they stand in the way of economic opportunities.

This is not really a statement about the nature of human motivation: rather it is a statement about the investigator himself— about the seriousness with which he proposes to inform himself about people's values and their perceptions of the possibilities of a situation.

This is indeed the point. The planner and the politician are not in a position to put *immediately* into the hands of the peasants the benefits which they say will accrue from their policies. No developer has the resources to operate continuously in the mode of charity: he has first to persuade people to help him by helping themselves. All that he can offer them on the spot is a promise of better things to come, if they do what he says. In other words, they have to trust him. He needs to have credit; any measure which is entirely new requires a large amount of credit; but the developer (even if he began life as a member of the community) has to operate from behind a mask and to that extent his credit is immediately diminished.

There is another difficulty in the cliché that 'every man has his price'. As a definition of the word 'price', this statement is true; but it is also trivial, because the planner has to know not merely *that* everyone has a price, but *what* is the price and what factors go into the reckoning. He is working in the dark so long as he does not know what benefits the people think they can realistically expect (as distinct from what he promises them), what things they expect they will have to give up, and the relative value to them of these benefits and costs. By no means all these sums can be worked out in terms of money. Indeed, some of the values are only with difficulty articulated in words; and the most fundamental of them all—the community itself—is expressed obscurely through the contradiction of egoism and altruism. Certainly situations like this do not lend themselves easily to quantitative prediction.

The planner's dream—and the myth which every competent planner tries to get into circulation in order to compensate for his inability to force people to do what they do not want to do— is that everyone is falling over himself to sacrifice his own interests for the good of the community. Accordingly, at least at the most public level, development plans are promulgated around the dogma that the interests of the community are supreme. It is only at the secondary level of implementation and through the mouths of secondary echelons of administrators that the possibilities of individual gain are suggested. I think these priorities are right, for nowadays not even the most rampant supporters of private enterprise can stomach a public contempt for the common good. But at the same time, as some of our material suggests, it seems to be a mistake to plan on the assumption that people will in fact respond to appeals for altruistic behaviour. At least in communities like those described in this book a plan which depends upon corporate and voluntary activity—in a framework, say, of co-operatives—is unrealistic and will fail.

This is not because the people of these communities are strangers to co-operative activity. Still today the people of Losa run a sophisticated system of irrigation by canals, and a generation ago this was true of many of the other communities. The people have always co-operated to exploit the mountain pastures. Finally, there is ample evidence of the delicate collusion required to cut down the reputation of upstarts. Indeed the very capacity to sabotage the plans of developers and reformers itself rests upon co-operation. But they do not co-operate with the object of modernizing their own communities.

This points towards a strategy for development, or at least an explanation of why things turn out the way they do. Robert Wade suggests that the success of the reform in central Italy in creating small farming enterprises is due partly to the fact that the plan did not require co-operative activity by the farmers. The functions which might have been performed by such co-operatives were in fact carried out by an external agency, endowed with sufficient resources—even to the extent of supplying cutlery. In other words, the line of development should be through those modes of activity suggested by the left-hand side of our diagram in Chapter 1. Where change has come about, it has been through the decisions of individuals and not through communal decision. The farming enterprises in Colombaio constitute one case. In Valloire the attempt at co-operative development failed and it has been succeeded by a phase in which individuals are finding their own ways of exploiting new resources in their environment, and so 'modernizing' their lives. Migration too rests upon individual decisions, although it does of course have consequences for the community: but there are no community decisions about migration.

Those sons of the communities who come back from the wider world and want to bring about modernization come to the conclusion that the place needs a 'shake-up'. As the mayor of

U

Auguste put it, his community needed a 'psychological shock'. What this means is that individuals and their families have to be shaken out of the net of community relationships in which they are caught. In more concrete terms this means diversification of jobs and of sources of income. This is exactly the difference between a community like Pellaport and most of the other communities described in this book. People in Pellaport, because they make their living in the same way, depend more upon one another than do the members of such diversified communities as Losa, Valloire, Colombaio or even Auguste.

The diversification of ways of making a living, which comes about through incorporation into a larger economy, automatically cuts down the frequency of exchanges, restricts the flow of information, and so increases ignorance about one's neighbour and thus promotes that paradoxical ignorance and indifference which decreases jealousy and opens the way towards various kinds of co-operation. It is only when people have been shaken out of the net of community relationships, that they begin to perceive the possibilities of forming associations, including some which transcend the boundaries of the old communities. At that stage they are themselves prepared to put on the mask of public service.

None of the communities described in this book have reached that point of development. Indeed some of them may never do so, because everyone who matters will have migrated to work somewhere else. Moreover, in most of them, it is not a question of shaking the existing population out of its present loyalties and relationships, but of waiting for them to die off and allowing a new generation to set up a form of living together which no longer has the characteristics of a closed community. Those villages in England, which are said to have a vibrant associational life, are staffed by people with diverse sources of income, living relatively private lives. In these villages the reforming pressure is to make inroads into the privacy: in the villages described in this book, at least until a generation ago, the struggle was to maintain some kind of privacy.

The kind of development which is needed is not community development, so much as a development which leads towards the destruction of community life. That is one conclusion. The second conclusion is that no social reformer or planner can afford to do without a systematic knowledge of the beliefs and values of the people whose lives he is planning to change. But—and this is the third conclusion—there is nothing to be gained by telling people to change the beliefs which they hold: beliefs only change in the light of experience. The planners have to provide this experience and—at least in the case of Valloire—they may do so as much through failure as through success.

In a word, peasant communities cannot move *as communities* into a twentieth-century economy. This is certainly true of the level of agricultural efficiency, for peasant techniques and the size of peasant holdings do not permit them to compete efficiently in the market. But it is also true at another level. The masked impersonality of a diversified society is wholly incomprehensible —and would in any case be unacceptable—to those who have been brought up to act as if men did not have the right to be different from one another.

NOTES

1. Some of my friends in Losa had a stock of such comment about *i meridionali*—the people from the South of Italy. They were said to be unwashed, unwilling to work and with minds that seldom rose above the navel. The point was sometimes clinched by listing the better known American gangsters of the mid-wars period—those of Italian descent—and then stating firmly that all such people were *meridionali*.

    The fairy-tale accounts given in *Middleton*, Chapter 5, may differ in idiom from the above, but they carry the same message. 'The most distant of these creatures, beyond the magicians and sorcerers, are creatures hardly human in appearance, who walk on their heads. . . . These people love to eat meat that is rotten, and "bad" meat such as snakes, frogs, hyenas and other night creatures.' (p. 237)

2. See *Coser*, pp. 67–71.

3. I recall the parents of boyhood friends giving the news, with pride, that their sons had been recommended for a 'stripe'. But they added, also with pride, that the offer had been refused because 'he wants to stay with his mates'.

4. 'Authority' is carried by an office and is not a characteristic of inter-actions between whole persons. In cases in which, without office, the words of one person are listened to with respect and his example followed, so that he becomes an informal leader, the appropriate word is 'influence'. In communities like those studied in this book 'authority' and 'influence' are not only different but also opposed. Influence very easily cancels itself: the informal leader has to lead without being seen to do so, since leadership implies inequality, and overt inequality destroys influence. This means that the range of command available through

influence is small and beyond a certain point the leader has no alternative but to dispense with influence and take on the mask of authority.

5. The tragedy and comedy of social ignorance emerges in the stories of pious Brahmin town-dwelling families, who hire an up-country Brahmin cook and after twenty years of faithful service, they discover that he was after all, an Untouchable.

6. The point is excellently made in *Szwed*, p. 96.

7. This term and some of the ideas in this chapter came from reading the typescript of an essay by Robert Paine. See *Paine* (3).

8. In the London *Times* of 22nd April, 1968 is reported a now notorious speech about immigration made by Enoch Powell. He began by comparing himself to the 'Roman', who seemed to see the river Tiber 'foaming with much blood' and the speech continued in the same portentous style, proclaiming the seriousness of Powell's purpose and staying just short of the point of caricaturing itself and so turning into comedy. Some time later, it fell to Mr. Hogg to speak on the same topic in the House of Commons. This speech is reported in the London *Times* of 24th April, 1968. Some of what he said is marked by a degree of levity which, at first sight, is very surprising considering the subject and the occasion. The humour displayed is, to put it as charitably as possible, of the 'curate's egg' variety (in fact, that is the joke used) and would have fitted well into fifth form debates of the 1920s and 1930s. The first unkind thought that crosses one's mind is that this was, after all, the House of Commons. But second thoughts do Mr. Hogg more justice. His argument was that immigration did not provide a problem so insoluble as to bring on the inevitable doom predicted by Enoch Powell and therefore a subject fit for the high prose of tragedy, but was rather a simple matter, to be dealt with by common sense and foresight and well within the capacity of ordinary men, with ordinary commonplace senses of humour. In other words, Hogg's style must deliberately have been designed to puncture an inflated occasion and turn a proclaimed tragedy into an everyday commonsense affair.

9. These labels are in use in English and there are fairly close equivalents for most of them in the languages of the countries in which lie the communities described in this book. The analysis which follows is intended to transform these terms into concepts which have significance across cultures: that is to say they can be used to ask questions about any culture, even those which do not have equivalents of these terms.

It should also be obvious that there are many other ways, varying from one culture to another, of indicating the degree of overt moral evaluation intended in the message.

10. See *Honigmann*, p. 280. In the area south of Salzburg the nice term for a baby conceived out of wedlock is 'child of the *alm*'.

11. The term 'gossip' in English is extremely flexible and easily gives rise to confusion. Of the English terms listed here, this alone has the connotation of malice. Even then the word is frequently used with an indulgent meaning, and people may speak with relish (and a slightly humorous self-deprecation) of 'having a good gossip'. Nevertheless, the dominantly evil connotations of the word mean that no-one can ever, in a serious situation, attach the label 'gossip' to what he is saying, since this warns his listener to discount the news and to doubt the sincerity of the news-giver. Consequently skilled gossiping is done in such a way that the speaker either conceals the fact that he is gossiping

or else behaves in such a way that no-one can possibly say that he is gossiping. The unskilled gossip leaves himself open to accusations of malice and consequently his words are ineffective.

12. See *Paine* (2), p. 514.
13. The phrase 'faceless bureaucrat' conveys exactly the masked quality of a single-interest relationship.
14. See *Moore and Tumin*.
15. See *Walter*, especially Chapters 4 and 5.
16. See *Lynch*, Chapter 5.
17. Appointment by election, of course, involves the sanction of the vote, which puts teeth into gossip. The downfall of Mayor Martin in Valloire provides an example.
18. See the argument in *Cancian*, p. 11. See also *Lopreato*, Chapter 1.
19. 'The State is one shape of this fate, like the wind that devours the harvest and the fever that feeds on our blood. There can be no attitude towards fate except patience and silence. Of what use are words? And what can a man do? Nothing.' *Levi*, p. 59.
20. See *Lewis*, p. ix.

References

ARENSBERG, CONRAD M. *The Irish Countryman*. Gloucester, Mass., Peter Smith, 1937.

Atti della Giunta per l'inchiesta agraria e sulle condizioni della classe agricola (The Jacini Enquiry), 1883. Vol. IX, p. xxv, Potenza.

AVARD. *Panchayat Raj as the basis of Indian Policy*. New Delhi: The Association of Voluntary Agencies for Rural Development, 1962.

BAILEY, F. G.
   (1) *Caste and the Economic Frontier*. Manchester: Manchester University Press, 1957.
   (2) *Tribe, Caste and Nation*. Manchester: Manchester University Press, 1960.
   (3) 'The Peasant View of the Bad Life', *Advancement of Science*, Vol. 23, No. 114, 1966.
   (4) *Stratagems and Spoils*. Oxford: Blackwell, 1969; New York, Schocken Books, 1969.

BANFIELD, E. C. *The Moral Basis of a Backward Society*. New York: The Free Press, 1958.

BANNISTER, D. and MAIR, J. M. M. *The Evaluation of Personal Constructs*. London and New York: Academic Press, 1968.

BARBERO, G. *Land Reform in Italy: Achievement and Perspectives*. Rome: FAO, 1961.

BARTH, F.
   (1) 'On the study of social change', *American Anthropologist*, Vol. 69, 1967.
   (2) *Ethnic Groups and Boundaries: The social organization of Cultural difference*. London: Allen & Unwin, 1969.

BLAU, P. *Exchange and Power in Social Life*. New York: Wiley, 1964.

BOTT, ELIZABETH. *Family and Social Network*. London: Tavistock, 1957.

BOULDING, KENNETH. *The Meaning of the 20th Century*. London: Allen & Unwin, 1964.

BOURDIEU, PIERRE. 'The sentiment of honour in Kabyle society', in *Perisliany*.

BROWN, ROGER and GILMAN, ALBERT. 'The pronouns of power and solidarity', in *Style in Language*, Sebeok, Thomas A. (editor), Cambridge (Mass.), 1968.

BURLING, ROBBINS.
(1) 'Cognition and Componential Analysis; God's truth or hocus-pocus?', *American Anthropologist*, Vol. 66, 1964.
(2) 'Rejoinder' (to Hymes and Frake). *American Anthropologist*, Vol. 66, 1964.

BURNS, ROBERT K., Jr. 'The Circum-Alpine Culture Area: A Preliminary View', *Anthropological Quarterly*, Vol. 36, 1963.

BURRIDGE, KENELM.
(1) *Mambu: a Melanesian Millennium*. London: Methuen, 1960.
(2) *New Heaven New Earth*. Oxford: Blackwell; New York, Schocken Books, 1969.

CAMPBELL, J. K. *Honour, Family and Patronage*. Oxford: Clarendon Press, 1964.

CANCIAN, F. 'The southern Italian peasant: world view and political behaviour', *Anthropological Quarterly*, Vol. 34, 1961.

COSER, LEWIS A. *The Functions of Social Conflict*. London: Routledge & Kegan Paul, 1956.

DJILAS, M. *Land without Justice*. London: Methuen, 1958.

DUMONT, L. *Homo Hierarchicus*. Paris: Gallimard, 1966.

FIRTH, RAYMOND.
(1) *Elements of Social Organization*. London: Watts, 1951.
(2) 'Social Organization and Social Change', *Journal of the Royal Anthropological Institute*, 1954.

FOSTER, GEORGE.
(1) 'Interpersonal Relations in Peasant Societies', *Human Organization*, Vol. 19, 1960.
(2) 'Treasure tales and the image of the static economy in a Mexican peasant community', *Journal of American Folklore*, Vol. 77, 1964.
(3) 'Cultural responses to expressions of envy in Tzintzunzan', *Southwestern Journal of Anthropology*, Vol. 21, 1965.

(4) 'Peasant Society and the image of limited good', *American Anthropologist*, Vol. 67, 1965.

FRAKE, C. 'Further Discussion of Burling', *American Anthropologist*, Vol. 66, 1964.

FRANCIS, E. K. L. 'The personality type of the peasant according to Hesiod's Works and Days: a culture case study', *Rural Sociology*, Vol. X, 1945.

FRANKENBERG, RONALD. *Village on the border*. London: Cohen & West, 1957.

FRANKLIN, S. H. *The European Peasantry*. London: Methuen, 1969.

FREEMAN, S. T. 'The social organisation of a Castilian village', *American Anthropologist*, Vol. 70, 1968.

GLUCKMAN, M.
(1) 'Gossip and Scandal', *Current Anthropology*, Vol. 4, 1963.
(2) 'Psychological, Sociological and Anthropological explanations of Gossip and Witchcraft: a clarification', *Man* (ns) Vol. 3, 1968.

GOFFMAN, E.
(1) *The Presentation of Self in Everyday Life*. New York: Doubleday, 1959; London: Allen Lane The Penguin Press, 1969.
(2) *Behaviour in Public Places*, New York: Collier-Macmillan, 1963.

GOODENOUGH, WARD H. 'Cultural Anthropology and Linguistics' in *Monograph Series on Language and Linguistics*, No. 9. Garrin, P. L. (editor). Georgetown: University Press, 1957.

GRÄSSLUND, PER. 'Harstena och Krakmarö', *Liv och Folkkultur*, V, Samfundets för svensk folklivsforskning arsskrift, quoted by Redfield, 1960, *The Little Community*, p. 108, 1952.

HALL, EDWARD T., *The Silent Language*. New York: Doubleday, 1959.

HANSSEN, BORJE. 'Fields of social activity and their dynamics', *Translations of the Westermarck Society II*. Copenhagen: Ejnar Munksgaard, 1953.

HOMANS, G. C. *Social Behaviour: Its Elementary Forms*. London: Routledge & Kegan Paul, 1961.

HONIGMANN, JOHN J. 'Survival of a cultural focus' in Goodenough, Ward H. (editor), *Explorations in Cultural Anthropology*. New York: McGraw-Hill, 1964.

HYMES, DELL H. 'Discussion of Burling's paper', *American Anthropologist*, Vol. 66, 1964.

KELLY, G. A. *A Theory of Personality—the Psychology of Personal Constructs*. New York: Norton, 1963.

LEVI, CARLO. *Christ stopped at Eboli*. London: Four Square Books, 1959.

LEWIS, W. ARTHUR. Preface in Epstein, T. Scarlett, *Economic Development and Social Change in South India*. Manchester: Manchester University Press, 1962.

LISON-TOLOSANA, CARMELO. *Belmonte de los Caballeros*. London: Oxford University Press, 1966.

LOPREATO, JOSEPH. *Peasants no more*. San Francisco: Chandler, 1967.

LYNCH, OWEN M. *The Politics of Untouchability*. New York: Columbia University Press, 1969.

MALINOWSKI, B. *Argonauts of the Western Pacific*. New York: Dutton, 1961.

MARRIOTT, McKIM. 'Caste Ranking and Food Transactions: a matrix analysis' in *Structure and Change in Indian Society*, Singer, Milton and Cohn, Bernard S. (editors). Chicago: Aldine 1968.

MAUSS, MARCEL. *The Gift* (Translated by Ian Cunnison). London: Cohen & West, 1966.

MIDDLETON, JOHN. *Lugbara Religion*. London: Oxford University Press, 1960.

MOORE, WILBERT E. and TUMIN, MELVIN M. 'Some sociological functions of ignorance', *American Sociological Review*, Vol. 14, 1949.

MYRDAL, GUNNAR. *Objectivity in Social Research*. London: Duckworth, 1970.

PAINE, ROBERT.
(1) 'What is Gossip About? An Alternative hypothesis', *Man* (ns), Vol. 2, 1967.
(2) 'In search of friendship: an exploratory analysis in "Middle-class" culture', *Man*, Vol. 4, 1969.
(3) 'Informal communication and Information-management' (typescript), n.d.

PERISTIANY, J. G. (ed.). *Honour and Shame: The values of Mediterranean society*. London: Weidenfeld and Nicolson, 1966.

x

PITT-RIVERS, J. A.
(1) 'Social Class in a French Village', *Anthropological Quarterly*, Vol. 33, 1960.
(2) 'Interpersonal Relations in Peasant Society', *Human Organisation*, Vol. 19, 1960.
(3) *The People of the Sierra*. Chicago: Phoenix Books, Chicago University Press, 1961.

RADCLIFFE-BROWN, A. R. *Structure and Function*. London: Cohen & West, 1952.

REDFIELD, ROBERT.
(1) *The Little Community* and
(2) *Peasant Society and Culture*. Chicago: Phoenix Books, University of Chicago Press, 1960.

ROSSI-DORIA, M. *Riforma Agraria e Azione Meridionalista*. Bologna, 1948.

SAHLINS, M. 'The sociology of primitive exchange' in *The Relevance of Models to Social Anthropology*, Banton, Michael (editor). London: Tavistock, 1965.

SANDAY, PEGGY R. 'The "Psychological Reality" of American-English Terms: An Information-Processing Approach', *American Anthropologist*, Vol. 70, 1968.

SCHELLING, THOMAS C. *The Strategy of Conflict*. New York: Oxford University Press, 1963.

SILVERMAN, S. F.
(1) 'An ethnographic approach to social stratification: prestige in a central Italian community', *American Anthropologist*, Vol. 68, 1966.
(2) 'Agricultural organisation, social structure, and values in Italy: Amoral familism reconsidered', *American Anthropologist*, Vol. 70, 1968.

SIMIC, ANDREI. 'The management of the male image in Yugoslavia', *Anthropological Quarterly*, Vol. 42, 1969.

SIMMEL, GEORG. *The Sociology of Georg Simmel*. Glencoe: The Free Press, 1950.

STACEY, MARGARET. *Tradition and change: a study of Banbury*. London: Oxford University Press, 1960.

STIRLING, P. *Turkish Village*. New York: Science Editions, Wiley, 1966.

SZWED, JOHN. *Private Cultures and Public Imagery*. St John's:

Institute of Social and Economic Research, Memorial University of Newfoundland, 1966.

TYLER, STEPHEN A. *Cognitive Anthropology*. New York: Holt, Rinehard & Winston, 1969.

WALTER, E. V. *Terror and Resistance: a study of political violence*. New York: Oxford University Press, 1969.

WHYMPER, EDWARD. *Scrambles in the Alps*. London: John Murray, 1871.

WHYTE, WILLIAM F. *Street Corner Society*. Chicago: Chicago University Press, 1965.

WILKINS, L. *Social Deviance*. London: Tavistock, 1964.

WOLF, E. *Peasants*. Englewood Cliffs, New Jersey: Prentice Hall, 1966.

WRIGHT, G. *Rural Revolution in France: The Peasantry in the twentieth century*. Stanford: Stanford University Press, 1964.

YOUNG, MICHAEL and WILLMOTT, PETER. *Family and Kinship in East London*. London: Routledge & Kegan Paul, 1957.

Index

ACLI, 266

Adams, Paul, 25n.

address, mode of, *see* naming

Africa: migrant labour in southern Africa, 30; secret societies in West Africa, 291

agencies, *see* state agencies

aggiustata, 34, 249

agricultural extension services, 38, 135–6, 137. *See also* state agencies

agricultural improvement, 38, 69, 135–6, 253, 274. *See also* land reform

agricultural loans, 38

agricultural techniques, 26, 116, 135–6, 186–7, 247, 274

agriculture, peasant, 212; decline of, 35–7, 119, 248, 253–4; industrialized farming in competition with, 33–4, 248; maximization of work opportunities in, 29, 30, 33–4; security of, 30, 35–6; subsistence, 251. *See also* mechanization; markets; land

Algeria, 20

Alps: Austrian, 139 et seq.; Cottian, 36, 39; French, 41 et seq., 69 et seq.; Maritime, 231 et seq.

altruism, 3, 4, 9, 21, 25n., 169, 173, 281, 283, 297; as a political resource, 22; mistrust of, 174

Ambedkar, Dr., 27, 40n., 293

apron, wearing of, 2

Arbeiter, 139; marriage of, 148

aristocracy, 54, 59, 66, 170

artha, 23

artisans, 214, 215, 216, 217, 220, 252, 254, 276n.

assessment, 7, 157, 158–9, 184; community membership and, 159, 282; ideal of equality as basis for, 153, 159

associations, 42, 118, 124, 148, 157, 167, 263–5, 275, 298; unwillingness to participate in, 266–73. *See also* co-operatives

Auguste, 119–37, 281, 298

Austria, 139–66

authority, 43, 75, 78, 89, 90, 91, 146, 175, 176, 179, 192, 207, 246, 250, 266, 268, 270, 283, 290, 291–2; consent to, 15; distinguished from influence, 299–300n.; legitimacy of, 210; of referee, 20; of *signori*, 236; personal gain and, 209, 267; reluctance to take positions of, 273

Avard, 40n.

avoidance, 1, 123, 150

bachelors, 202; as traditionalists, 58

Bailey, F. G., 24n., 25n., 104, 118n., 173–4, 277n.

band, village, 266, 270, 273

Banfield, E. C., 68n., 270, 276n.

Bannister, D. & Mair, J. M. M., 108

Barbaro, G., 276n.

barley, 36

Barth, F., 211n., 276n.

Bauer: changing conditions of work of, 145; marriage of, 148

bavarder, 287; distinguished from gossip, 1, 122–3

behaviour, social, *see* interaction

beliefs, *see* world view; values

Blau, P., 25n., 99–101, 102, 114, 116, 118n.

Blaxter, Loraine, 25n.

bonne volonté, 124, 125, 126, 137, 138